NORMAN HASTINGS:

Through My Eyes Too

Tales from a Leicester Boardman

DEDICATION

To Norman's Grandchildren

Glyn Stephen Hastings

Jennie Marie Hastings

Graham Roy Mason

Rory Edward Mason

Philippa Frances Jane Mason

Chloe Louise French (nee Hall)

CONTENTS

ACKNOWLEDGMENTS

Many thanks to Gill (Mrs Google) Eagles, Ian Brierley, Shirley Talbot and Joanne Birch for their help and technical support, and to John Shenstone and Danny Hastings for being the best sounding boards a cousin could have.

Names appearing in this book are entirely fictitious to protect identities

Chapter 1: The End of School Days

School days, so they tell us, are the happiest days of our lives. In my case, certainly not so! However, my school days taught me a few tricks that were to stand me in good stead for later in life, and most certainly the old saying 'you set one to catch one' stood me in very good stead when I later became a School Boardman, or in modern parlance, an 'Education Welfare and Attendance Officer.'

But judge for yourself and read on...

According to 'the book' in my day, children left school at the age of 14 years. Not so in my case for on or around 31 July when I left school for the last time, I was still only 13 years old, my birthday being 5 days later.

I don't think there was anything special about my being allowed to leave a little earlier than I should have, although even I recognised that throughout my years spent in senior school I could quite easily have been described as 'brain dead' by the long-suffering staff who tried so hard to put knowledge into my thick skull. What a sigh of relief must have gone up when they saw the back of me after so many seemingly wasted years.

A few days later, and almost unrecognisable in civilian clothing (as opposed to school uniform) here I was, queuing alongside my former class mates at the local labour exchange to collect a small blue card which stated I was now exempt from further education by virtue of me being no longer of statutory school age.

Standing out from everyone else I spotted dear old 'Gilly' who I regarded with some amusement and, dare I say, affection. This was due to an incident in my second year of Moat Boys Intermediate School when the classics' teacher (Billy Boden) was recounting a story of how an ancient Greek (or other) had sculpted a marble statue of a beautiful woman which was so lifelike he fell in love with it! At this point Gilly, who happened to be sitting next to me, had whispered,

'I bet he made a hole in her!'

Unfortunately, our Billy had spotted the exchange and had ordered,

'Share the joke with the class Gilbert!'

I was mortified and sat there in a cold sweat! Any other mortal in his or her right mind would've thought of something, anything! The ensuing silence was dreadful. My mind was working overtime and I silently willed Gilly to think of something, say anything, but please don't repeat what you did say!

I don't know who was getting redder. Gilly, who was wracking his brains (what few he had) or our Billy, who was fast losing patience. Finally, and with nothing to fall back on, out it came,

'Please Sir, I said, I bet he made a hole....'

Let us be merciful and draw a curtain over what happened next!

I found what was written on my blue card quite amusing for what it said was I was now exempt from further education. Further education?! That was a laugh for I'd not even reached average in what had been on offer in the years 1938 –

1941, but to regress.

Shortly before my school leaving date all the other school leavers and myself had been interviewed by a lady who, we were told, worked for the Youth Employment Service and it was they who would fit us into suitable jobs for each individual boy's ability and aptitude. I was duly interviewed but having no idea whatsoever as to what I wanted to do for the next 50 odd years, said I would like to work on the railway. This was because a chum of mine, Jim, who'd left school a year previously, now worked for the local Railway Station and Jim assured me that the job didn't test the 'mentals' too much. As a result of all this groundwork, when my letter arrived it said an appointment had been set up for me at a local Accountant's office where I was to be trained in accountancy! Even I had to join in with my Form Master's near hysterical laughter when I showed him the letter!

'I thought you wanted to be an engine driver?' he chortled, 'Well, at least they nearly got it right as this firm of accountants are just across the road from the station! Never mind, the Youth Employment Service is noted for putting square pegs into round holes!'

I duly presented myself for interview, in school time of course, and was asked a few questions such as,

'I take it that as you were sent to us you have a particular aptitude for arithmetic?!'

Which had me telling fibs straight away with,

'Oh yes Sir'.

The job was mine, however, mam had made a few enquiries about this particular firm and what came back didn't convinced her,

'No, no, you're not working for them!'

So that was that. I was out of a job and hadn't even left school.

Just before the leaving date, the final exams came up. I was in a cold sweat for, although the numbers in class had dropped due to the Christmas and Easter leavers departing earlier, I knew I would still occupy my usual place in the exam tables which meant I'd be bottom of the class! But then a piece of luck came my way and it came about in this way.

Whenever the Headmaster was called away for any reason each boy in turn was told to sit in the secretary's room when she was out and listen for the phone. Today it was my turn! I had class work books to occupy me but being nosey I started to poke around the office to see if anything as improbable as an unexpected half day holiday was on the cards! There wasn't. The Secretary's overflowing waste bin caught my attention next and, stooping down to push the offending papers back into the waste basket, something caught my eye. They were the upcoming Maths Test papers that had been rejected for various reasons after spoiling whilst going through the Roneo duplicator. Hurriedly I sorted out a complete set of the papers and pushed them into my pocket. That night I found my pal Jim (from the Railway) and he worked the maths out whilst I studied how it was done. In those days all working out had to be shown. Just putting down the answers would've led to a full investigation as to how the answers had been arrived at. Mission accomplished!

Now for History and Geography! I confess I did what every cheating schoolboy has done right back to the year dot. That is I wrote dates etc., on my wrists and shirt cuffs, omitting, of course, 1066, for every schoolboy knows that one date. The Geography paper was slightly more difficult, but I managed. When the results' day came I felt a smidgeon ashamed at finding I was now third from top of the class rather than my usual place of bottom. Even the Headmaster came in to congratulate me at my final year's progress and I distinctly heard him say to my Form Master,

'The boy's an obvious late starter.'

From the look on my teacher's face (for he knew me of old) I could tell he was suspicious and thinking,

'Late starter be buggered; he cheated! But how?'

The other test I was most proud of was 'Arts and Crafts', in which again, I was marked high. It came about in this way.

At the start of my last school year I was with my class in the Metalwork room bemoaning my bad luck. The Metalwork master, who'd previously been absent due to 'war work', had now returned and the tranquil days of skiving, were gone. Some of the boys, even with his nibs being absent, had quietly gotten on with various projects, but I hadn't. Scrounging around in the scrap box where all the discarded previous efforts were dumped, I found a badly misshapen copper bowl. I was about to throw it back in with the other waste when I realised it had possibilities. You can believe it or not but for the rest of that school year I wandered about the metal work room gently hammering out all the dents and little imperfections from my bowl. I even found a discarded base which, at a pinch, fitted the base of the bowl although I had neither the skill or inclination to solder it to the base properly. Come the time to 'get your work marked' I was called forward and my bowl and base (still unattached) were scrutinised from all angles.

'I bet you're really choked you haven't had time to finish the base to bowl soldering aren't you squire?' I was asked.

'Oh yes Sir, but time has run out, has it not?!' (the nerve of this boy!)

So, I'd finished with any sort of schooling. Or had I! Some words come to mind that perhaps sum things up perfectly when thinking of or indulging in formal state provided education. These are that 'my education was interrupted only when I went to school.' Profound words but very true when taken in the context of social life.

At this time my immediate family consisted of just me and mam. The rest of her brood were away:

The eldest, John Edwin (Ted) was in the Army having volunteered his services as soon as war was declared. At the time of Dunkirk, him being in the Medical Corps, he was sent to Dover where, with a rubber ground sheet draped around his shoulders, he would go deep into the bowels of the rescue ships that brought back the dead and wounded and, with the injured or corpses draped over his shoulder, he'd climb up the steep ladders and bring them ashore. Next, Ted had to sort out which of the dead had lost a limb or such and, with thick clips/staples he'd fasten a limb back onto the corpse ready for decent burial.

Maisie was serving in the WAAF (Women's Auxiliary Air Force) on the barrage balloons. We roared with laughter when she recounted a story about the time a sex maniac nicknamed the 'Yardley Ghost' had been on the prowl. The WAAF were billeted in Nissen huts with outside toilet facilities. Terrified to go outside during the night to use the toilet the girls had used a washing bowl to pee in throughout the night. The next morning one of the girls who'd come in late from leave recounted how, hot and tired from a long train journey, she'd nevertheless had a quick wash in the water left in the bowl! When the girls told her what type of water was actually in the bowl the poor girl simply said,

'I wondered why I couldn't work up a lather with my soap!'

Ronnie was working on a farm many miles away from us and I missed him terribly. Ron was lovely and would occasionally send home a 'bunny' he'd shot to help eke out our meagre meat ration.

The 'boot & shoes':

With no job to go to it was left to mam to take on the role of Youth Employment Officer and so I tagged along behind she who had always worked in 'the shoes,' and was duly presented at a local boot and shoe factory where, against nil competition, I was taken on as a warehouse boy cum trainee packer. Sadly, I never quite got the hang of tying a 'figure of eight' slip knot. I think it was the bit to do with the left over right (or was it the right over left?) that threw me. Whichever it was I found that by pulling on the string end that should've tightened the noose around the stack of shoe boxes, I pulled the whole lot undone leaving me scrabbling around on the floor under the accusing glare of my immediate superior, picking up both boxes and shoes, whilst at the same time trying to match the shoes by sizes.

Now, a word about my superior packer: In all the time, well actually the very short time, I worked in 'the shoes', I don't think that miserable old so and so said one kind word to me. Mentally I thought of him as 'old constipation chops' for the simple reason his screwed-up face reminded me of someone straining hard! I did, however, learn which button needed to be pressed in the lift to take me up to the next floor which was a shrieking screaming horror of a place full of noisy machinery, one of which that had little gas jets alight on which the shoes were quickly pulled over to get rid of minor threads and imperfections.

The room stank of the toilets located in the corner, but I have to say the male operatives were a friendly lot. Even friendlier was a young girl who worked in the packing room. She took a definite shine to me, as demonstrated by her singing a 'Carmen Miranda' song that went, 'I, I, I, I, I, I, like you very much', and each time she made a point of brushing past me.

Hard luck gel! Like most boys my age I'd been left in no doubt that any contact with a person of the opposite sex could mean babies! I could only look and dream but not touch! Just as well really, for one week after starting the job I was ready with my coat on to go home for my dinner when a lorry pulled in which needed unloading. Without being asked I offered to stay on and help only to be told snidely by 'old constipation chops',

'No, no me laddo, if you're not sitting at the head of the table when the victuals are ladled out, there will be hell to pay!'

This touched me on the raw and without further ado I told him what he could do with the job and the lorry. (and with the latter sideways in) After only one week I was again looking for work!

Engineering:

Next, I worked for a small engineering firm, and once again it was mam who got me the job. Honestly, I think she used to have nightmares of me being unemployed. The boss was one of God's Gentlemen who, prior to starting up in 'precision engineering' had worked as a stoker in a local dye works but the war had given him opportunities and he'd had the guts to take a chance.

The only chap in the place until I started working there was Jim and it was he who was bringing the money into the business through his skills as an engineer. This meant Jim could order me about with no objections from our erstwhile boiler stoker as I was to find out on virtually my first day when Jim handed me five shillings and told me I was to go the corner of such and such a street where 'Gertie' would meet me. Having satisfied myself that 'Gertie' really was 'Gertie' I was to hand her the five shillings and 'get a receipt'. I was to find out later that Jim had put Gertie 'in the club' and the child was now 6 months old.

In my next few months as a trainee engineer Jim added to my 'Facts of Life' knowledge by recounting details of his sexual liaison with Gertie during cosy tea break chats! It made me fantasise about what 'IT' would be like if only I dare... but I daren't!

As this was about all I was learning here I decided it was in my best interest to look for work elsewhere, and so in spite of mam's protestations, I handed in my notice!

Bread delivery boy:

Christmas had passed and the weather was deteriorating. It was the time of year anyone else, other than this idiot, would've looked for work as close to a hot radiator as possible! Say 'hello' to an idiot, dear friends... 'Bread round delivery boys wanted' ran the advert, so I applied and got a job at the Co-op bakery.

On the first morning I turned up at 6am as instructed where I was introduced to my immediate superior, 'Sid', who regarded me with the deepest suspicion and told me to 'stand there whilst I fetch the horse and delivery cart'. As I did so a lad a year or so older than me sidled up and asked,

'Who've you got for a mate then kid?'''

'Some bloke named Sid.' I told him.

'Oh Christ! Bugger your bloody luck' said my new acquaintance, 'I had the old bugger all last week and he nearly sent me mad. All he can talk about is his daughter who was jilted at the alter by her fiancé. Mind you, with him as a prospective bloody Pa in law, I reckon I would've done a runner as well!'

Our conversation ended there with the emergence of Sid leading his horse and bread cart. Kitted up with a brown smock and a leather cash satchel draped around his neck, we set off. We also had a 'float' so we could give change to those who 'paid' daily for their bread. This was not coin of the realm but the silver coloured oval discs of different monetary values purchased with the weekly groceries at the local Co-op stores upon which 'divvy' was paid at the end of the year. I didn't know until then that horses are first in the 'who can fart the loudest and the longest stakes!' Being January and war-time the early morning was a deeply depressing time of the day. The streets were empty of traffic and thank goodness for it because every so often the iron rimmed cartwheels would run into the tramline grooves and the whole 'kit and kaboodle' would pull to one side. Fortunately, to counter the early light snow and ice, steel studs had been screwed into the horse's hooves.

Our first stop was up a cobbled gateway at the side of a cinema at the back of which was a bakehouse where cakes and pastries were made. It was warm and well-lit due to the blackout curtains and shades still being in place, and I was glad to get some of the early morning chill out of my bones. As though by magic my erstwhile friend popped up again,

'Has he started to tell you about his daughter yet?' he whispered.

'Give us a chance mate' I whispered back, 'I've only known him a few minutes.'

'A few seconds is usually long enough' he replied and then looking furtively around, my new friend pushed a large, still hot from the oven, jam bun into my hand, warning me not to let anyone see me eating it. I didn't.

Fully loaded, we again set off, arriving at our first street for deliveries. I was to deliver down the one side and Sid down the other. I went down a long entry and rapped smartly on the door which was opened by an elderly grandma type of lady.

'Good morning, Madam, do you need any bread today?' I asked.

'Oh, what a nice lad' came her reply, 'You're a big improvement on the other cheeky little devil! What about a nice hot cup of tea, ay?'

To this day I don't know what made me say it but say it I did....

'Oh, that's very kind, but I'd feel so guilty drinking a hot cup of tea whilst my mate, Mr Sid, is just as cold and thirsty as I am!'

'Then fetch him over, you thoughtful boy' she said, and I duly obliged. So, there we sat, Sid and I, right in front of a blazing fire, drinking that sainted lady's tea. Sid, I might add, was regarding me with real respect for, up until then, I don't think he'd ever had a tea spot. I was home and dry, and if you want further proof of that then let me tell you that hardly were we back on the cart when Sid leaned back, lit a cigarette and began,

'The tragedy in my family is my daughter was jilted at the alter!'

I loved that job and quickly found I had a knack of getting on with my customers. Sid was happy too, even more so when, upon cashing up at the end of each working day, my 'pay in' was always spot on. But all good things come to an end eventually and the writing was on the wall. Just a week after starting mam was taken into hospital gravely ill. Our house was closed up and I was sent to lodge with my Aunt Annie and Uncle Wal. The distance to my workplace was doubled and due to the early morning start and with no public transport that early in the morning, I had to walk. This didn't go down at all well with my Uncle who, after a week or so of getting up with me at 5am in the morning began to lament,

'There's not much point in going to bed at night if I have to get up this bloody early to see you off to work!'

Pressure was put on from all sides to 'pack the job in' and get a job that started at 8 o'clock!

When I told Sid I was leaving, I thought he would cry.

'My life's one long tragedy' he lamented, 'no sooner do I get a first-class lad like you than I lose you!'

He was placated somewhat when I told him he was the nicest bloke any youngster could hope to work for, and I meant it. I'd not developed any strong feelings for the horse however, so didn't even give him a pat when passing, hoping his extreme flatulence was not catching for it was most embarrassing chatting up the daughters of my customers and watching them double up with laughter as the brute farted and farted and farted!

Oh yes, a leaving present! I was given a piece of fruit cake kept back by Sid especially for me to take home! Housewives would've fought over that particular commodity with it being the war years, and the big boss who set me on told me,

'You can come back at any time son! You've been first-class!'

Now it was me who was nearly shedding tears. Four jobs in five months, not bad I suppose!

Factory errand boy:

I started in my new job based in the packing room whilst also doing the firm's errands on a bike with a basket. It was all very interesting. I took my orders directly from the cashier each morning around 10 o'clock when I would take into my charge a large leather wallet in which were cheques sent to the senior firm, plus some small petty cash which I also had to deliver to the parent company in town. Although I was based in the packing room I regularly came into contact with staff from the office. I was in the peculiar position of working for both but not truly belonging to either. I was soon to decide where my loyalties lay. 'Up the Workers!'

The cashier from the office called me into his room one day and asked,

'Do you know where such and such a street is?'

As it happened I did, so he handed me a sealed envelope, holding it out with the tips of his fingers as though contact with me might contaminate him.

'The address is on the envelope. Just hand it to the shopkeeper and he'll know what to give you.'

I completed my errands and, leaving his job until last, finally arrived at my destination. I was surprised to find it was a shop rumoured to sell 'men's things' - a shop men slid into, rather than entered, as you will see.

Having been given the low down by Engineer Jim on the 'birds and the bees', I already knew what 'men's things' were.

I handed over the sealed envelope to a male shop assistant who wore spectacles with thick glass lenses but even then he needed to hold the note contained within right up against his nose to read it. He disappeared from view only to re-emerge a moment or so later resealing the same envelope, which he handed to me. I took it and left, tossing the envelope into the bike basket before setting off back to base. I was pushing hard on the pedals going up the cobbled street when I noticed the envelope which had been juddering around in the basket, was coming unsealed and the contents peeking out. This was a box some 8 inches long and 3 inches wide which, being nosey I stopped my bike and liberated from the envelope. I lifted the lid and inside, reclining upon a bed of white powder (French chalk) lay what we more common kids called 'a froggie'! A red, fully extended, all ready for action, contraceptive! The rubber it was made from was so thick I guessed at once it was washable, and it did rather cross my mind that wearing a thick monster like that whilst performing the 'act of love' (or in streetwise jargon - having a poke) would be like paddling in the sea wearing 'wellies'. I replaced the lid but no matter how hard I tried that darned envelope flap would not seal down again so I was left with no choice but to take it into the cashier's office just as it was. I was all ready to bluff out what I knew would be an interrogation as to why the envelope was open but thank goodness the office was empty, so I left it on his desk and ran.

Back in the packing room I checked to see if 'Perce had had another fit in my absence. Perce was an epileptic and his turns horrified and yet fascinated me. I suppose due to the war and manpower shortages the company were glad to employ anyone who could even stand up occasionally. Normally, the first indication we had that 'Perce had 'gone off' was the sight of a pair of feet sticking out from under a bench, juddering and jumping about. Another character in the packing room was Tom. Tom was a bit of a 'Jack the Lad' who's favourite target was Mary, a young woman who worked in the next room. Hardly would she appear before Tom would invite her into his love nest, a space he'd made in the crates and wooden box room known only to our hero, for the entrance was cunningly concealed. However, any searcher could easily find the entrance by following the strong smell of Saint Bruno pipe tobacco to which Tom was addicted. He smoked this even though several signs stating 'Smoking Strictly Forbidden' were clearly displayed. In answer to which Tom would simply retort, 'F*ck 'em!'

I was just recounting the 'froggie' story to Tom when the internal phone rang and I was ordered to come upstairs as the cashier wanted me! I went in fear and trepidation to the office where his nibs sat glaring up at me.

'I made it quite clear in the letter you took from me that the envelope was to be sealed down when it was returned. What have you got to say to that?'

'Please Sir, I don't know about that. I took your letter into the shop and the man handed it back to me just as I put it on your desk.'

'Did you look in the envelope?' was his next question.

'Look inside Sir?' I replied, 'I didn't Sir, I didn't even notice the envelope was open until I put it on your desk!'

He stared at me for what seemed to be hours, and then said,

'Alright, you may go.'

I went at a rate of knots.

A day later the cashier came into the packing room for something or other and would you believe it, that prat Tom stood laughing at him. Of course Tom was asked,

'What are you laughing at?"

Tom made some silly excuse but by the way his nibs glared at me, I knew he'd guessed I'd not only seen inside the envelope but also told Tom, who I now knew could not be trusted to keep a confidence.

One of the office men seemed vaguely familiar to me. He was a big bloke who, when not working, seemed to spend a lot of time telling Lucy (a very sexy office girl) that he'd 'like to give a good tanning', or making other such threats that, even to innocent me, carried sexual undertones. It was all a big act to disguise his true sexual orientation as I found out one day when, working alone in a side room, our friend came in and, seeing me up a step ladder, reached up and grabbed my 'goolies'. I kicked out backwards, catching him in the face, thus telling him in no uncertain terms 'hands off.'

Following this my mind went back to when I was 12 years old. I was sitting in the local cinema watching the film 'The Great American Broadcast' starring Alice Faye, my favourite heartthrob. A chap next to me had asked 'excuse me, do you have a light?' I'd replied in the negative. Ten minutes later, this bloke took out a cigarette and lit it. Next, he asked 'would you like a piece of chocolate?' It was wartime and chocolate was rationed, but I said 'no thanks.' This bloke then began to 'otch' about and as he did so, he draped his raincoat over his and my lap. Then it started. He put his hand on my thigh and slowly started to inch it higher and higher. Would you believe it. It was just about here my dream girl, Alice, appeared on the screen wearing a vest which only just covered her shapely bottom. I jammed my elbow down onto my upper thigh trapping his hand between my leg and under his mac. He could go no further but in fighting for my virtue he'd made it impossible for me to extract the greatest pleasure a twelve year-old boy could get from the film. The lights went up for the interval and the man grabbed his mac and went elsewhere, no doubt to look for another innocent boy.

Yes, I'd recognised him. The office bloke and the dirty mac operative were one and the same person.

I was later moved into the offices as an office boy but couldn't stand the snobbishness of those who in my view were in there just to dodge the Forces. One day I was given an awful 'rollocking' in front of everyone in the office after standing up to the biggest dodger of them all, 'Tom,' but the final straw was being ill for a week with chest trouble and not being paid. Was the cashier paying off that old score? In went my notice.

Before I left my employment as 'office boy' I had one more duty to perform. Working in the main factory as general 'dogs bodies' were 14 year old twin brothers who were very, very poor. They were always anxious to please and with the exception of an obnoxious bully who was a full year older than them, were generally left to get on with their work. On this particular day, the twins' lives were being made hell and I decided to remonstrate with their tormentor. For my pains I was told,

'Mind your own f*cking business or I'll punch your f*cking head in!'

Now, I hate fighting but I've never ever run away from a bully such as this character. 'Right!' I said, 'after work, on the park, let's see who's gonna get their head punched in!'

That evening we were on the Spinney Hill Park trying to knock the living daylights out of each other. Just as a spectator called the warning 'look out, here comes the Parky' (Park Keeper) I let one go, right on the end of his nose! He bled like a stuck pig. Fight over, he ran one way and I ran the other with the Parky in hot pursuit! He'd no chance of catching us though, after all he was nicknamed 'Old Biscuit Feet' by all the kids who used the park!

Builder's labourer:

Whilst glancing through the 'situations vacant' column in the local rag, a local lad I knew told me he was being 'called up' and his boss, a jobbing builder, would be wanting someone to take his place. I hadn't a clue what a builder's labourer would need to know or do but I went to the boss's house to be interviewed.

I was promised that if I worked hard he'd have me indentured (apprenticed) but with recent memories of another such promise (as an 'apprentice engineer') I took those words with a pinch of salt.

On my first day, riding on an old bone shaker of a 'sit up and beg' bike, I peddled some 4 miles to where I was to meet the 'brickie'. I was to labour for dear old Ernie. The first thing Ernie did after I introduced myself was to grope down into the deep recesses of his brown bib and brace overall from whence he produced a very battered but shiny tin from which he extracted a Park Drive cigarette. Holding this in his right hand he placed the end between his already well moistened lips and twisted it slowly round and round, so the end was thoroughly wet with his spittle.

'Why do you do that Ernie?' I asked.

'For the simple reason lad that if I don't and go to take the fag out of my mouth quickly, then I'm liable to pull half my lip off with it!'

Having smoked the occasional cigarette myself I knew he was quite right and painful it can be, leaving one with a very sore lip indeed. A lesson learned.

Another piece of 'brickie lore' which was drummed into me time and time again by Ernie was to 'always keep the bricks wet as they stick together better.' In fact even today, decades later, when passing builders putting up walls I cannot resist saying, 'keep wetting the bricks mate!' This advice has often brought, with no malice intended, a response of 'why don't you p*** off and mind your own 'expletive' business!'

My builder boss was cashing in on the shortage of skilled men, most serving in the Armed Forces, although he seemed to do damn all himself! The money was pouring in from the efforts of my mate Ernie and old Bill, who must've been nearly 80!

Bill was never too proud to tell anyone interested that he'd always been and still was, a labourer, although from what I'd seen he was as good as any time served man, and as nice as Ernie was. Bill was full of advice and one of his favourite sayings was, 'don't sing anything as sad as 'tah rah rah boom dee aye'; sing something cheerful like 'don't bury me deep'.

At odd times I was sent to assist Bill and to see him scaffolding a house using only great long poles and rope was an education. One property was a very high, four-storey building that Bill, his grandson and I were to 'point up' right to the roof. However, when we got up to where the slope of the roof met the brickwork we found holes which showed where birds were going into the roof space to nest and we could hear the young chicks cheeping inside. To cement these holes up would be, to our minds, 'murder of the innocent' so we left the entrances open. The scaffolding was finally taken down and that was that... or so we thought!

A week later the boss came tearing round to where we were working,

'Why did you leave those holes for the bloody birds to get into the roof?' he screamed.

Both myself and Bill's grandson feigned ignorance.

'The birds must've dug the mortar out again boss,' we said.

'Bloody liars' he retorted, 'you did it on purpose! Now I've got to ladder up there, or rather you're going up, and fill those bloody holes in!'

We had to go with him but watched as he lashed three ladders together and raised them up to the roof. He then mixed some sand and cement together and, turning to old Bill's grandson said,

'Right, up you go!"

At this he was met with 'Not on your bloody life boss! It ain't safe!'

Now it was my turn...

'Right, you can go up!'

'Not on the pittance you pay me I'm not' I replied.

He had no choice but go up himself! I'm darned glad it wasn't me up there, and just to liven things up me and the other boy kept shaking the ladder and calling out,

'Tell you what boss, the wind ain't half got up! Hold on tight now! We'd hate to have to tell your missus you fell and broke your neck!'

The main part of my job was mixing up the 'three and one' for Ernie (ie three of sand and one of cement) whilst in between times throwing gallons of water over the bricks to keep them wet! Honestly, with each stack of bricks you could hear a hissing sound as they sucked the water in.

Every brick had to be 'handed' off the lorry and the boss would go stark raving bonkers if even one brick was chipped. There was none of this business of tipping them off as is quite common practice today. Instead we'd throw them to each other four at a time, side by side. My goodness, some of those brick sides were so damned sharp they'd cut like a knife!

Mainly we were building low brick walls at the front of houses to replace the iron railings taken for the war effort. The walls were about four-and-a-half-foot high and topped with blue bricks laid edge on to make a nice pattern. I remember having to put every ounce of sand through a riddle, thus removing the small stones that might otherwise mar the smooth mortar.

'Can you paint, you useless bugger?' thus spake my boss one day, 'Only I've got a job for you!'

Now, as it happened, I'd done a bit of painting at school and in my innocence I thought this was what he meant, otherwise I wouldn't have answered 'yes boss' so eagerly. Without further ado I was dragged off to a three bedroomed semi-detached house, shown a ladder and a pile of grotty old paint tins, and left quite alone with the parting words of his nibs, 'You can paint this bugger then!'

Can you imagine anyone other than my boss leaving a 15 year old boy alone and unsupervised to paint a whole blasted house? Well, as told, I painted the bloody thing and my boss was overjoyed, as was the lady of the house which now 'stood out' in all its newly painted splendour!

Had that money grabbing boss of mine dared to advertise 'painting by time served tradesman' on the front of my masterpiece I would've demanded a rise but sadly he didn't. What I did get was yet another monstrosity of a house to paint which, being three storeys high at the front and four storeys at the back in a sunken yard, finally put paid to me as a craftsman painter.

Here I was on the top of the tallest ladder with no-one 'standing' the bottom rung. I held on like grim death with one hand and had a paint brush in the other! As the wind got up I looked down and thought, Oh dear, oh dear, oh dear, it's a very long way to fall!

To cut a long story short, I managed to finish the job, but as far as I was concerned my neck came before the boss's profits! I had to agree with the swine though when he shouted,

'You've got more bleeding paint over yourself than the bricks! And look at the bleeding pavement!'

Perhaps my comment of 'it's very colourful, isn't it' was the wrong thing to say and I'm sure the next job the boss gave me, of helping old Bill clean out a 'backed up' sewer pipe, was just to make a point!

Together, me and Bill lifted off the square manhole trap. I for one wished we hadn't, for the dirty water below, containing that which I'll leave to your imagination, had come right to the top of the inspection chamber. Bill made no comment and simply lay full length on the slabs alongside with a great deal of groaning and grunting then, with a short length of rodding bamboo, began to see just how deep the s**t was! It was very deep, so deep in fact he had to ask me to roll his shirt sleeve up and still he hadn't reached bottom! Finally, with the pipe leading out located, further lengths of bamboo rodding were screwed on and the rods, one after another, vanished into the scummy water until, with a loathsome sucking noise and the rapid disappearance of the you know what, SUCCESS!

Slowly Bill stood up and stretched his aching back, then smoothed down his 'Bruce Bairnsfather' (of Great War fame) moustache. With his immaculate self restored, Bill started pulling out the rods, humming as he did so whilst wiping off what was sticking to them with his bare hands. Finished, he wiped his gory hands down the sides of his brown overalls and without further ado, apart from a 'time to eat, boy,' he reached for his old lunch bag, dug out a hunk of bread, an onion and some cheese and, using his pocket knife, began to cut off and feed small pieces into his mouth!

Although Ernie was rather contemptuous of Bill, I liked the old boy! Bill was never afraid to tell the boss what he thought of him and the boss put up with it, probably because he knew that with the men away from home fighting for King and country, old Bill was a pearl beyond price.

Ernie, who was pushing fifty, told me he'd gone to America prior to the Great War and when work was short he'd worked as an extra in films but with the outbreak of War he'd joined the Army and fought on the Western Front. I saw no reason to doubt him. Although eager to know about his exploits I was to be disappointed for Ernie, like other ex-soldiers, had been mentally scarred by all he'd gone through and would only talk about places including the terrible battles in and around Villers Bretonneux.

It was from Ernie I learned many of the ditties the soldiers sang: 'You've got a kind face you old Bastard, you ought to be f*cking well shot, or tied to a public convenience, and left till you f*cking well rot!' (this was for the Sergeant Major) Another was 'Mademoiselle from Armentieres, Parley-voo, who hadn't been kissed for forty years, parley-voo'.

I have to say here I'm sure Ernie was singing these ditties whilst his mind was back in the trenches. Often his eyes would flood with tears for no reason I could see. Of course, the tears could've been for his late wife as Ernie was a widower but, first and foremost, to me he was a good mate. He never got cross or raised his voice if the 'mix' was a bit sloppy or thick.

It was that man again; the cloud upon the horizon,

'You! Come on with me! Let's see if you can bugger this job up!'

I bit back a retort and off we set, arriving at an empty house.

'Now,' said the Gaffer, 'I want you to whitewash this ceiling and paint the living room door. Can you manage that? The whitewash is mixed so do the ceiling first.'

Off he went and I began whitewashing the ceiling as instructed. On completion it looked good, very good, but as the whitewash began to dry, greasy patches started showing through the large ornamental plaster ceiling 'rose!' What the heck?!

I painted it again but with the same result. After four attempts it still looked a mess and then the penny dropped. Originally, the house lighting had been gas, and over the years the grease from the gas had contaminated the plaster. What to do?

I managed to find some bits of old soap, washed the rose down and tried again. It was still a mess. Next, I found some sugar soap amongst the dribs and drabs the gaffer had left, so I washed it down with that and tried again. It was hopeless! Seemingly the rose would have to come down and a new one be fitted, or it be left off altogether as many in those days did. Two days later and I was still on that blasted rose! Then the 'bad penny' turned up.

'What the f*cking hell have you been doing?' he demanded.

'Getting more and more fed up!' I replied. 'This rose is full of gas grease and if you think you can do any better, here's the f*cking brush!'

This just left the door to be painted.

'I've mixed the paint for you,' said the Gaffer after calming down.

May I just say at this point that in wartime Britain paint was at a premium. You couldn't just buy it like today and so what I was presented with were the dregs from all the old part used paint tins he could dredge up, and I mean dredge up! In fact to this day the nearest colour I could put to that paint was the colour of the 'sludge' old Bill had rodded out the sewer!

With the boss gone and after washing down the door with sugar soap, I started painting, determined that the so and so would have no cause for complaint over my painting skills. The paint went on like a dream. Upon completion it looked gorgeous and when his nibs returned he was thrilled, so thrilled in fact it crossed my mind that maybe I should ask him for a rise! Of course, his answer would've been 'NO' so I didn't bother.

My part done I went back to Ernie who, in my absence, had been paired up with old Bill's grandson!

Ernie welcomed me with open arms and muttering,

'I tell you what son, if I'd had to put up with that insolent little sod one more day, I'd have packed the bloody lot in!'

My state of euphoria lasted a week and then my nemesis was screaming insults at me once again.

'That bleeding door you painted! The bloody paint ain't dried yet!'

'But it looked lovely, boss! You even said the gloss finish was a masterpiece!'

'Well, it ain't dried! What did you do to that paint?'

I'd had enough...

'Hang on' I said. 'You mixed the blasted paint! All I had to do was wash the door down with sugar soap, wash it with clear water, let it dry and then, using your paint, the paint that you mixed, paint it! So, don't you bloody well blame me!'

That momentarily shut him up, and then he said,

'I strained it, I put some driers in it, I put some thinners in and stirred it well! It looked fine!'

Here the penny dropped!

'Hang on Gaffer,' I said, 'Where did you get the thinner from to put in the paint?'
'Why?' he said, 'It was from that sauce bottle with thinner in I brought from the store I keep at home.'

With this he went into the kitchen of the house in question and produced a sauce bottle half full of what he said was 'thinner'. I hardly dared tell him, but I had to.

'No wonder that paint hasn't dried, boss,' I said, 'That isn't the bottle you brought from the paint store, that's an old bottle I got out the dustbin. I took it down to the local bike shop and put some oil in it to oil my bike wheels. You put my lubricating oil in that paint. No wonder it won't dry!'

Just for a moment I thought he was going to kill me but I'm still here, so he didn't!

He had to wash all the paint off himself and I was never again asked to do a bit of painting!

In fairness to the Gaffer I have to say that although up to now it would seem he and I were always at logger heads, I think each of us had a sneaking liking for each other. He was the sort of a bloke who would do nice things, things you would least expect! Also, at the drop of a hat, he would come out with the most outrageous sayings!

For example, whilst standing watching me pulling hard at a grossly overladen wheelbarrow he would have me near hysterical with laughter with his 'that's it young man, pull as if you're pulling the bloke next door off your sister!'

(This was one of the few printable sayings, and even this one's been edited!)

I was with the Gaffer one day and we were walking through the town centre when coming towards us was an elderly gentleman who my boss addressed with the greatest respect, even going so far as to call him 'Sir'. The elderly man was very smart and wearing an overcoat trimmed with what looked like black fur on the collar. He wore a Homberg hat and his shoes shone like glass, but were they shoes? He seemed to be wearing spats! The most noticeable feature though were his eyes, for they seemed to be slightly out of true; one looked slightly one way to the other. Even to me, the old boy spelled 'money!'

As the two were talking the old boy pulled out a gold cigarette case, even though he was already smoking a cigar, and offered one to my non-smoker boss. No sooner had he accepted a light than the boss clipped his fag and slipped it to me. (see what I mean about doing the occasional nice thing?) The conversation finished and we separated. Waiting until we were out of earshot the boss said,

'That was one of Old King Edward VII bastards by one of his fancy women! He gets a pension from the Crown!'

Ernie had sent me into town to pay his union dues. The union man was a chatty sort of bloke who asked me if the boss had arranged for me to be indentured. I answered in the negative, so he gave me some advice:

'Son, if he doesn't have you indentured then you'll be a dogsbody for the rest of the time he employs you! Tell him straight – Indenture you or stick your job!'

I got all the papers together for being indentured and gave them to my boss to read. Little did I know until years later when talking to a brickie who'd later worked for the boss that the Gaffer could neither read nor write. The writing was on the wall! (only the boss couldn't read it!)

I'd been given one of the rottenest jobs I was ever to be handed. The house in which I was now was empty and awaiting the arrival of the plasterer who was to plaster the kitchen. My part in all of this was to prepare the bare brick kitchen walls for the plasterer to 'lay it on' which meant I was given a small tool which looked not unlike a hammer with which to knock chips out of every brick in that damn wall. Nowadays they have a special adhesive which is painted on.

By the end of the morning my hands were covered in blisters whilst every so often I was spitting brick dust on the floor. By knocking off time my hands were bleeding and I'd still only chipped one side of the four walls. This decided me. Looking through the local paper every night became a ritual as I wanted 'out' but this time I wanted it on my terms.

'Join the Army as a boy apprentice and be trained in all aspects of motor engineering. Apply to your nearest Army Recruiting Office' said the notice! My luck was in, for the Army Recruiting Office was just around the corner from where Ernie and I were working. Was this what I was looking for? It sounded about right because, daft as it sounds, whilst so many men who I'd come into contact seemed to do nothing else but scheme on ways to dodge the forces, yours truly couldn't wait until he was old enough to be 'called up!'

I told Ernie what I had in mind and with no hesitation he said,

'Go for it boy, if that's what you really want!'

Without further ado after first washing my face and combing my hair, I set off. I entered the door marked 'Entry' (well, you would, wouldn't you) and found myself in a highly polished hall with two tables set out with various forms all ready to deal with the expected rush of applicants, of which I seemed to be the first. Where was everybody? The place seemed empty.

I looked for a bell to ring... no luck... so I shouted, 'anyone home?' No reply! Next, I hammered on the desk, making enough noise to wake the dead. Believe me, I was in that empty hall for over 10 minutes, shouting, whistling and for good measure, singing Ernie's theme tune... 'You've got a kind face you old bastard!' Nothing! With the 'balls up' at Dunkirk and Singapore now explained, I walked out. If that was the Army then stuff em!!

It was Friday! The traditional day our wages were paid! Late as usual, the man with our pittance of a wage turned up. Ernest was paid first and then me. Now, the week before I'd stayed on for a short while to help unload bricks from a lorry that'd been involved in an accident. As many of the bricks were covered in blood my boss had told me he would grant a bit of overtime. This worked out at four old pennies or two new pence in today's money. I counted the contents of my wage packet no extra four pence! As our wages were made up by the boss's wife

I felt I needed to point out the mistake.

'Boss, your missus hasn't put that bit of overtime in my wages!' I began.

'Is that all you buggers think about!? Bleeding money!' He screamed back!

That did it!

'All we think about?' I shouted back, 'Why, you tight fisted, Army dodging sh*t!
I'm doing a man's work on slave labour wages! You want bloody shooting! You
can stick your lousy job!'

I thought he was going to have a go at me, but I was already holding a shovel to
defend myself. He looked to Ernie for support, but Ernie was on my side. I could
only trust myself to say,

'Have my tickets (cards) ready for next Friday!'

I then went home.

Several days later the following week, my last week, the boss came to where I
was labouring for Ernie and tried to engage me in conversation but I just ignored
him. Come Friday I left.

I didn't see the boss again for another twenty years and then one day, cycling
home, there he was with another chap fitting a stone doorstep to a property. He
was having difficulty fitting it in and was pulling away as hard as he could. How
could I resist it! I shouted out as loud as I could,

'That's it Gaffer, pull as if you're pulling the bloke next door off your sister!'

Chapter 2: Training for the Merchant Navy

Tail between my legs I went back to my old boss in engineering. He pointed out I'd left of my own accord but was willing to take me back on. Since I'd left a new partner had joined the firm. He was a qualified engineer and I quickly saw that whatever money he'd put into the firm he was determined to get it back tenfold as quickly as possible...... and I was the means he'd use to achieve that goal. From somewhere he'd acquired a 'Ward Capstan' lathe. It was second hand as the good stuff went to the bigger firms but was too good to dispose of, and so it came our way, for, small as our firm was, it was still contributing to the war effort. The 'capstan' was set up and I went through the series of movements, i.e. pull this lever out... turn this wheel... shove that rod in... turn this other wheel... put the drill through... pull that lever... adjust the flow of suds (cooling fluid) ... start sequence again... During this procedure the new partner stood over me with a stopwatch, timing me so he could work out how much to pay me on piece work. Here we go again! Because what I turned out was earning me money based on my production, I worked like a mad man, but always in the strict order outlined above. By the third day I was absolutely whacked out because, believe it or not, on retiring to my bed at night, I was doing the whole blasted sequence in my sleep!

Again, all the promises came to nought, for the money I was earning didn't match up with what I'd been promised. Once again I saw I was wasting my time but then salvation loomed upon the horizon.

It was Saturday early evening and I was listening to the wireless. The programme was called 'shipmates ashore', a programme devoted to the Merchant Navy and hosted by Miss Doris Hare, who later in the 1970s was the mother figure in the television comedy 'On the Buses'. My ears pricked up, for mention was being made of the Merchant Navy training ship which took on 'boy entrants' aged around sixteen years to train for the catering or deck departments. The courses lasted from six weeks to two or three months. An address was given, which I duly noted down, and I wrote off for an application form. Not only did the form arrive within a week but also enclosed was a brochure showing happy smiling boys wearing blue working gear or blue striped blouses which I learned later were called 'piss jackets!' Why? Don't ask me!

By this time mam had remarried and moved out and I was living with my sister Maisie. Maisie had been discharged from the WAAFs after marrying Stoker Petty Officer Les Foreman and now had a young baby. Little did Maisie know that within a year poor 'Les' would be lost at sea during the D Day landings, going down with his ship HMS Pylades.

I took the form to my doctor so he could certify I was breathing and was accepted into the Merchant Navy. Now to tell the boss! His reaction?

'No, my lad, you can't go! You're in a reserved occupation and more useful here rather than messing and buggering about singing, 'a life on the ocean wave'.

That did it,

'I'm going to appeal!' I said, 'I want to go to sea, and I'm going to sea!'

Maisie, bless her, supported my stance, in fact it was she who pointed out whilst vetting my application, that the doctor had put a wrong measurement for my chest expansion, and so with her support we went off down to the appeals section of the local employment exchange. We were ushered in and at first the chap we saw was adamant,

'Your employer says he wants to keep you and so I must refuse your desire to leave him.'

With so many lousy, frustrating jobs behind me, I just stuck to my guns.

'Mister' I said, 'If you don't say I can leave to go into the Merchant Navy, then I'm telling you now I will refuse to go to work. I am not going back!'

The gentleman appealed to my sister,

'Can't you make him see reason?'

At this point I suddenly realised the board money I paid to Maisie must've been a tremendous help as she was only getting a pittance from the government and had a small baby to provide for. Nevertheless, with no hesitation she said,

'If he says something then he means it! He's only being used as cheap labour; I know just how little he earns!'

Then she played a card I'd never even thought of playing...

'When he was a little boy of seven, he had to go into the Sanatorium with consumption. If he went to sea it would be a far healthier environment than him working in that smelly enclosed engineering barn of a place!' (all of this was

36

true)

I was given permission to leave the engineering.

A week or so later I got my orders plus a train warrant to join the training ship Vindicatrix berthed at Sharpness Docks in Gloucester. I was up early on the day I was to join her and walked across Spinney Hill Park which was deserted, it being so early in the morning. I confess to thinking whether I was doing the right thing, and then all doubts resolved I set off more confidently for the station with just a small plywood case my brother in law had made in his spare time at sea. I didn't know it at the time but Les was already dead.

Change at Birmingham, change at Gloucester, change at Berkeley Roads, into Sharpness along with several other boys who'd joined the train at various stations along the way, to be met at Sharpness and escorted back to the docks by the Chief Steward who chatted quite easily with us as we walked.

We were to find out in due course that in the Merchant Navy there were no 'bullshit' Officers being addressed by their rank, Chief, Third, Second, or whatever. The Merchant Navy was a civilian service and thus not subservient to military laws. It's worth noting however that the slaughter of our Merchant shipping during both World Wars was appalling. Had these seamen refused to sail and not brought in the food, ammunition, tanks, guns, clothing etc, then the Wars would've been lost. Based upon the numbers of men engaged, the Merchant Navy had the worst casualties of all the services. Over the years I've heard many ex-Servicemen spilling a line over the appalling conditions they had to endure upon first 'joining up' but for myself, I will simply tell the truth as to how it was for me.

The new entrants were lined up against a hut just inside the gates of what was to prove to be the land part of the camp whilst our names and personal details were checked off against a list by the Chief Steward. Amongst other things he was in charge of ordering the food allocated to the Merchant ships and making out the daily menus for the ships cook.

The Chief Steward was assisted by his wife and one of two girls who popped in and out of the office hut, never once making eye contact with we appreciative boys. We were duly informed no contact was to be made with the office girls and as to the local girls no contact was to be made during training! They thought we were all reform school throw outs anyway!

With everyone duly accounted for we received a few words of welcome before being led off to one of a few newly built huts where we laid out our kit on very new bunk beds. No complaints so far.

In a boisterous group we were then walked through the camp. Merchant seamen never marched for, as I was told later, 'you can't get the buggers out of the pubs long enough to teach them!'   We went down a slight, rough slope and then, as we started to edge our way along some lock gates, we saw her - 'The Training Ship Vindicatrix' afloat on the Sharpness Canal.

With not much time to take it all in we were led up the gang plank, turned right past some obvious serving hatches and saw stretching before us, a long mess deck containing scrupulously scrubbed tables and long forms on which to sit.

The mess tables were laid with plates upon which were thick slices of gammon and two large 'boiled in their skin' potatoes, interspersed with jars of yellow piccalilli, (take as much as you want lads) plates of bread & butter and big mugs of coffee to wash it all down.

With full tums and congratulating ourselves at having put away a repast such as some of the lads rarely, if ever, saw, our guide invited us to return to our hut, 'so as to write and let your folks know you've arrived safely!'

We fell for it, didn't we! Those new entrants with no paper to write on were given sheets by those who did. The letters were collected with most, if not all, extolling the catering arrangements, 'arrived safely, food is marvellous etc.' The trap had been set and fallen into, for, although supper being two slices of bread and dripping and another mug of coffee was perfectly acceptable, breakfast the next morning was not. What I got, as did every other new entrant of my group, was a bowl of milkless, sugarless porridge followed by a plate with one piece of bacon so salty it looked like it was covered in white frost, plus two 'boiled in their skins' potatoes. I cut into the first potato and it was rotten all the way through, whilst the second potato was only partially rotten so I was able to salvage a small amount. To be fair the mug of coffee was drinkable providing you didn't normally take sugar. Sent back to our cabin to prepare for the coming day I just had the time to scribble,

'Send food... starving! We were conned!'

Those tins previously containing dried national baby milk for baby Michael were a godsend for sending what bits of food the family could dispatch to keep our body and souls together.

Next step in the process was baring our arm for a smallpox vaccination, and Edward Jenner, the physician and scientist who developed the vaccination, had been born just along the road in Berkeley!

Next, as the clothes we'd arrived in weren't suitable for sea training purposes and Merchant Seamen didn't wear a 'provided by the State' uniform, work clothes had to be provided. Every boy who opted for the catering department was provided with two 'piss jackets.' These were short, striped, long sleeved, buttoned up, linen work coats, then two pairs of denim type work trousers, a pair of thick, black serge trousers (which were three inches too short in the leg), a white serving jacket which was the only decent bit of kit provided, a peaked cap and finally, if memory serves me right, a pair of thick black shoes. We also got a small kit bag with draw string to keep them in.

These items were a blessing for some of the boys as they'd arrived with virtually nothing. They had no change of clothes, no pyjamas and slept in the raw, they didn't even have a comb or toothbrush. Poor beggars! As lousy as the food was to many, to some it was a feast.

To give a bit of background history, 'Vindi' had started life as a sailing ship in the 19th century and during World War I the German Navy used her as a rest and recuperation ship for U-boat crews. Taken as a prize of War by Britain she was berthed in London and used as a sea training ship until 1939 when she was towed to Sharpness for safety. Only in the last week or so of training did the boys sleep on her. This was in very tinny, two tier bunks which rattled. As for Sharpness itself we didn't see very much of the place. Coastal ships coming in from the River Severn mainly berthed there.

'Vindi' was berthed on the canal and at the side of her was the traditional tow path, approximately two metres wide. Next was a dry-stone wall and over this wall was the River Severn thus, by tossing a stone under arm from the deck of the ship, the stone would land in the River Severn.

Catering boys had little contact with those lads who'd opted for deck duties. Those boys wore a black top and black woollen hat, and had a longer stay before being tested and passed on to the Merchant Navy pool offices in the sea ports.

Except in the huts, the toilets used by trainees could be found almost opposite the gangplank leading up to and into the ship. These were in a long, low, barn like, brick building and consisted of a long plank with holes cut into it at intervals under which could be seen large pans to receive whatever it was that came down. As you can imagine not a lot of time was wasted in that smelly place, although I can clearly remember one of our group in there for some time. He was a big fair-haired lad who was suffering from 'the 'Vindi's,' a particularly virulent form of diarrhoea, and claimed to be directly linked with the 'Vindi soup' into which we all maintained, as in the song; 'Anything Goes!' That poor blighter went in to his martyrdom at 9am and was still in there, fast asleep and worn out, at 11am.

In class we boys had to learn the quarter points of a compass, but as we never saw a compass, that wouldn't have been much use had we been torpedoed. We also learned how to 'step a mast' but that wasn't any use as we never had to do it.

41

Lifeboat construction... clinker or carvel, or flush or overlapping planking? Did it really matter? Afterall, would you stop and ask,

'Is this clinker? If so, I'll keep swimming as I prefer carvel!'

Finally, we had to learn the parts of a sail in small boats. These I promptly forgot and when called before the dreaded Captain Angel, stammering and stuttering as I was, he kicked me out of the exam room and confined me to ship until I did know the answer. This didn't upset me too much for on the reset I easily passed.

I was now coming to the end of my time as a trainee and all that was left for me to learn was how to set a table for Officers eating in the ship's saloon and which side to serve from. Having completed that I was sent to work out my time along with several other boys in the Galley.

At last I was to be near real food but was I hell! The Cook kept the keys to the storeroom close to his chest though I fear most of the food allocated to the ship for us boys never arrived, it likely having been 'flogged' on passage.

Cooking in the Galley was done in big steam cauldrons which looked not unlike big round bottom drums with lids screwed down and held by several large butterfly nuts. The Cook's 'piece de resistance' was suet duff, the recipe of which was kept a closely guarded secret until now. I will now reveal it to you, oh most fortunate of readers:

Prepare several large, empty, catering size corned beef tins, avoiding as you do so the sharp, jagged, edges, as the rust around the top could give a nasty infection.

42

Next, take a large amount of flour and carefully add a few lumps of lard or at a pinch, some of the fat from the Officers' dinner joint.

Mix with water and throw in half a handful of currants and mix thoroughly. If you find a few cockroaches have found their way into the mix don't worry as when cooked they closely resemble currants.

Pop into the steam cauldron and sit back, occupying one's thoughts with the looks of pure pleasure on the trainees' faces when they see the feast, all topped off with the watered-down treacle or molasses placed before them!

Our time on the ship was very nearly up and to finish us off we left our hut for the last time, carrying our kit to stow it down below on the Vindicatrix proper. Seeing the below decks for the first time frightened the life out of us, as I suspect we frightened the life out of the cockroaches that must've been upset by our presence, but we had to put up with it.

With less than three weeks to go many 'Vindi' boys, including myself, sent home a request to borrow money to buy a uniform because all we had to show we were Merchant Seamen was a kit bag on which our names and large MN were stencilled. In Sharpness was a shop which sold clothing and other goods to seamen calling at the port. Now, whilst the owner, an elderly lady, could measure the chest, waist and arm length, the inside leg measurement presented a problem and so anyone wishing to be measured needed to take another boy with him. It was this boy who groped up the crotch with one end of the tape measure whilst the lady took the measurement at the other end!

Nearly 50 years later I went back to Sharpness and could've cried. Everything was gone! All that was left was the brick lavatory block which was now used as a storage facility by the boat owner using the mooring where 'Vindi' was berthed prior to being towed to the breaker in the 1960's.

By chance the shop where my uniform was measured was still there and I got talking the chap who now lived at the property. It transpired he was that lady's nephew. I recounted the 'bring a chum to measure your inside leg' and he thought it hilarious having never heard this before. He assured me his Aunt was still alive and living in another area, and promised that when he next saw her he'd remind her of it!

As a result of this visit, all those years later, I got in touch with a Roy Derham and along with him and other 'old boys', a Training Ship Vindicatrix Association was formed and commemorative tablets placed on the brick wall of our ex latrine (but now store room) and in the Sharpness church.

So, dear reader, if you're ever going down the M5, when you come to the Sharpness/Berkeley turn off, take the time to visit Berkeley Castle and then go and look out, as so many young boys did, over the canal and the River Severn, and think of those children of the Merchant Navy who never came back. R.I.P.

The countdown to leaving 'Vindi' had begun. I was called in to Captain Angel's room for the re-sit of the test I'd failed some week or so before. He sat there looking just like a picture of someone's favourite Grandpa, all snow white hair, white moustache and pink complexion but it was there the resemblance ended for he was a fierce old bugger. He touched in turn the points of a lifeboat sail, daring me almost not to know, but I'd done my homework knowing full well that should I fail this attempt, I would be kept back when the rest of my group had passed to do another week or more until he was satisfied. I passed. Re-emerging on to the deck I heard a strange whistling noise coming from a clear sky. I looked up as did others to a shout of,

'Look at that aeroplane, it hasn't got a propeller!'

We'd just seen our first jet!

We didn't have a passing out parade, but everyone leaving was given a travel pass plus a few other papers, and with kit bags over our shoulder we passed through the gates for the last time as trainees. We boarded the train at Sharpness, alighting at Berkeley Road Station ready to catch the next train on. It was here several of the group left us and we next alighted at Gloucester, or was it Bristol? Certainly, most of the group were from the Bristol and South West areas. For myself and two others our destination, as stated on the rail warrant, was London St Pancras. That journey seemed to take hours. The carriages were packed with civilians and servicemen, several of whom had climbed up into the meshed overhead luggage racks and were fast asleep. Black out regulations called for very dim lighting in the carriages, a rotten sickly yellow colour, and conversation gradually died down as the evening progressed. With the length of the war time journey we London bound boys had to undertake, one would've thought we'd be let out earlier in the afternoon, but no, we all went out together. Mind you, it was nice to see the occasional young female as the only ones we'd seen for six weeks had been the two office girls who, up to our leaving, still hadn't raised their eyes to us.

A shedding of steam, a rattle over points that caused the carriage to sway and roll, a gradual slowing down and we were into St Pancras. The time was so late that all the tube trains had stopped running, likewise the buses. I didn't have money for a taxi yet my eventual destination in the East End was Dock Street. Here I would find the shipping pool office and, so I'd been told, a Merchant Navy hostel which would accommodate me until such time I was found a ship. Not far from the railway station I saw a sign, 'Service Hostel.' I went in. There was a man at a desk.

'Please Sir, could you give me a bed for the night until the tubes start in the morning?'

'Sorry lad' came the reply, 'This place is for servicemen only!'

'Please Sir, I am a serviceman; I'm a Merchant Seaman going to the Dock Street pool office!'

'Sorry lad, we're full up!'

Were they, I wondered, or did he have it in for Merchant Seamen as so many did, believing Merchant Seamen were overpaid simply because being a civilian service we received danger money! What these people didn't realise was that every item of clothing for civilian use as well as our sea-gear had to be bought by ourselves, and that's why upon entry we were given a thick wad of clothing coupons, and that wasn't all! If torpedoed, as so many were, two or even three times, all gear lost was replaced out of our own pocket, and here's the real shocker... Right into World War II, immediately a ship was sunk by enemy action, as soon as the poor survivors took to the boats or dived into a blazing sea, their wages were stopped,

46

and they were deemed unemployed. As for the big wages, well, I'd been earning more as a trainee engineer than ever I got per week in the Merchant Navy, and all the time I was at sea and in a war zone for weeks at a time!

I came back onto the street to thuds and bangs in the distance spelling an air raid. What to do? Along came a policeman in a black helmet with 'Police' stencilled on the front.

'Now then young man, what are you doing out at this time of the night? Don't you know there's an air raid on?' he asked.

I explained who I was and that I needed someplace to lay my weary head until the morning. He was great! He led me along several streets until we finished up at yet another forces hostel. He came in with me and stayed until he was quite sure I would be accommodated. I was taken up a flight of stairs and into a long dormitory type of room with a very dim night light glowing. All around the room were occupied single beds. The occupants, with it being so late, seemed to be fast asleep, some moaning, some groaning, some calling out, others snoring, and now and again a few loud farts were to be heard! For Pete's sake what a racket! My guide and mentor led me to a bed close to the door through which we'd entered and indicated a bed.

'You can sleep in this one, son' he whispered, 'and as you obviously don't know the drill, what I suggest is you sleep in your clothes, have that kit bag in bed with you with your arms wrapped around it for safe keeping, do not take your shoes off without you put them under your pillow, and all being well when you wake up in the morning you will still have all your gear intact! Goodnight!'

A nod being as good as a wink I did just as he suggested, the only difference being that I fed one of my shoe laces through the button hole in my shirt and then tied the other lace to it, and so I slept, very soundly I might add, my legs wrapped around my kit bag and my arms cuddling my shoes.

Next morning I saw that my fellow sleepers were all forces personnel. Breakfast wasn't included in the accommodation and so I set off to find Dock Street, Aldgate East, via the tube, which for me with no idea of the geography of London was an adventure in itself.

Some kind soul put me right as to which line I needed for my destination and, now seated and speeding on my way, I had time to look around and take in what was going on around me, noticing that the language I was hearing from all sides was not English! Next, I noticed that some of the men wore funny shaped hats and had long ringlets hanging down from their heads. I sat pondering, but by the time the station sign said 'Aldgate East' I still hadn't sussed it! I got off the tube, and so did most of my fellow passengers, but who were they? Eventually I found out. Aldgate East was the east end of London and this was the area settled in by the Jews.

A fairly long walk down Leman Street brought me to the pool office. I don't know what I expected to find but what I did find was a dusty looking front office. Inside were bare floorboards and sticking up from these were iron railings leading, one at a time, to desks over which were signs saying Catering (me), Deck (seamen) and another sign pointing up some stairs which said 'Engine'. I got in the short queue for catering and straight away was asked by a disreputable looking guy behind me, 'got a fag mate?' I said no. I did have one but I was onto the cadgers

48

and as far as I was concerned he was one!

At the desk I handed over the various pieces of paper given to me before leaving 'Vindi.' I was told to book into the Flying Angel hostel across the road then go to a certain address to have my photo taken for my Seaman's Discharge Book. Then I was to come back and I'd be sent home for a few days leave.

Returning from leave I had time to look over the Flying Angel Merchant Navy Hostel. There was a commissionaire in the front entrance hall and the foyer wall had several large swordfish adorning the walls. The place was spotlessly clean and the single bed cabin I was shown into had a single bed, wardrobe and bedside cabinet containing the one necessary bedroom item, to-wit, a chamber pot! However, with the bathroom just across the corridor this wasn't needed.

For the few days I was to be 'on the pool', I became friends with another young 'waiting for a ship' seaman who showed me his seaman's discharge book and demonstrated how Merchant Seamen always went out on a 'trip', never a 'voyage' for that description was for passengers only, and there were few passenger ships sailing out of London.

All around the East End were bomb damaged and burned out 'blitzed' buildings. Even today in many parts of the capital, rows of houses with whole or part flat roofs can be seen that date back a hundred years or so, the original roofs having been blown off by bombs during the Blitz.

Having done our duty for the day, which was to report to the pool office to ask 'have you got a ship for me yet?', my new chum and I went on walks. We saw the Tower of London as it was before the powers that be 'tarted' it up thus destroying forever the brooding menace the Tower conveyed. We stood looking at a small fenced off area at the back of the Tower which was littered with all sorts of discarded bits and pieces and, on reading a small plaque that would've been so easy to miss, we realised this was the spot where over the centuries most of the executions took place.

All along the side of the River Thames could be seen burned out warehouses that for years had received and stored imported goods from all over the world. Most of them now were shells but some could be identified as being storage places for spices because, as the flames consumed them and their contents, the aromas were burned into the very brickwork so even if your eyes were closed you were transported to the fragrant east. In many of the open cellars and cleared areas, yellow wildflowers were growing. We were told that the seed from which these sprouted would've lain buried in the ground for hundreds of years.

Without much money to spend, most of our wanderings usually found us in some small café or forces canteen. Up to now my uniform was still in its wrapping for I'd heard from several sides that wearing the uniform was 'swanking' but our little silver badge, worn so proudly in the lapel of the jacket, gained us entry with no questions asked. The exception was a Jewish club. Leman Street and the immediate area was a very popular Jewish area, and here we were told in no uncertain terms to 'clear off!'

Life on the ocean wave:

My mind was anywhere but in that pool office when I pushed my discharge book, still with virginal clean pages, through the grill and waited for the usual 'nothing today, come back tomorrow.' Instead I got,

'I've a 'deep sea' signing on this afternoon. Do you want it Galley Boy?'

Did I want it? Too bloody right I wanted it! Deep Sea? Yes, definitely! No pissing around on crappy little coasters for me, sailing up and down the east coast, take your own victuals! I wanted 'foreign!' The North Atlantic, the convoys, and by golly if they signed me on then that's what I'd get! That afternoon, for the first time, I went upstairs in the direction as pointed by that 'Engine' sign and into a large room with a lot of people lined up. Among them were several very Arab looking men, some of whom had cloths around their neck with one end in the corner of their mouths, but more about them later. Words were spoken by a very Naval looking uniformed man.

'I am the Captain etc., etc.'

Names were called and job descriptions quoted, some of which were new to me... 'Donkey Man... Trimmer... Scullion etc etc. Then my name was called 'Galley Boy!' After I'd signed the book a rotund, jolly looking man came up to me.

'Is this your first trip son?' I was asked, to which I affirmed it was.

He told me he was the Chief Steward of a 5000-ton general cargo vessel built in

1939, that he was in charge of catering arrangements on board the ship, that the ship was a happy ship, (most important this) and how he would've introduced me to my immediate superior, the Cook, but he, the Cook, had no need to sign on as he'd sailed on the previous trip and never signed off. I was told to report at a certain berth at the Surrey Commercial Docks the following morning.

I was so excited I doubted I would get any sleep that night, knowing the next morning I would see my first ship! After a good breakfast I enquired how I could get to Surrey Commercial Docks and was told to 'get a taxi', which I did, arriving at the dock gates very shortly after. As soon as I was allowed in and after asking where the berth was, I sniffed and smelled the aroma of new wood for Surrey Docks was the eventual docking place for timber at this time. I found my ship. She looked, and was, huge! There she lay, tied up and clean and bare of any deck cargo, painted in war time grey. The only identification to confirm she was indeed my ship were her name boards high up on each side of the bridge. Hesitating and nervous, I walked up a steep gangplank. She seemed deserted apart from a little old chap wearing a peaked cap and uniform jacket who was sitting on the corner of one of the ship's sheeted down hatches. I later discovered he was the Chief Engineer, nick-named by some 'wag' as 'old frosty bollocks'. However, he was nice to me,

'Please Sir, could you tell me where to find the cook?'

Now, doesn't that tell you how green I was, asking the Chief Engineer where I might find the cook?! He pointed out the general direction I needed to go and on entering a long narrow Galley I was greeted with a very Geordie voice asking,

'Where the f*ck have you been till this bloody time, son?!'

This was my first introduction to Harry the Cook whose skills, by rights, should've earned him the title of chef rather than cook! Let me say here and now lest you get the wrong idea about him, Harry was one of the nicest blokes you could ever wish to meet. He was in his twenties, very outspoken but he never bullied, and if the pressure was on he would always help me out! Harry had an assistant named Danny, a Londoner, who was just learning the trade. Actually, it was a miracle Harry was so normal as I later found out his previous ship had been hit by a German buzz bomb whilst in dock, and then being towed up the river with poor Harry on her, she was hit by a second! Would you believe it! I think knowing the force of these terrible bombs had it been me I would've been crawling up the wall.

So, my first day passed with me sitting outside the Galley peeling and preparing potatoes, cabbage, carrots etc. whilst sitting on a long metal plate covering high pressure, steam heated pipes. This was no hardship though as the heated pipes meant I had the warmest bottom in London!

Feeding time over I went inside to a large metal trough of a sink where I ran in cold water which was heated to scalding by a thin copper steam pipe. This was more problematic as the steam pipe could quite easily take the skin off your hands.

After washing up saucepans and other cooking implements it was time to 'get your head down!' This was part of the catering department ritual as we had a 6am 'turn to.'

Harry led me to our department's accommodation which was immediately under the lifeboat deck. In the middle of the said deck was the store of potatoes housed in a slatted open-air locker. Harry led me through a door and over a raised sill which was to keep the sea out when she shipped a 'green one.' This could cause the deck to be flooded to the depth of several feet, as I was shortly to find out. The plate over the first door on the right said 'Hospital'. This was to be my home for the first trip. Inside it was painted pure white with a red deck, and in the corner was a small lavatory cubicle. Instead of traditional bunks there were raised metal beds each side and the whole ensemble was completed by a couple of single wardrobes. Very nice! It was explained we were carrying more staff than usual, hence the use of the hospital cabin. I slept for an hour (2pm – 3pm) and then turned to for another bout of washing up!

Every meal was dished out to the crew in large metal mess tins by a junior crew member, affectionately called 'the Peggy.' Afterwards, we catering staff adjourned to a small mess room situated amid-ships in the main officers and bridge housing, port side, close to the Officers' and Captain's accommodation, where we joined the Bosun and Chippy (carpenter) for our meals.

Our food was fantastic, especially as we were used to war time rations at home. A typical breakfast was cereals or porridge, curry and rice, ham and eggs, toast if you wanted it, tea or coffee. Lunch was soup 'a la Harry,' meat of the day (beef, pork or mutton), boiled spuds, sometimes baked cabbage or beans followed by spotted dick or semolina or rice pudding, with coffee to follow. As for supper, who the hell wanted supper after all that lot?! J. and J. Denholme of Glasgow (the owners) did us proud.

After two days tied up alongside in Surrey docks the tugs came for us around 7.30am. I was so excited as gradually, with engine room bells ringing in answer to the bridge commends, we were inched into the centre of the dock. From my position I could look across and up to the back of the bridge and see the activity as heads popped up then disappeared, checking that all was well, as slowly we were guided through lock gates that would lead us into the River Thames proper. I remember going to the ship's rail and looking down on the gathering people waiting to cross over as soon as we were clear. I felt very nautical and dare I say, very superior, after all, was I not going off to war whilst all they had was their 8 – 6 jobs?

Eventually we left the narrow parts of the Thames and emerged into the wider Thames Estuary, and I saw for the first time the red sails of the Thames barges which made me wonder were these the 'red sails in the sunset' of the popular 1930's song?

We sailed up the east coast of England and anchored for the night off the port of Methil on the east coast of Scotland. Laying off at anchor for our overnight stopper made me realise that the war time blackouts left much to be desired because as we gazed at the distant shore we could see faint lights dotted about. By the time we 'turned to' next morning we'd been 'up anchored' and on our way for several hours. Cook Harry told me we'd be going around the top of Scotland, turning west and then south. Our destination was 'Loch Ewe!' This was the convoy gathering point from whence we would eventually set sail across the dangerous waters of the North Atlantic.

The sea had been very kind and I wasn't at all queasy. We entered the Loch entrance which was protected by two 'boom' vessels who, on seeing us arrive steamed one to the left and one to the right, pulling aside as they did so the great chains stretched across to prevent any 'U' boats from getting in. The Loch was a scene of tranquillity. Several vessels had already arrived, but so vast were the stretches of the Loch they seemed to take up no room at all.

The whole place seemed deserted with no sign of habitation around its banks. We lay in there for about a week as the later arrivals steamed in. They seemed, to my untutored eyes, a right motley lot. Some were smart and freshly painted in the North Atlantic grey, while others looked as though it was only the all over rust that held them together. Placed where I was I could hear the comments of the older crew members who seemed able to identify individual ships even from a mile away. Such comments ranged from, 'she's a good un' to 'that one's a hungry bastard' indicating the shipping company was either very good, or one to refuse to sign on with.

With the convoy gathered the boom was pulled apart and we sailed out. Each ship knew just where her place would be in the convoy and which ship carried the Convoy Commodore, the man in overall charge, who was usually a retired Naval Officer of at least Captain rank. It was the Convoy Commodore who made the decisions.

The Naval escort came into position and off we went heading north, hoping to dodge the submarines lurking below the waves once the convoy was picked up. At first it was great but then, sitting outside the Galley peeling the spuds, I began to feel queasy, then I started to sweat. I started to pray, 'Dear God, make this bloody ship stay still!' Make no mistake about it, sea sickness is the most terrible of sicknesses! You just want to die! So there I sat, the warmest bum in the convoy with a bucket containing spuds waiting to be peeled, a bucket to hold the peelings, a bucket in which to put the peeled spuds and, between my legs, another bucket into which I was being violently sick. The ship was rolling hard as we were in ballast which means carrying no cargo and so sailing high. The buckets kept overturning and the contents swilled around in the scuppers. The Chief Mate told me that if I blocked those self-same scuppers with potato peelings then he'd personally throw me over the bloody side! I was in a mess, but then out of the Galley popped dear old Harry the Cook.

'How's it going then Son?' he asked.

In answer I dry retched, having nothing left in my stomach to bring up.

'Hang on' he said and went back into the Galley, emerging a moment or two later to hand me a handful of those square cracker biscuits.

'Keep pushing these down you' he advised, 'and don't be afraid of being sick. It'll pass after a time. However, one thing I must warn you about...' Here he paused for dramatic effect then went on... 'It isn't so much the sickness you need to watch out for but just remember, when you're throwing up, if you feel a lump of gristle at the back of your throat then swallow it quick because that'll be your ring!'

If anyone fails to understand this advice, may I suggest they ask the nearest Sailor!

I kept going until 'get your head down' time and then had a sleep which seemed to help a little. The cabin boy who occupied the twin to my bunk in the hospital cabin was also a first tripper 'deep sea' although he'd done previous trips on a coaster, London to Shields. Now in the same shape as myself he swore,

'Never again! From now on I'll even steer clear of the canoes on the local park!'

We were ill for about a day. The 'please Lord, let me die' type of ill and then it passed.

With time now to look around and take note, I saw that the convoy we were part of covered miles of the sea! There were new looking ships of around 10,000 tons loaded, as well as rusty old buckets that looked as if they should've been scrapped years ago, but no, there they were shooting out clouds of black smoke that could be seen for miles whilst the poor frantic stokers down below were shovelling like maniacs in an attempt to give their skipper the knots demanded by the destroyer escorts who were themselves dashing around, as one cynic on our crew put it, 'like tarts dashing up and down Lime Street looking for some poor sailor to pass her 'dose' on to!'

Smoke was every convoy's nightmare as it could be seen for miles. It was easy for the oil burners, all they had to do was open a tap a little more.

The aforementioned Chief Mate passed by and, obviously forgetting the threat he'd made should I block his scuppers with potato peelings, he actually asked me how I was liking the sailors' life? When I had the chance to observe him more I saw he was usually a quietly spoken Scot who loved poetry, and with a sailor on the wheel during his watch who appreciated poetry, the two of them, rank forgotten, would often spout poetic gems to one another. If a particular piece could be helped along with gestures by the Helm Man, then Mate would take the wheel as the poem was delivered. Sadly though, the Mate was an alcoholic. Put whiskey in front of him and he wouldn't rest until the bottle was empty. Full of whiskey he was to fall asleep at the meal table several times and the Captain would quietly order the Second Mate to fetch two of the crew to carry the near unconscious Mate to his bunk. What a shame!

Apart from the engine room officers all the rest down below were Arabs, formerly from Aden but now living, many of them with English wives, in North Shields. They were a very quiet, well-behaved bunch of men who never seemed out of sorts, and never ever did I hear any of the white crew make disparaging remarks about them.

These then were our Arab stokers, greasers and donkey man. A great bunch of lads!

Occasionally, we could see and hear depth charges going up around the convoy as Adolf's lads tried to get among us but the escorts were first class!

The first casualty within the ships came when a crew member of a general cargo vessel not far from us, died. Word had it he was in his sixties and he'd been on the sea all his adult life. Hardly an army dodging bastard as many Merchant Navy critics would have you believe. Came the appointed time for him to be committed to the sea his ship sailed full speed ahead through the lines of the convoy until she was well out in front of us all and then, guarded by a lone destroyer, she stopped. The plank was then up-ended and down he went to the bottom of the ocean,

'Nothing of him that doth fade. But doth suffer a sea-change into something rich and strange.'

The Galley was separated from the main bridge structure in which the Officers, the Captain and Chief Steward had their cabins. Also here was the catering staff mess room, main saloon, and pantry in which the food was served out, having been brought over from the Galley. Set in the floor of the pantry was a hatch and steps leading down into the storeroom.

Harry was now descending those steps to fetch up supplies for the next meal, but some idiot had put a small shelf over this hatch and on this shelf an even bigger idiot had placed an empty bottle. Harry was halfway down the stairs when the ship rolled sending the bottle crashing down upon Harry's head. The first I knew of this was when crewmen ran past me, coming back a few moments later carrying Harry, as white as the proverbial sheet and with his head swathed in a blood-soaked towel. The Chief Steward was unable to stop the bleeding so the skipper was sent for! A signal was flashed to the Convoy Commodore who contacted the Destroyer escort, 'Doctor urgently required!' Within half an hour a Destroyer came alongside and lines were passed between the two ships. When I say alongside, don't take me too literally as there was quite a space between us. Harry was carried onto the deck and lashed into what looked like a long straight jacket. Should the line snap whilst being passed over between the two ships he would float, head upright. Hooked on, the transfer started, and we held our breath as slowly, Harry was hauled from our ship to the Destroyer. Mission accomplished the lines were cast away and to the whoop, whoop, whoop of the

Destroyer, our two ships separated.

It was two or three days later and I was up on the boat deck with my head in the slatted potato locker when I heard various and assorted whumps and whangs which I didn't need to be told indicated the Destroyer escorts had picked up submarines in the vicinity. Not wanting to miss any of the excitement I emerged and surveyed the mass of ships around us. Now it's a strange thing about being part of a large convoy but although things 'hot up' quite often nothing can be seen, and this proved to be the case on this occasion.

It was mid-morning on a bright, near sunny, day. We were in the Gulf of the St Lawrence River and the sea was calm with nothing to be seen to port or starboard – land wise that is! Looking out across the deck to port I noticed something which drew my attention. No, it wasn't a submarine but a line of what seemed to be spume, easily missed from deck level, which was coming closer to the ship. As I walked towards the ship's rail the very faint line reached the side of the ship and vanished.

'Strange' I thought as I walked across the deck, only to see the thin line re-appear on the starboard side and quickly disappear into the distance. I lost sight of it and was returning back to the spud locker when I heard a 'bang' in the far distance. Running back to the starboard side of the ship I saw a Corvette (Canadian I was told later) way over on the other side of the convoy, slowly come to a standstill with smoke coming from her stern. It was then Joe Pratt here finally twigged that what he'd thought was a thick spume trail was in fact a torpedo and had our ship been lower in the water cargo wise, I wouldn't be here now. Upon arrival at our destination we were told the Corvette had been towed up to Quebec and was salvageable. We had no idea how many of the crew were killed.

Slowly, hour by hour, the land drew in upon us the further up the St Lawrence River we sailed. Most of the convoy had dispersed to sail to other Canadian ports and we seemed all alone as we sailed past some of the most colourful land I'd ever seen. It was nearly 'Fall' and the trees were a riot of colour. Past Quebec, gazing out at the heights which General Wolfe and his troops had scaled, a seemingly impossible achievement, then onto 'Three Rivers', our destination, which lay just below Montreal, to load timber.

Three Rivers had a lovely clean and welcoming seamen's mission presided over by 'Charlie', one of the nicest blokes you could ever wish to meet. That is, unless you were rowdy and a trouble maker in which case you soon discovered that: A) Charlie had been a boxer and B) Charlie wouldn't be messed about! This was Charlie's domain and woe-betide any seaman who thought otherwise.

Most of our time was spent in the seamen's mission which sold bottled beer and had a juke box which was much patronised by me playing, 'Is you is or is you ain't my baby' and 'Down in the Valley' over and over again. I visited the local cinema once and was amazed to find the music in the intermission was provided by a lady on a piano! It was coming out of this cinema I witnessed an incident that proved just how stupid some ship mates could be!

A western union boy delivering to a block of flats left his bike against the kerb. Along came one of our crew who, seeing the bike was unattended, grabbed hold of it and rode off down the street laughing like a maniac! Upon our return to ship

I found our idiot ship mate had pulled the bike aboard using a heaving line and was secreting it in our bathroom to take back to England as a souvenir! We all turned in but two hours later the culprit, ashen of face, woke us up with the news that the Canadian Police had started searching the ship tied up in front of us looking for the bike. We told 'matey' to get that bloody bike out of our bathroom as no way were we 'carrying the can' for his stupidity! What did he do? He took the bike onto the deck and threw it over the side. His logic being 'no bike; no evidence!'

It was in the mission hut I saw an incident that turned my stomach. I'd gone into the toilet for a pee where I found one of our seamen, a real 'Spring Bok' hard case, with a young seaman from the ship tied up forward of where we lay. As I watched, the young chap held his hand out, fingers extended,

'Spring Bok' took each of the fingers in turn and broke them, three in all. I thought I'd pass out. Later, I heard that the young chap was being mercilessly bullied on his own ship by several crew members and wanted 'out'. He couldn't be paid off with only half of the trip being completed and if he jumped ship he'd lose all his wages. His way 'out' was as a distressed or 'injured' British seaman!

To the side of the land on which the mission hut stood were several very nice houses. Walking past one evening I saw a very nice girl of about sixteen standing at the gate of her home. I winked at her and she blushed and giggled. The next night ditto. On the third night I tried to chat her up only to discover she was a French Canadian and spoke only French. I spoke only English. But we manged. I'd decided to ask her to the pictures, but that night Charlie called me over.

'You've been getting friendly with that girl over the way,' he stated.

'Why yes. I'm hoping she'll come to the pictures with me,' I replied.

Charlie looked worried,

'Listen kid, back off. The English aren't flavour of the month with the French Canadians and anyhow, her old man's a racketeer. Take my tip, don't even look at her.'

I took his advice, thinking there was enough danger at sea without having a blasted gangster after me. She was lovely though.

So, we said farewell to Three Rivers and, with holds stuffed full of timber and the decks piled high with ditto, we set sail for the UK and some home leave!

More war time trips:

It was time to go back to the ship. The letter said, 'Join at Sunderland' and my discharge book was marked 'V.G' (very good). The Chief Steward and Harry were pleased with me! After another tiring wartime train journey I arrived at the dock side and there she was. It was like coming home.

I went aboard, deposited my kit, and went into the Galley. It was about 10pm and there, instead of Harry, stood an old guy stirring a large square tin in which he was making gravy.

'Hello. Who are you?' he asked.

'Me? I'm the Galley Boy!' I replied.

'I'm the stand in Cook,' he offered.

As he was talking and still stirring the gravy, I noticed a large dew drop was forming on the tip of his nose.

'I've had a long journey, so I'll go and get my head down,' I said moving towards to doorway.

Still stirring the gravy, the old fellow turned his head towards me and, as he said 'Right, don't be late in the morning' I saw that the dew drop was gone, and there was only one place it could've gone! I made a mental note not to have gravy on my dinner the next day!

Things were cooling down submarine wise in the North Atlantic and the trip would've passed by without comment from me except we hit the very belter of a North Atlantic storm. To give you some idea, although we were part of a very large convoy, the waves reached such a pitch of viciousness that when the ship's bows went plunging down into the roughs of one of these monster waves, we were so deep down the convoy might not have existed! On each side of the ship were walls of water so high the only way to look was up. Then the next wave would lift the bows and up and up and up we would go until, at the peak of that wave, we were looking down at the convoy.

And roll!! Well, you wouldn't believe it! I peered into the Galley, the floor of which were of quarry type tiles, swimming in water, even though (as every door on the ship had) there were raised combings to stop any water shipped from coming in. As I watched, and I was hanging onto the door frame, poor Harry, who by now had re-joined the ship, plus the new assistant Cook, unable to find a hand hold and wearing rubber soled Galley shoes, were skidding from one end of the Galley to the other accompanied by miscellaneous pots, pans etc. After a short time when things had settled, Harry asked me to go amidships to the Chief Steward's room and ask him for a side of meat to cut up for dinner. I had a stretch of open deck to cross with just a hatch in between. With the meat slung over my shoulder, (and it was heavy) I started back. Just as I reached the hatch, I heard Harry's voice,

'Look out son! She's shipping a green un!'

The ship, rolling badly, had leaned hard over to starboard and now at the end of the roll was beginning to fall away like an express train to port. From the corner of my eye I saw Harry's face framed in the Galley porthole just as he slammed it to. I looked up and there, all ready to break over the ship, was one of the highest waves I was ever to see, and it was going to break over me! I knew with certainty that if it did, then I was a goner! Instinctively I dropped the meat and dived, wedging myself behind a stanchion that went up to support the two-foot-high side of the hatch. The wave broke upon the deck just as I'd foreseen and I was under feet of sea water hanging on like grim death! Still rolling, most of the water returned back to the sea via the scuppers and I was still getting my breath back when I heard,

'He's gone over the f*cking side I tell you! He was right in the way when that bloody wave broke and he's not there now! He must've gone over!'

66

'Gosh, man overboard!' I thought, 'I wonder who it was!'

With water pouring out of my ears, I stood up to be greeted by Harry, who emerged from the Galley, with,

'You c**t! We saw you standing there just before the wave broke and the next minute we looked, you'd gone! All we saw was that meat floating in the scuppers!' 'Nice' I thought, 'a near death experience and for my troubles I get called a c**t!'

We arrived at St Johns, New Brunswick, Canada in deep snow, and went outdoor skating on a frozen park lake with a couple of girls we met up with. (Olive and Jean) The ship then sailed to Cape Breton Island where we slept ashore for one night whilst the ship was fumigated to kill off the cockroaches, then it was up to Halifax, Nova Scotia! Would you believe it, when going into the main post office the first words I heard were from a lady in front of me who said,

'How long will it take for this letter to get to Leicester, England?'

I'm only sorry I didn't tell her, Leicester? I know it well!

On the return journey back across the North Atlantic we started from Halifax, Nova Scotia via the Newfoundland Banks which were notorious for dense sea fogs. For days we were in convoy sailing almost blind through the seemingly impenetrable wet fog whilst all around us the other ships, like us, blasted off with their sirens every few moments. A most mournful sound. The only visual sign of their presence were the large boards towed behind them on long lengths of line. The boards kicked up a white disturbance on the sea surface and were just visible to the seamen stationed in the freezing cold bows of the ship. With the fog finally dispersed it was off to England, home and beauty.

Now we've had enough of war stories and so although the incident I'm going to recount happened during the war, I promise you that not a bomb, mine or torpedo is going to be included in the story.

I was in the midship pantry helping the 2nd Steward dish out food for the Captain, two of the mates and two radio operators when one of the seamen from down aft appeared at the door to the midship's hatch, going absolutely bonkers, cussing and swearing that 'this meat' (which he held out for our inspection) was all f*cking fat! Now, why he was complaining to us I don't know, for after being prepared in the Galley and served out into large mess tins for the seamen and firemen by the cook, the food was carried to these two messes by the nominated 'Peggy', and so neither the second Steward nor I were implicated. I had a quick glance into the mess tin and the meat seemed perfectly ok but I ventured no comment, not wanting to get thumped, for this chap was really doing his nut.

Along came the Chief Steward.

'What the hell is all this shouting about?'

'It's the f*cking meat!' said our visitor from aft again, 'It's all fat, and Board of Trade says........!'

The Chief Steward stirred the meat in the mess tin with a fork before declaring,

'Away with you man, there's nothing wrong with this!'

He might well have saved his breath. This chap was a 'sea lawyer' of the worst kind and was not going to give an inch. By this time the meat and gravy had begun to congeal and it didn't look at all appetising.

Whilst this was going on I was still serving out for the Officers in the saloon just across the alleyway when the 2nd Steward came in.

'Look out, the Captains coming! He's heard all the commotion and wants to know what the hell is going on!'

At that moment the Captain came in.

'Just who's making all this damned racket?!' he demanded. 'We can't hear ourselves think in the saloon!'

'This f*cking meat is too fatty and Board of Trade regulations say...'

The skipper fixed him with a steely gaze, stirred the meat in the tin and gave his verdict.

'I can see nothing wrong with this, in fact it's exactly the same meat we're eating! Now get back aft and let me hear no more of this nonsense!'

Our lord and master had spoken, and anyone else would've taken off like a rocket! The Captain was an ex Royal Navy Officer, complete at all times in full uniform, unlike most Merchant Navy Captains who were complete with bowler hats and looked as though they'd been dressed by a seaman's charity. We were proud of our Skipper for he gave us a bit of class. But did our own 'Fletcher Christian' heed the Skipper's warning?! He did not, and still argued! The Skipper had had enough.

'If you don't get back aft, I will log (fine) you out of your wages when we pay-off!'

At this the Seaman started to argue.

'I've got my rights and you've got no...' but that was as far as he got.

'You're logged' said the skipper.

'Logged? F*cking logged am I?' Was the reply and now, beyond all reason, he took hold of a half full tureen of soup being kept warm on the hotplate for second sitters and upturned it all over the Captain's head. You never saw a mess quite like it. That seaman took off like a scalded cat whilst the Skipper went to his day cabin to change. The rest of us just dissolved into hysterical laughter!

At the end of the trip we were 'paid off' and on the bad lad's book was entered the amount of his logging. In the space for conduct was written DR (decline to report). That on its own is as bad as you can get but there was more. Against DR was added 'Recommend this man be discharged into the Army.'

Was he? I don't know, but I bet had the Captain found out who it was on those silent, blacked out nights at sea who shouted, 'Have you got the f*cking soup out your ears yet skipper?' there would've been two loggings to record!

On the anniversary of V.E Day I wrote a short account of where I was on the last day of the European war. The North Atlantic. Thinking back all those years set my mind working and I remember thinking about that last 'war-time trip.' Note, we always went on a trip, and never a voyage or operation as our Royal Navy comrades did!

I consider the details of our adventures worth recounting as to do so will prove we Merchant Seamen had more to fear than the turbulent seas or Adolf and his Nasties.

We were in convoy, of course, and it was early in 1945 as we set off 'North about' across the North Atlantic. All was quiet apart from a few bangs in the distance. Eventually, having separated from the rest of the ships, we sailed into New York harbour where we lined up in the saloon to be photographed and have our fingerprints taken. Very shortly afterwards we received a New York dock pass which contained these identifying details. As the ship needed her bunkers replenishing we moved alongside the coal wharf and the bunker hatch covers were removed. We, the crew, were once more called into the saloon and asked 'how much of a 'sub' (advance against wages) did we want.' Armed with our dock pass we were then allowed to go ashore.

We two ship's boys 'Galley' and 'Cabin' soon found ourselves with older crew members in a bar and silly, silly, were persuaded (although it didn't take much) to drink American Rye with beer chasers. During this session the bar tender realised we were underage and the two of us were slung out onto the street to the cheers of our shipmates. Let me emphasise I wasn't drunk, just 'tiddly'. 'Cabin' decided he was going back to the ship but with the night still being young, I set off to see the sights. Fine at the time but an hour later I realised:

a) I was hopelessly lost.

b) I had no idea where the old ship was tied up.

What was I to do? Easy, all I had to do was find a policeman! I looked around! Plenty of people but just like England if you needed a copper you could never find one! I decided to ask a passer-by for directions!

The first person I approached pushed me out of the way. The next couple ignored me completely! I swear I would still have been standing there had it not been for two young, 'Bobby Soxer' girls who, to my appeal of 'please could you direct me to the nearest Police Station as I'm lost,' giggled, took one arm each and took charge. I remember we went down some stairs and into the subway. We got on a tube train (they refused to let me pay) and shortly afterwards we emerged into the street to stand in front of a large building which they indicated I should enter. I stepped forward then remembered the girls and turned to thank them, but they'd already gone! In all that time, apart from giggling, they'd never said a word!

I went in like a lamb to the slaughter. It was a large room with bare wooden floor, a desk on a plinth facing me and behind the desk, instead of a wall, a stretch of steel bars, obviously 'to the cells!' Sitting at the desk was the biggest policeman I'd ever seen and as he stood up I saw he wore a black shirt, black breeches and black diagonal leather Sam Brown type belt with a black holster in which a huge black gun poked out. I explained my predicament 'Sir-ing' him as hard as I could.

'That's OK kid,' he said. 'How about you sleeping it off in one of my home from home rooms back here and we can sort it out tomorrow!?'

Sleeping it off?' I may well have been tiddly but I certainly wasn't drunk! I think my English accent and politeness had confused him!

I began to slowly back away and as he made no attempt to detain me I fled into the night. Now what to do? Nearby I saw a drug store so in I went for a cup of tea whilst I rethought my strategy. I hesitated just inside the door and a lovely young lady behind the counter, seeing I was looking a bit lost, called,

'Can I be of assistance?'

I started to explain my predicament but hardly had I got out 'well, actually I'm a...' when that dear soul exclaimed,

'Hey, you're a limey' and before I could order tea she broke in with,

'If it's tea you want kid, forget it, our tea's lousy. The coffee's OK though!' (Which made me think 'so what the hell was the Boston Tea Party all about?')

I explained I was lost and had no idea where my ship was berthed. Would you believe it, that lovely young woman took over! I was handed a free cup of coffee whilst she went over to a wall mounted phone. She dialled a number and handed me the phone with a whisper, 'It's the US Customs!'

'Yeah?' said a voice on the other end.

'I'm sorry to bother you but could you please tell me where my ship is tied up as I seem to have lost the address?'

'Are you nuts?' said the voice 'We don't give out that sort of information. Don't you know there's a war on?!' and with that the phone was slammed down.

'No luck?' asked my new friend and mentor.

'No,' I said. 'He just asked me if I didn't know there's a war on!'

Laughing, she tried another phone number and this time it was the US Coastguard on the other end. They were equally abrupt but before the phone was slammed down, I blurted out,

'Look, if you don't tell me where my ship is I'll just kip down here, and if she sails tomorrow without me you'll have a distressed British seaman on your hands! Now, do you tell me or don't you? And for your information the war you seem so worried about is a thousand miles away and I've just been in it! How about you!?'

I got the information! She was at the Weehawken coal wharf.

My new friend wouldn't take anything for her time and trouble and came outside with me. Indicating a bus stop just over the road she said,

'The bus will take you right to the wharf you want. Now, are you OK for the fare?'

I assured her I was, thanked her again and we parted. She was great!

A bus soon came and the driver was smashing. I was the only passenger so stood chatting to him as we drove along. Fine! Fine! Fine! Until... the bus stopped to pick up another passenger. It was another crew member and he really had been on the rye whiskey and beer. He got on the bus, saw me, and his face lit up.

'Hey 'Galley' he greeted, before being violently sick all over the front two seats of the bus. I wanted the earth to open and swallow me. That poor driver! I knew most public vehicles carried a sack of sand for such eventualities so immediately offered to get it and clean up but was told to 'leave it! I'm going into the depot after this run anyway.' The rest of the journey was in silence and thanks to that drunken fool my former new friend wasn't so friendly!

We said goodbye to 'little Ole New York' but not before seeing a huge burned out hulk of one of their aircraft carriers being towed in. It was a racing certainty the Japanese bombers had had a field day, and frankly, one wondered whether it was worth towing all the way back from the Pacific.

Once again, alone and unescorted, we sailed down the East coast of America very aware the seabed was littered with wrecks of ships. This was the U-Boat's second 'Happy Time' killing area for it took the Americans a long time to realise that leaving their coast lit up with no attempt at blackout, simply silhouetted the defenceless merchant ships and 'Bang, Bang, Bang, mate, that's your lot...!'

The Stokers, Trimmers, Greasers and Donkeymen we carried in the massive coal-fired boiler and engine rooms were Arabs. We got on well with them but quite unwittingly they were the cause of an incident. Why we stopped off at Norfolk, Vancouver I don't know, but whilst tied up that first evening we were not allowed out of the dock. However, we could visit the dockside canteen, which four of us did. In we went to find several of our Arab friends already there. We ordered refreshments and I called out,

'Hey Ali, Mohammed, come over and I'll let you buy me a big drink.'

They laughed and started to come over to us, crossing as they did so a two-inch wide line painted on the floor.

'Get back to your own side' shouted the canteen manager, 'this side is for whites only. You Arabs can stay on that side!'

That did it. These lads were our crew mates and could always be relied on so we told the guy to stick his Mason-Dixie line and walked out.

We sailed south, destination unknown, still alone and in dangerous waters. Our American allies then supplied us with a dirigible or airship as an escort which allowed us one good night's sleep. He didn't stay long however and soon after was replaced by a fighter-bomber. He got bored flying around us, and was making us dizzy I might add, so began making mock strafing attacking dives on our ship, some very close indeed. Now our Captain, a very no-nonsense type, brought out from retirement, ex Royal Navy skipper (and I do mean NO nonsense) called the 'Sparks' to the bridge and ordered him to send a signal to our friend,

'Our DEMS Gunners are now manning the ship's Oerlikon guns and if you endanger my ship once more, I will order them to shoot you down!'

And so we said farewell to our American friend as, make no mistake, the Skipper meant what he said!

Still we sailed, with the weather getting warmer and the seas bluer, and then we were told we were off to Cuba to collect sugar for the UK!

Nearing our destination, we were surprised when the ship dropped her bow anchor and we just lay, seemingly in the middle of an empty sea. Then along came a tugboat full of Cuban Grandees and their wives who were to come along as our 'Freebee' passengers for the few hours ride to our eventual destination. I can only imagine the effect this noisy and nosey bunch of Cubans were having on our unsociable skipper, but I guess he just had to put up with them. For myself, I rather enjoyed the smell of opulence and cigars that enveloped them, seemingly like a cloud, but what I didn't like was them treating us like their servants.

A few hours later we reached our destination and any thoughts of enjoying the seamier delights of Cuba went overboard with our passengers, for we were anchored so far out the shoreline was just a blur. This very 'cheesed off' crew were merely told we'd be loading sugar in sacks from barges and there was no shore leave! That was that then!

I was standing in the port side gangway watching our guests preparing to disembark into another tug drawn barge when the Chief Steward came bustling along. He was absolutely raving!

'Just come here and see what those dirty buggers have left for us to clean up!'

Whilst on board the passengers had been using the toilet next to the Chief's cabin and not used to modern plumbing had thrown the toilet paper onto deck floor. Adding to this at least one person had been sick so I'll leave it to your imagination as to the mess we now were required to dispose of.

'I'd like to teach those dirty buggers a lesson' said my immediate boss.

'Would you Chief?' said I 'Only, I have an idea!'

I went into the pantry and picked up the 'gash' bucket which was three-quarters full of the debris from the saloon officers' meals, old coffee grounds and tea leaves. Carrying this bucket of 'gunge' I went portside and peered over, looking aft, where the tug was just beginning to pull away with our friends towed behind in the barge. We had only our bow anchor down which meant the ship's head had swung into the wind. Lovely! I upended the gash bucket and the stiff breeze took away the contents, and so to shouts of rage and shaking fists the brilliant whites of the late visitors became speckled with debris. But then other voices joined in the shouts of outrage and looking up I saw the wrathful faces of the ship's Officers glaring down at me from the bridge. 'That's it' I thought, 'This moment of madness is going to cost me at least the logging of five quid off my wages when we pay off!' But it didn't, because although I never knew for sure, I suspect the Chief Steward showed the Skipper the filthy mess...before telling me to clean it up! I settled for that.

The barges came out and our winches, greased and oiled, got to work as we began to load sacks of brown sugar. As we were so far from land the Cuban dockers were required to live aboard, sleeping on the deck. Not only did they bring the sugar but also small bottles of white rum to trade for our cigarettes. (I believe their cigarettes were made from cigar tobacco). The dockers also brought a pig aboard which they fed with our scraps, and we referred to as the Bosun's young lady!

That rum was a mistake...

It was evening and my cabin mate and I were sitting on our bunks discussing the day's events. I was sitting closest to the door, side on to it, and Blondie, my mate, sat facing it. Suddenly the door was kicked open and the Third Engineer, looking very menacing, stood there. Not a word was said and with no warning at all he lurched across the cabin and tore the electric fan, screws and all from its shelf on the bulkhead and threw it as hard as he could at Blondie's head. The fan shattered into small pieces. To my dying day I maintain that had it hit him Blondie would've been dead. In those few split seconds we could see from the Third Engineer's dead white face and glaring eyes he was mad! Raving mad drunk on that rum! The force of the throw had taken him off balance and without a word said Blondie and I ducked under his arms and were off. We ran onto the deck and shot up the ladder to the boat deck where, in the darkness, we crawled under a lifeboat and lay there, trembling and terrified whilst the Third Engineer rampaged around screaming how he was going to kill us. There's no doubt he was off his rocker because Blondie was his mess and cabin steward and they were the best of friends! That is until the rum arrived.

After things had quietened down and the ravings and shouting could no longer be heard, Blondie and I crept out and tiptoed into the alleyway off from which lay the various catering crew cabins, the first being the cabin used mainly for extra hands although designated 'the Infirmary.' The door was slightly ajar and we could hear the oddest sounds emanating from inside. We peeked in and would you believe it? Inside stood the Third Engineer, tightly grasped so he was unable to move, by two burly seamen, one on each arm. In front of Third stood big Jimmy, the twenty year old apprentice due soon to take his Officer exams, and as hard as he could he was punching Third on the jaw trying to knock him unconscious to stop him getting into further mischief. The sound of the blows sickened us but bothered Third not one iota! He was laughing and jeering at them.

We'd had enough and left, thinking it was all over but it bloody well wasn't for half an hour later we were running for our lives yet again, and I really mean that, for close behind us was the Third Engineer once again and this time he had the ship's axe and he meant to use it on us!

With Third close behind we burst out of the port alleyway close to one of the bunker hatches right under the nose of the Captain. We froze, as did Third, but then still completely mad drunk, he came more slowly forward with the axe raised. Slowly the Captain's hand came up and I saw he was holding the largest service revolver I was ever to see. Very, very quietly he said,

'Put down that axe or I will shoot you!'

Still that madman advanced! The Captain's hand moved slightly and I heard a click as the revolver was cocked. The sound must've penetrated the alcohol fumes in Third's brain for, oh so slowly, the axe was lowered. From out of the shadows stepped the Second Engineer and several crewmen who quickly put the manacles on our friend's wrists before half carrying, half dragging him away. What happened next, I heard later. Third was taken to his cabin where more manacles were put on his ankles then he was lashed to his bunk. The cabin door was locked from the outside and he was left shouting and screaming threats. Early next morning the door was found forced open and Third, still drunk, was located down in the engine room where he'd put a hacksaw in a vice and was trying to saw the manacles from his wrists. They certainly don't make them like our late Third anymore. (thank God!)

Now we were once again in 'Little ole New York' but anchored out in the bay. We had a lovely view of the Statue of Liberty but at times it seemed we were on a floating seabed of contraceptives, toilet paper et al which all seemed to indicate our American Allies favourite pastimes. I hope they've cleaned up their sewage disposal system since then.

We set off once again. Now we were the convoy's Commodore ship. 'Sparks' was rushed off his feet, as was the Chief Steward. Flags were shooting up and down like a fiddler's elbow but the general feeling among the 'hoi polloi' was one of relief; our ship being right in the middle of all the other ships. This was when hostilities ceased!

We broke off and for the first time sailed home up the Channel which up to then had been closed to our ships due to the invasion transport going across. I will never forget in the area around Dover and the 'sands' the heart-breaking sight of all those bombed, mined, and torpedoed ships sticking out of the water, nor the thousands of brave Merchant Seamen, some only young boys, who lay in those steel coffins.

And so, for us, the war was over – or was it? On the evening of the day peace was declared officially, a small convoy set sail from Fife in Scotland. Later that night explosions were heard out to sea and a few hours later shocked and bleeding Merchant Navy survivors were being brought ashore. Did someone forget to tell Adolf's lads? We will never know!

Peace time trips:

And so with the war over I decided to take a long leave from the sea, but having the quiet of peace time under my belt, I decided to write to the shipping company to see if my former ship was back in the UK from her first peace time voyage – Bergen, Norway. She was, and the company sent back to tell me I could join her where she was berthed. She was in dry dock in the Tyne having her bottom scraped.

Out of the dock we tied up alongside in South Shields and I made many friends including Mary, a lovely girl who worked at the Shields Post Office. All too soon we were pulled out into the river and a trip began that started out to the west and brought us back in from the east. I will just touch on the ports we visited giving details which may be of interest.

First, was the Panama Canal. How can I describe the tiny little cars that pulled the ship through each lock! Up the steep concrete ramps that had steel cog bars set into them and into which the large cogged wheels under the cars 'meshed' giving the traction to pull us forward into each lock in turn until we were raised so high that at one time we seemed to be on top of a mountain looking down upon the forests.

Coming out of the canal we turned and sailed up the Pacific coast of America arriving in Vancouver, a town with a large Japanese population engaged, I was told, in the salmon fishing and allied industries. Here I befriended Shirley M and her family who welcomed me into their home. They lived in a flat and the heating was provided by upending a bucket of sawdust into a slow combustion stove. I've never seen such a stove since.

After Vancouver we set off again and arrived in Singapore. It was late at night when we anchored out on the bay and so didn't see much but the next morning, having time to look around, (although we never did get ashore) we found that tied up alongside was a tug boat manned by Japanese sailors. I have to say they were pretty impressive, smart, clean, stocky little blokes, but the skipper was a caricature of a Japanese Officer! Very tall, thin, and buck toothed, with one of those little peaked cloth caps so often seen in the war pictures. Again, we set off, this time arriving in Bombay (now Mumbai) having sailed through a sea covered in Portuguese Men of War jelly fish. They were enormous!

Beggars were everywhere in Bombay. Give them just one 'Anna' (money/coinage) and the whole mob would descend, calling out,

'Buckshee sab (not Sahib), no mamma, no papa Buckshee sab.'

In one of the main streets we saw a huge public fountain in the basin of which were dozens of Indians having a bath. Just along from this we saw an Indian pull a cobra from a basket and, having got the promise of a few rupees from the gathering crowd, he then extracted a mongoose from another basket and before you could say 'bingo' the mongoose and snake were trying to kill each other! The mongoose won but the showman pulled it from the snake's neck before the snake expired, no doubt so it could fight another day! The same evening whilst walking along minding our own business, my cabin mate and I saw a great crowd of Indians racing towards us chased by two Royal Navy sailors who were out of their minds with homemade hooch! (alcohol) Well, they must've been, mustn't they to chase such a crowd armed only with old broken-backed chairs! We stood well back to let the mob go past, wanting no part of the mayhem, but then saw several members of the Bombay police, creeping up behind the two. The police made their move by first jumping onto the backs of the drunken idiots and then having brought them down they began to belabour them with their long batons. Our two friends were knocked out cold. The policemen then stood back as the mob, having gained courage, came running back and began hitting the prostate forms of the two with long sticks and Lathi. It was obvious the police intended to do nothing to protect them when, seemingly from nowhere, a British Army Sergeant appeared shouting,

'Get back you bastards, leave them alone!'

He then turned to me and my mate and said,

'You two, help me get them up!'

The authority in this one British Squaddie's voice was such that the mob stood back muttering and waving their fists threateningly. Somehow, we got those two to their feet and holding them up we began to drag them towards the dock gate which, thank God, we could see at the end of what seemed like a very long road. Thus, we went in, line abreast, the two held up between us, still out cold.

With the mob still hurling insults at us as we went in, the Sergeant hissed,

'Don't look back at them,' ......and so what did my daft mate at the other end of our line do? That's right, he looked back! That did it! A great howl of hate went up from the mob which had by this time doubled in size and they began running after us. I was terrified for the two were dead weights and already my arm supporting the one between me and the Sergeant felt as though it would drop off.

We ran as best as we could with the mob filled with murderous intent hot on our heels. The Police? Oh, they cleared off!

To this day I can remember the dock we were running for. 'Alexandria dock... blue gate' manned by British and Indian soldiers. The three of us were on the point of collapse when the dock guards, on seeing what was happening, came running out and lifted our burdens from us. We beat the mob by only a few feet and as we dashed into the sanctuary of the dock itself the gates were slammed shut. Those gates were thick solid wood and about ten feet high but even so, we stood inside seeing them bending inwards as the mob pressed against them trying to get at us. An hour later re-enforcements arrived and the mob dispersed.

We asked after our drunken friends two days later and were told they were 'still out.' Those damn fools could've got us killed! Apparently, they'd visited the 'out of bounds' Grant Road where prostitutes sat behind barred windows and allegedly made booze out of dead dogs and rotten potatoes. Let's hope that's all they got in Grant Road for V.D was rampant. Is it any wonder Grant Road was banned to all Service personnel?!

So, we said farewell to Bombay and set off again on our travels. It's worth saying at this point that we were now engaged on doing what Merchant ships had been doing for centuries unless interrupted by war etc, that is to set off to ports all over the world, picking up and unloading cargoes wherever they could. No time scale was set for the length of any trip. It could be one, two, or three years' duration depending on availability. Pre-war living conditions and food were often vile, but not for us. We had the National Union of Seamen behind us!

Soon after 'up-anchoring' we ran into a Pacific/ Indian Ocean 'snorter' of a storm. The sea went mad! We pitched, tossed and rolled so much that at times I wondered if she would ever roll back. Off watch/ duty, I did what I did in the north Atlantic and purchased a tin of cigarette tobacco and paper from the Chief Steward's stores and for hour after hour when the storm reached its peak I rolled cigarette after cigarette while hanging onto my bunk, praying the ship wouldn't roll right over. After things had quietened down and the screw (propeller) had stopped lifting out of the sea due to the steep angle she went in, nose down, I went onto the deck to find several crew gleaning a harvest of flying fish that had glided aboard in the hurricane force winds. They tasted great.

Next stop was Durban, South Africa. A beautiful country where the police carried knobkerries. (sticks with a hard, round ball on the end) Here the local church took the ship's company on an outing into the Natal. The scenery was lovely and we had a game of cricket where I split my trousers so badly I had to walk around like a cricket umpire with my shirt tied around my waist. This amused the local natives who came to serve the picnic food. Arriving back at the sponsor church I declined the services of a rather angular young woman who then proceeded to show me into a back room where, after supplying me with needle and thread, I started repairing my trousers. Busily engaged, the door was thrown open and in came the local Parson demanding to know what I was doing sitting there with no trousers on! As he wasn't wearing a dog collar or had other means of visual identification, I told him to 'hop it' (or words to that effect)

Durban was lovely but smiles seemed to be few and far between. On the last night as we stood waiting for the ferry on a landing stage, several bare-chested Zulus wearing traditional costume strolled up and began chanting whilst rhythmically raising their legs up and down, and before our very eyes Africa came alive!

Off we sailed again, through the Suez Canal and into Alexandria. The Suez Canal was lovely if looking at sand for hours 'rocks your boat' but two events stick in my mind:

Some of us went into a restaurant for an evening meal. It was very good, but in every company you'll find a silly bugger, and we had one with us. Having eaten and sitting back waiting for the bill, one of our company said, very quietly,

'Well, that's it then; now we do a runner!'

Honestly, I couldn't believe my ears, but that's exactly what he did. He stood up, or rather leapt up, and ran for the door of the restaurant at a rate of knots. Only having enough money for our own needs we ran after him, and so into the night we raced with several Egyptian waiters in hot pursuit. I don't think their hearts were in it to try to catch us because several of the lads were big strong seamen. We got clean away.

Then, on the way back to the ship I passed a shop that had a very nice handbag in the window which I decided my recently widowed sister would love. In the shop, having seen the asking price, I started to haggle but the shop owner was obviously a cut above many of the Egyptians we'd come across and he told me the price was what he wanted. Take it or leave it! The bag was well worth the money so I bought it. As it was a very cold night, and it does get very, very cold at night in Egypt, I pushed the bag through the front of my shirt with one end sticking out so it was obvious I wasn't trying to conceal it. As we were walking through the dock gates an Egyptian Officer wearing one of those red Tommy Cooper type fezz hats came out of the dock gate office. Grabbing my arm, he pulled the handbag from my shirt and without saying a word walked back into the office. I went straight in after him and demanded he give the bag back but he refused. At this I went 'dead bolshy' and informed the world at large, and that greasy bugger in particular, that I was not going to move until I got that bag back!

As for Alexandria as a City you can keep it! It was all dirty (pornographic) books and bum boat men who having sold you items would send young boys up the side of the ship to pinch them back again. On top of that were the horse drawn gharries pulled by poor starving nags with every rib showing because the owners neglected to feed them properly. Even our Arab crew men didn't have a good word to say about the Egyptians!

So, we said farewell (and bloody good riddance) to Alexandria, which is a sentiment I'm sure would've been echoed by the restaurant proprietor had he known we were leaving! The next stop was 'Bone' in French North Africa.

After an uneventful trip we came alongside at 'Bone' and were rather surprised to see a large crowd of the locals jumping up and down on the quay side where we intended to berth. In our ignorance we thought they were gathered to welcome us in but as the pilot pointed out,

'No lads, they're waiting for you to try and go ashore so they can cut your throats!' We stayed aboard.

We only stayed for a short time in Bone, just long enough to load iron ore (more about this later) and then off we went again, this time to Tripoli Harbour. Everywhere one looked could be seen the bomb blasted wrecks of ships sticking up out of the sea. By golly that place, Queen of what was to have been Benito Mussolini's empire, had really been pasted. The statue of Romulus and Remus still stood but the statue was the only bit of interest in the place. We sailed out of the 'Med' and anchored for just one night in Gibraltar Harbour just in time to see one half of a ship being towed in. I heard later they found another half of a ship and welded them together.

Iron ore is a nasty commodity to carry in a ship's hold, especially if going through the Bay of Biscay which is notorious for great slow rolling waves hitting a ship on the beam, or side. Careful loading has to be observed otherwise if too much of the stuff is low down in the holds the ship reacts like a huge pendulum, and she rolls, and rolls, and rolls. Gradually the rolling builds up until you think when she's right over, 'Christ, she isn't going to come back!'

By the end of this trip I needed to look around and take stock. I soon realised that by going deep sea I'd not done myself any favours promotion wise. Had I gone, as so many lads had, on the coasters which just sailed up and down mainly the East Coast, London to the Tyne, then my seaman's discharge book would've had many entries... two days up, two days load and unload, two days down... sign off... next ship, sign on. Solution? Go short trips and get rated!

My final trip was on an ex German prize of a warship delivering Ford vans from Dagenham to Copenhagen. At the end of this trip when the time came for me to 'sign off' I did so without any regrets as I hadn't formed any real attachment to the ship. Now officially 'paid off' I decided that the old adage usually applied to Merchant Seamen of 'having no friends, no family, no money and being wanted by the police' no longer applied to me, so I left the Merchant Navy and went home.

Norman Hastings aged 18 years

Chapter 3: Back to Civvie Street and Engineering

Needing time to adjust to civilian life I got myself a mundane job as a machine setter in a box factory, but now my old nemesis stepped in. My eldest sister, Mabel, a girl of 21 years, had died of consumption in 1935 and just a few months before her death I was found to have a cavity on one of my lungs caused by this deadly disease. I was admitted into the local hospital for consumptives (on Groby Road) and ordered 'absolute bed.' for three months. I was one of the few lucky ones to get over the 'the scourge of the white death'. It was while I was in the hospital King George V and Queen Mary celebrated their Silver Jubilee and I, along with my cubicle mate, Frankie Jordan, being children, were awarded the Silver Jubilee medal. I lost mine but years later managed to replace it through a coin and medal dealer. It was because this nemesis cast a shadow over my life I made the decision that until a cure was found for this killer disease, I would not form any close relationship with any female. No way would I marry, fall ill and pass this disease onto my partner or children. It was a promise I kept.

Working indoors was a shock to my constitution and I soon felt very much under the weather. I went to our family G.P who handed me a sputum test bottle and ordered me to 'come back in two weeks for the result.'

I went back as told and, grave of face, he told me,

'The sample contained a large number of T.B bacilli. I'll try to get you into hospital as soon as I can!'

A month later I was admitted to my old ward in 'the hospital for consumptives' and two weeks after this, following further tests, was told the disease was in remission. What got to me most was the fact most patients were ex forces and wearing uniforms although the majority had never been abroad or seen any active war zones. Every week a paymaster came in and paid them their forces wages, and yet Joe Soap here, war service and in active war zones, was trying to manage on a few shillings a week of sick benefit. I will tell you this though, I would not have changed places with those poor devils. More money or not I don't think many of them lived for very long. Consumption was a killer.

I went back to the factory following convalescence but regularly scanned the situations vacant columns in the local paper. 'Trainee branch mechanic/ engineer wanted. Apply to.......' I applied for, and got the job at Roneo Vickers, a well-known office machinery company. I was told I'd be working outside the showrooms and workshop as much as indoors and I'd be my own man so long as the customers using the machines were satisfied.

I was handed a rail voucher to get me to London as I was to be accommodated in a hotel with other trainees whilst being trained at the firm's training school in Southampton Row. Our teacher was a lovely old chap, a typical London businessman with bowler hat, rolled umbrella, and smart grey overcoat. The course was easy although some nine or ten machines needed to be partially stripped down, reassembled and tested.

I returned after one month to the local branch with a good report and at once ran slap bang into the sort of managerial thinking that so many times brought work places out on strike. The Branch Manager, almost at retiring age and wishing to put that day off by bringing in a little more in the way of business, insisted that the service reps, four in number including myself, should work alternate Saturday mornings for no extra money although the terms of our employment stipulated a five-day week! The service reps, all married men with children, had no choice but to agree and I was forced to follow suit. A typical job I was expected to undertake went like this:

It was 5pm on a Friday evening and one of our customers at Northampton rang in to say their machine had developed a fault and the customer needed to run off thousands of copies of a timetable for distribution on the Monday morning. I arose on the Saturday, caught a bus to the local railway station and boarded a train to Northampton. At Northampton I caught a local bus to the main bus depot offices. Here I mended the machine and stood by until the job was 'run off'. I then caught a bus back to the railway station, took a train back to my base city and caught a bus back home. Total time on the firm's business 8 hours!

My reward? In a whisper, because I don't think the manager wanted anyone else to hear his largesse, he said, 'put a late evening meal down on your expense sheet old chap!' What was a late evening meal worth? 4 shillings and 6 pence, or as it would be worth today, approximately 24 new pence. To be fair, they did pay me for the fares expended.

Time passed, and I was now established at the engineering branch in my home town of Leicester. I didn't realise how invaluable I'd become until Mr P, the supervisor over all mechanics and who I'd take out with me on his periodic visits to the branch, right out of the blue sent me a letter from, of all places, India! In his letter he said,

'I'm currently touring India and Pakistan. On my return I will be asking for applications from branch mechanics willing to come to India and train native labour to service and maintain the Company's products. I have you in mind for this most prestigious post. Should you be willing to take the job then please write to me at Head Office saying so and the job is yours. An inter-house memo will be sent to each branch for the branch mechanics' attention. As soon as you see it make formal application and the job is yours. Company policy says these posts must be memo'd.'

Two months later and still no memo had been given to me. Then Mr P came to the branch. He was rather short with me but we went out for a drink that evening and he began,

'You rather let me down. When you wrote and said you were willing to take on the India job I did all the ground work ready for the 'off', but you didn't respond to the memo, why?'

'For the simple reason I didn't see any memo!' I replied.

To say he was annoyed was an understatement. The next morning I found him waiting at the Branch as soon as I arrived.

'Come along' he said, 'I intend to have this out with the branch manager!'

Upstairs we went and into the manager's office.

'You were sent a memo that specifically stated it was to be shown to your branch mechanic. It was to do with India. Now I'm told your mechanic wasn't given this memo, why?'

The manager went red.

'Well, you see, salesmen are two a penny. Service reps only have to clean and oil our machines, but good mechanics cannot be got for love nor money and our mechanic would, in my opinion, be irreplaceable.'

That old bugger cost me a job that would've had me made for life!

I soon found that two thirds of my duties were to do with keeping the customers happy once the customer had purchased one of our machines, and I had the knack of doing this. Witness the following:

It was around 1950 and the salesmen were making a killing as war time shortages were still being felt, and so some of the sales side were not above telling a few 'porkies!' 'Mal' a salesman, came to me on this day saying,

'We have a problem! (Notice the 'we!') I recently sold a machine to a firm and now I've been told the machine isn't doing what it should be, and if 'you' can't put it right the machine will be thrown out!'

I was taken to one of the largest pet food suppliers and my salesman friend, instead of coming in with me, parked two streets away. It was strange he didn't come in with me but I soon found out why. I was taken through into the general office, a palatial room with the deepest of deep carpets, and was left standing by our machine whilst 'She' was fetched out to me. 'She', it emerged, was one of the first Harvard USA trained 'time and motion' experts and as soon as she loomed up I knew why 'matey boy' was skulking around the corner. With no preamble or introduction, she began with,

'Your salesman sold us this machine stressing it can do 150 copies per minute. I have timed this and it's only doing 120 copies per minute.'

Displaying a large stop watch she continued,

'I expect to return in 10 minutes and find the machine running off the claimed 150 copies per minute!'

I was in a cold sweat as these things were geared to a maximum of 120! Left with a clear ultimatum I began to tinker with belt, pulleys etc and by some miracle got the machine churning out 145 copies per minute. When she returned 10 minutes later I had my answer ready.

'If I gear the machine up any faster, every time the office door opens the draught will cause the paper copies to fly all over the place!'

I omitted to tell her this could be avoided by turning the machine round so the 'feed side' would be facing the draught. Even so, having packed my bag, when leaving the office, I chanced to look back. The machine was now going so fast the completed copies were flying up into the air, draught or no draught, with the office girls leaping up to catch them looking just like the 'corps de ballet' doing 'Swan Lake!'

The old manager died and a new manager came to the branch. He seemed a reasonable sort of a chap and so I tackled him about the unpaid work each alternate Saturday morning. After I'd explained, a look of horror crossed his face.

'Oh my God, cut it out at once,' he said. 'If the factory down at Romford find out you chaps have been coerced into working extra hours for no extra overtime, we'll have the lot of them out on strike!'

With that Saturday morning work was stopped, dead!

I was regularly being called out to firms and factories all over the East Midlands. Some I enjoyed going out to but others I dreaded. First among the latter was a Mental Hospital in Northampton. The building was a late Victorian place set in its own grounds. My visits went like this: The call would come into the office and what was usually said was,

'The printing machine is only inking down one side!'

Until I cracked the problem I'd be frankly puzzled, for this type of breakdown was being reported even though I'd reset the inking rollers just a few days before. Every door and gate had to be unlocked and locked in this place. I'd walk down the lane to the prefabricated reception block and knock on the door then out would pop one of the supervising male nurses who would smile and say something like,

'Not you again?!'

After seeing his door was securely locked he would then cross the lane with me, unlock the gate into the recreation exercise yard, push me inside and lock the gate behind me. So, there I'd be in a large exercise yard surrounded by the inmates. One I remember very clearly and it was obvious his mind was completely gone.

'1914 Mans, 1915 Lens and Loos, 1916 the Somme......'

At one time I'd asked one of the attendants why was he shouting out World War I battles only to be told the patient was a GPI. Asking what this meant I was told he'd caught syphilis whilst in France during the Great War and never had it treated properly because of the shame. GPI meant General Paralysis of the Insane. Another old boy parading around the yard was clothed in a thick padded type of boiler suit which he was constantly plucking at. I was told he would reduce his suit to shreds in three days at the most. Some patients would be screaming, others muttering and one chap used to creep up behind me and jump on my back! Caught unawares I usually thought I'd have a heart attack!

In the building where the printing machine was set a male nurse who gave patients some simple instruction would point out that the ink rollers were completely out of 'kittle' and I would reset them using special gauges. It was during this last visit I dreamt up a scheme which the supervisor agreed to. He left the workroom whilst I concealed myself behind a store cupboard. Ten minutes elapsed and I was about to give it all up as a waste of time when I saw one of the patients who'd been in the next room under another supervisor, creep in, sidle up to the machine I'd spent 10 minutes setting up, then start to twist the setting bars on the inking rollers. Satisfied, he crept out again. Problem solved!

During one of these visits the attendant asked if I'd like to be shown around. I said yes please. We went through, ward after ward, with door after door being unlocked and then locked behind us. It was heart breaking to see how many mentally ill people had been locked away as they were too ill to be allowed out into society. Finally, we went through a door and emerged into a cobbled yard, open to the sky but surrounded by the tall hospital buildings. It was deadly quiet and what shot through my mind was I'd been transported back to the 19th century. Suddenly a scream rang out. A blood curding 'make your hair stand on end' type of scream! All the fiends of hell seemed to be contained in it and I just looked at my escort, lost for words. Very quietly he said,

'That's one of our worst cases. Locked away, never to be approached without three of us in his padded cell and even then he wears a special harness to prevent him harming himself, and us!'

I was never so glad to leave a place.

Not all of my outside visits were as bad as that one however, and I soon found I could get on with the customers ranging from the Chairman of the Board to the office boy or girl. I was, dare I say it, good at my job!

Often whilst working on this or that customer's machine the operatives or departmental managers would come and chat to me recounting incidents or happenings in the daily life of their firm. For example:

The boss of this shoe factory was a Czech Jewish gent who was often to be seen storming around his factory berating any worker who just happened to raise his eyes from the job as the boss went past. Going into the yard cum loading dock area the boss saw two men sitting at the side of the yard having a smoke and picking winners from that day's 'Racing News'. The boss went spare,

'I don't pay idle buggers like you pair to sit around doing bugger all' he screamed. 'Get your bloody stuff together and wait here. The pair of you are sacked!'

With that he stormed off to tell the cashier to go and get their clock numbers so their wages could be made up. To hear is to obey and our friend in the wages department did as his lord and master instructed. The departmental manager then approached the pair, still sitting there with their mouths open, and said,

'You're a pair of idiots! Fancy letting the boss catch you out like that! Now I have to sack you!'

The two mouths closed with an audible 'click'.

'You can't bloody sack us' said one 'for the simple reason we don't work for that mad man! We're sitting here waiting for the cart to come then we can get on with emptying the dustbins! We're dustbin men!'

One of the largest factories I serviced was in stitches over this other true story:

The Board of Directors were having a meeting and all the top brass were present. Needing a paper from the work's office the Chairman rang down with the instruction, 'Send the Office Junior along with it; no need to come yourself!'

Now as it happened the office junior was 'Cowboys and Indians' mad and it just so happened the doors into the conference room were of the bar room swing door type. Seeing these the lad tucked the called for paper under his arm, then kicked the swing doors open and dashed in making like a cowboy pulling his trusty two six shooters from their holsters, shouting, 'Stick em up!'

The whole room went quiet and then as one, every member of the Board of the largest factory, probably in the City, stood up and raised their hands above their heads. Lovely!

Then again, all of us on the outside staff, service and mechanics, got the odd awkward beggar. This one was the Chairman's Secretary. I fell foul of her simply because having been called out to see why the print was very faint down one side of the paper, and this was usually because the ink container needed more ink, I lifted one of the offending sheets to see whether the faintness was left or right of the page. Hardly had I had a chance to even look at the print when the paper was snatched from my hand and I was snappily told,

That's private!'

I began to explain I wasn't interested in the contents of the said page, when she snapped,

'You're banned!'

Bloody hell! Being banned was a first for me!

When I got back to the branch the boss was not a happy man.

'How could you upset a customer like this one?' he asked.

He was still going on about it an hour later when the chap he'd sent straight after me to placate the woman came back with his tail between his legs. He'd been banned as well! In all that woman banned every outside rep in the place and then the day came, as I knew it would, when she rang in needing a service rep or mechanic. The boss was called to the phone to tell her,

'I'm terribly sorry Miss Queen but you've banned every one that works for us!'

Now she had to think fast for she may have been the boss's secretary but that machine needed attention. Her boss wouldn't like it if he knew that with each one of us banned by her the only way out would be to buy another expensive machine. She had to eat dirt!

'Oh well, you'd better send that first chap' she said.

We had to start all over again but not quite, for I now had the measure of her!

Her continual complaint was that the machine was too heavy to turn by hand but it was an electrically driven machine! The operator only needed to turn by hand once to turn out a copy for checking. See what I mean by an awkward beggar?!

Of course, things happened in the branches as well! Reggy was a Manager of another branch of the firm. Reggy looked like he'd be a beggar to work under but like all branch managers he went in fear and trembling lest sales dropped and the wrath of Head Office fell upon him. He'd taken on a new salesman whose performance was not coming up to scratch and so Reggy called the man into his office and warned him,

'If you don't pull your finger out, you'll be out!'

When nothing much happened in relation to this poor bloke getting new business he got another warning!

Now, Reggy could be quite nasty and this warning was delivered without mincing words. Still hopeless, so the poor bloke had to go! Reggy called him into his office and really laid into the chap. He could've just said 'you're fired' but no, Reggy being Reggy he just had to rub it in. Whilst he was ranting and raving the soon to be former salesman reached into his left-hand pocket and took out a newspaper which he very carefully, almost tenderly, laid out and smoothed on Reggy's desk. Next, he reached into his right-hand pocket and took out a one-pound tube of our oil based black ink. Slowly he unscrewed the cap of the tube and slowly squeezed the entire contents all over the newspaper. By now Reggy was panicking,

'What are you doing you fool? Get out of my office.'

Slowly, oh so very slowly, our friend lifted the newspaper at each side and up ended it all over his seemingly, by now, paralyzed manager, or should I say 'former manager!'

I had problems of my own for one of our salesmen disliked me intensely, mainly I think because he was quite a short chap and I was over six feet tall. It all stemmed from the fact our salesman friend thought I should load and unload his car whilst he stood and watched. Now, I pointed out quite reasonably I thought, that whilst I was more than prepared to help him load & unload I was in fact the branch mechanic and not his beast of burden! Matters came to a head one evening when again he came storming into the showroom demanding I unload his car. I refused, saying I'd be quite happy to help him but I wasn't going to be his 'skivvy.'

Now, as it happened, the branch manager was a new chap and my friend decided to push for a confrontation. He turned to the new manager and said, 'Did you hear that? Now, either he goes, or I go!'

The manger's reply was, 'Really! So when will you be giving me your notice?'

That finished it and ever after it was, 'Would you give me a hand to unload my machines, please?' When I eventually left the firm this same man sent me a Christmas card every Christmas for several years!

Chapter 4: Marriage and family life

I married in 1952. I was 25 years. Accommodation was at a premium and houses within the scope of my finances were few and far between so my wife and I did as many couples did and moved into rooms.

Soon after my wife became pregnant but as our landlady now decided our rooms were wanted we had to find alternative accommodation. Our luck was in when I saw a small, two bedroomed, terrace house being advertised for sale and I made an offer. In my favour was the house being in a development area so I wasn't surprised when my offer of £250 cash was accepted. I borrowed £50 from my brother, another £50 from my in-laws and mam loaned me the outstanding £150. This was all paid back within 5 years. So, in 1953 my wife and I, along with our new infant son, took up residence at 26 Gordon Street, Leicester.

Norman in 1953 with wife Joyce Hastings (nee Hart) and Stephen

We lived in Gordon Street until 1962 and in the interim years were joined by two daughters. Although the redevelopment of the area was not due to take place for a few years yet, our decision to 'get out' was based on the number of 'pimps' and prostitutes who were systematically taking over the district.

The Council purchased 26 Gordon Street from me for £200 and we were rehoused at 56 Gedding Road, Leicester. This house had three bedrooms and a long back garden. It was a happy home, a family house, and we lived there for 25 years, first as tenants and then owner occupiers.

Chapter 5: 1967 Education Welfare and Attendance Officer

I'd been a group Scout Leader at Mayflower Methodist Church, which our family attended, for over a year. I'd never been a Scout myself but had been asked to take on the job because the troop Scouters had not stamped out bullying. This meant 'cubs' coming up into the troop were not staying long as they were being picked on. I'd agreed to see what I could do as my own son was a Scout in this troop but what I hadn't been told was the troop Scout Leader was planning to leave as was the Senior Scout Leader. This meant I was left in charge of nearly 30 Scouts and 6 Senior Scouts without having a clue. All appeals to the sponsoring church brought only one volunteer forward and so finally I contacted the local university and a mature student, an ex-Scout, also pitched in. Between us we managed to keep the show on the road... just!

In addition to the scouts I was helping out once a fortnight at a club for discharged prisoners (The Anchor Club) which was a great help for what was to transpire later, as you will see.

The years had been passing and I was now approaching the ripe old age of thirty-nine. My children were growing up although still at school and I realised that if I asked myself whether I wanted to stay with this firm for the rest of my working life, the answer was a resounding, 'No!' This was the time of big business mergers, and 'hatchet men' were becoming a fact of life and moving in all over the country. What helped me decide was the top man at my firm dying after a stroke. Within three months loyalty and service meant nothing. However, I never dreamed my voluntary work would give me such a tremendous advantage when finally making up my mind to get out.

I saw the post of 'Education Attendance and Welfare Officer' advertised in the newspaper and in went my application along with the stipulated two referees' names! I put down the church minister and my stalwart helper who, unbeknown to me, was on first name terms with the Chairman of the Education Committee. I was invited for interview along with other candidates but as usual with these processes whilst cordial we were all rather tense. The Department's Chief Officer stipulated he wanted someone 'willing to do what had to be done' and I was asked about any service record. Naturally I spoke of my time as a Merchant Seaman which brought about the obvious question of rank! I couldn't resist,

'Actually, I did rather well! I worked my way up from Galley boy to Cabin boy!'

The ice was broken and I got one of the two posts advertised.

I knew something of the history of the old time 'Boardman' appointed as he was to get the children of the labouring classes into the state provided teaching institutions. The upper-class children were already being catered for in the public schools (fee paying of course) but the plight of the poor down the years was tragic. The workhouse test was part of our history and still very much in living memory. The sick, dispossessed, widowed and orphaned had only the workhouse to fall back on and once inside the Master's word was law!

Mother was separated from father and children from parents depending on the whim of whoever was in charge at the time! Those who could work were often farmed out to the factories or mill owners. Others were sent down the mines.

Little children had to drag heavy coal trucks, their limbs were broken, some had their eyes knocked out by drunken overseers and bullying older children throwing lumps of coal at them to wake them should they fall asleep due to exhaustion. In the factories, unfenced machinery and shafting ripped off arms, and the belts and shafting, all too often unfenced, would throw the tiny wasted bodies around like rag dolls once a child was caught up.

Gradually, thanks to the philanthropists, humanists and the like, Parliament was forced to act and a start was made to extract the most vulnerable from the rotten discredited system. Concentrating on the children, and with the popularisation of education, pressure from those already mentioned plus the new Parliamentary legislation, school places were made available, first to a few and then all children, usually from five up to fourteen years. To save money many early schools were built so the infants were on the lower floor, next up were the juniors and then at the top, the seniors. This explains why children moving from junior to senior spoke of 'going up'. For up they did go, whereas others, the less academic, went 'down'.

Provision was made for free school meals and nurses for the deserving poor. Now we had clean, airy & warm classrooms and signals were set for Education to Go, Go, Go! Well, not really, for the dear little children, often with the connivance and assistance of the parents, stayed away in droves thus adding a new word to our language... Truant!

But why didn't the children always attend school? Easy, if the local farmer or land owner wanted extra field hands at harvest time then they used the local kids! It was the same in the factories. If cheap labour was needed then here it was, and thousands of the little buggers were glad to add a few coppers to the family income. Common sense really!

To try and get the kids into school various schemes were tried and tested. One was payment by results, but not for the kid, for the teachers! If attendance reached a satisfactory level full capitation was paid. If it did not come up to scratch then money was withheld. School Boards were formed consisting of local worthies to help and advise Head teachers on all matters pertaining to the running of the school. One idea was the setting up of a School Attendance Officer, hereafter called 'The Boardman'. It then followed, as surely as night follows day, that if attendance was down the Boardman was sent post haste to round up the kids and woe betide any kid who wasn't on his death bed or screwed down in his or her coffin when his nibs came thumping on the door! Where money and the creature comforts that money could buy were involved the staff in schools in those days showed the same dedication to the children as the staff in the schools today show, well, some of them anyway! 'Get the buggers in!'

For myself, the one and only brush with the Boardman came when I was seven years old and living at 1 Morton Road, Leicester. The previous Saturday I'd been discharged from the Sanatorium having been confined for three months with consumption. (TB) My lot had been 'absolute bed' and I mean 'absolute!' That Monday, two days after returning home, a knock came on the back door. I answered to find a tall man with a round, peaked, hat. Unmistakeably 'The Boardman!'

'Aren't going to school today laddie?' I was asked.

'Please Sir, no Sir, I only came out of the Sanatorium on Saturday and I have to see the Doctor again Sir.'

'Yes, yes, I know all about that.' said my visitor, 'but your Headmistress wants to know when you'll be returning to school!'

That did it! In my life the Headmistress at my school was the be all and end all, sited somewhere between God Almighty and the Holy Ghost, who sounded pretty spooky as well and always put the 'wind up' me!

I began to cry and the Boardman was trying to shut me up when my sister, Mabel, a hopeless consumptive with, had I but known it, only a few short months to live, arrived at the door. She'd dragged herself down the stairs to see what was making me cry, and at once picked up the yard brush and advanced. He, deciding that discretion was the better part of valour, fled down our entry and made off on his bike. This was my only contact with the service as a child.

32 years later, when a 'Boardman' myself, I was to ask my Chief Officer, who'd let slip he used to work on the district where I'd lived as a child,

'Do you ever remember going to a house on Morton Road to be greeted with a frail slip of a girl brandishing a sweeping brush at you?'

The Chief swung on his heels and marched off. I think he remembered!

With my resignation submitted I left the employ of the Office Machinery company after serving the statutory one month's notice. I swore I would never

113

go back but, wanting to scrounge some various and assorted screws, nuts and bolts, I popped in to the branch one lunch hour. Seeing the storeman I asked,

'Is the boss around? I don't want him seeing me on the scrounge!'

His answer was,

'No! Soon after you left the firm a man came into the showroom, walked into the boss's office, told him to hand over his car keys, empty his desk of all personal possessions and then 'get out!'

He'd been sacked on the spot! Now do you see what I meant about hatchet men?! Who'd been a naughty boy then!!

My appointment as an Attendance Officer was initially for a probationary period and I arrived at the Central Education Office fully equipped with bicycle clips and a bike. In those early days all visiting was done by these means. A cycle allowance (and we provided our own two-wheeler) was paid monthly. Knowing no better I parked up in the side yard taking care not to scratch the Director's car, and went in through the main front entrance where a charming young lady greeted me. I was led through winding corridors, losing all sense of direction, and made a joke along the lines of hoping I could find my way back! To this my guide replied,

'Don't worry, this is the front way in! You Officers use the back entrance!'

This wasn't overt snobbery for, as I was to find out later, our way in was easier for getting to our office via side roads. In fact, one of the older, more experienced Officers put it much more succinctly...

'Of course we're at the back! Isn't that where you always find the arse holes?'

My new Chief greeted me briefly before taking me into the Attendance Officers' room which was placed as far from the front as humanly possible without actually siting the Officers' desks on the road outside. This, possibly the oldest part of the building, had probably begun life as one of the early schools of the City. Witness the high vaulted ceiling and the high narrow windows, obviously well used over the years and smelling of that dry, musty, aroma of layer upon layer of polish!

The room was tightly packed with desks. Again, these were very old, the type that in the good old days were meant to be 'stood' at rather than 'sat' at. Witness the stools in front of each desk that had blocks on each leg to meet the height at which the desks stood. Two of the room's walls had these desks around them whilst a double row of facing desks ran down the middle of the room to provide seating for something like 20 people, although as I stood looking around I could see only 3 or 4 men going about their office business, and one of those had been delegated to look after the 'new boy' for a day or two and show me the ropes!

Leicester Children's Department circa 1966

The Chief took me to a desk in the corner of the room and, picking up a piece of card upon which was glued a section of the map of the City said,

'This is your desk and this is the map of your district. I'm throwing you in at the deep end!'

Off the Chief went only to be replaced by my mentor who reassured me with,

'Don't worry, Lad, everything will fall into place! This is your desk and these boxes on top contain your district census cards, one for every house, which you'll need to keep up to date. Just keep your Head Teachers happy and the job's a doddle!'

With that he looked at my map,

'Ah! You've got a bit of 'rough' in this district, but you should be alright.'

I learned later that an Officer's district was his domain only, and as such I was not allowed to go onto any of my colleagues' districts, nor they upon mine, without the express permission from the Officer responsible for the said district, and that should a complaint be made against an Officer, be it made by a Head Teacher or parent, a full and impartial investigation would be made at Director of Education level, which seemed reasonable... as I was all too soon to find out!

The start of my new career coincided with the schools being closed for the long, mid-summer holidays. Accompanied by the Officer assigned to me, I spent the mornings on my district establishing whether the details on my census cards had changed in any way. I had to check the street name and number against the census card, knock on each respective door, introduce myself then have the name of the occupier confirmed. Details of any new arrivals (babies) were duly noted on the card but should the house have changed hands I was to establish where the former occupants had moved to and where the current residents had previously lived. In the afternoon the information gained was carefully transposed onto our office records with particular reference to new babies so we could tell our Infant School Heads what their intake would be each term during the next five years. Any changes of address and the census cards were swapped with the Attendance Officer for that district. We never lost a family.

The day before the schools reopened after the holidays, the Chief spoke to me again:

'Can I rely on you to go into each of the schools in your district and introduce yourself?'

As God is my witness this was the only training I received!

This district had three Infant Schools which I visited twice a week to pick up 'visits' (I was also on call for emergencies), three Junior Schools (ditto), one Senior Boys' and Girls' School (to visit every day and be available for emergencies), one Senior Grammar School (girls only) and one Special Needs School. (twice a week for pick-ups)

The area had a bit of a reputation for giving whoever had dealings with it trouble with a capital 'T' and problems with a capital 'P', but I always found the residents to have a marvellous sense of humour and the God given talent to laugh at themselves! They rarely took life seriously and, given the chance or even half a chance, they'd 'nick' anything that wasn't nailed down!

In the main the properties were part of a large council estate built in the 1920s/30s to house families who'd been uprooted and dumped en masse from huge slum clearance areas in the inner-city. I can think of no other words to describe their displacement. In those inner-city areas they'd plenty to see and do but here they were like fish out of water! No bright lights and no shops to trade at. The community spirit was gone. Is it any wonder it all fell apart? The locals even had a name for the district which proves my assertion of a sense of humour... 'Dodge City!' No other adopted name could've better described it but, to be fair, whilst their living accommodation ranged from very good to 'Oh my God,' I had little if any problems settling in, mainly because I could always laugh at myself and at the attempts of those bent upon 'extracting the urine', and I was always able to keep a straight face whilst some of the most outrageous 'cons' were tried out upon me. The clincher was a lesson I'd learned many years previously… never, never, never get a client trapped in a corner, and I don't mean physically. Always leave room for manoeuvre for if you do trap them with no way of escape they can only come out the one way – straight through you! This advice paid off, for when I eventually retired after twenty-three years of dealing with some really tough characters, only once did I feel physically threatened and that was a set up.

At this point I ought really to describe the duties of a School Attendance/Education Welfare Officer. They included, besides those previously outlined:

- Assessing for free school meals and clothing.
- Ensuring children with verminous heads went to the clearing clinic.
- Checking after a few months that the free clothing had not been sold to get Dad his beer money.
- Contacting the Senior School Medical Officer to see what alleged medical reasons for non-attendance were genuine.
- Writing prosecution briefs for Court action in non-attendance cases.
- Serving summonses on parents (and don't forget to duck).
- Prosecution in Magistrate and Juvenile Courts.
- Attending case conferences.
- Liaise with Children's Department, Probation Service, School Nurses etc.
- Investigating child sexual/ physical abuse.

- Advising parents of pregnant daughters, gender confusion and matters needing help from other authorities.
- Office census cards.
- Finding missing families.
- Escorting children to special educational needs 'out of town' schools.
- Study for three-year Social Studies certificate.
- Undertake 'any other' authority business.

Who was it who said being a 'Boardman' was a cushy number?! Oh yes, and once a month we delivered the salary cheques for the Headmasters and teachers.

In addition to our daytime duties, if Officers weren't able to contact a parent to let him or her know their child or children weren't toeing the line at school, we were expected to go out at night or weekends to the parent's home, place of work or even their favourite pub, just to let them know what was going on.

I was never, ever officious and wouldn't even consider prosecuting a parent without seeing him or her at least four times but when the 'crunch' did come I could truthfully say I'd tried my very best and failed!

On my first day alone on my district, without a clue as to the layout of the area, I set off on my trusty bike, pedalling through what seemed to be a grey concrete jungle. The roads were littered with broken bottles, discarded fish & chip wrappers and general debris. I remember I was wearing a grey suit, and had my briefcase, courtesy of and provided by the Education Office, attached to my handlebars so as to leave my right hand free to carry the bundle of free school dinner and clothing application forms that I had to find the time to deliver and fill in until the schools had completed their first few days and settled down with the new intake.

I very soon realised I was clearing those streets faster than a flag seller in Aberdeen on flag day! Everywhere I went, all ready to call out greetings to the locals, they, before I had the chance to even open my mouth, were vanishing through doors, up entries, and into back gardens faster than the blinking of an eye. I felt very unwanted.

On arrival at the first address I found the occupant leaning over a very sparse privet hedge in deep conversation with the next-door neighbour and although not a betting man myself, I could see that the subject of mutual interest was the local horse racing guide.

The rusty gate hinges creaked as it opened, and the pair looked up to see yours truly advancing towards them with his hands full of free dinner/ clothing forms. Panic! Without a word passed between them they both shot into their respective homes and slammed the doors.

I knocked, but nothing!

I hammered the door and this time a response, for the letterbox flap was lifted from the inside and a pair of eyes peered through the slot.

'What do you want?' said a child's voice.

'Is your Dad in?' I asked, seeing as how the chap I'd seen might well be the lodger!

'No he ain't!' Came the reply, but I could hear muted whispering in the background.

'Well, is your mam in?'

'Hang on,' said the child's voice.

The eyes vanished and the letter box flap fell back down but behind the door I distinctly heard a woman's voice tell the child,

'Tell him no, I've gone out'

Up went the flap again.

'No, she ain't in, she's gone out.'

I decided to play the game...

'Go and ask your mam when she'll be coming back.'

As good as gold the letter box flap fell down again so the question could be asked and in reply I heard,

'Cheeky bleeder!' from a woman's voice and a man's voice adding, 'Tell him to piss off!'

I decided it was time to call the game to a close so I lifted the letter box flap and called through,

'School dinners, free school dinners!'

The door flew open and I was greeted by a couple with happy smiling faces that nearly, I swear, lifted me inside the house. A chair was hurriedly dusted off for me to sit on and I began the ritual of filling in a form for free school dinners: Mother's name, father's name, all the names and dates of birth of the children, schools attended, and finally why they weren't in school today!

'They need school shoes Mister.'

I reached for another form.

Mother's occupation, if any, and father's occupation? Up to now Dad had been prancing around making sure I'd got every detail down correctly, but at this his eyes rolled and he leaned backwards grabbing his lower spine with both hands and, with an expression of deepest agony upon his face, declared,

'It's me bleeding back! I can't work but will those miserable buggers at the National Assistance Board believe me? No!'

It was some of the best acting I'd ever seen, so good in fact, I nearly offered him my chair!

Next, we got on to the family finances. Out came the rent book, the tally man book, the family allowance book, the social allowances books, in fact so many books were presented to me that I couldn't resist,

'Christ Missus, you've got more books here than they've got in the local library!'

Business completed, I was ushered to the door and with the whole family waving 'ta rah' from the front gate, I mounted my trusty old bike and set off down the road. Near to the bottom of the road I heard a news vendor calling, 'Racing results, get your paper! Latest results!'

A second later I was nearly knocked from my bike by father rushing past at a rate of knots! I swear he went so fast that if he'd been a runner in the two thirty at Kempton Park then he would've been led into the winners' enclosure, bad back and all!

Oh yes, just before leaving the house I'd pulled father to one side and asked why he'd run inside to hide when I'd arrived. His reply was,

'It was that bundle of bleeding forms mate! 'Me and the neighbour thought you was holding a 'nap' hand of summonses and you were going to serve them, or some of them, on us!'

Problem solved!

A few days in and the feeling of 'Ye Gods, what have I let myself in for' had, in the main, passed! I'd been into each of my schools, introduced myself, and been commiserated somewhere along the lines of 'You'll be sorry!'

The J family:

One of the first families to become a 'regular' for visitation purposes were a family I'll refer to as J. I found them to be a likeable lot who seemed willing to go along with me although I felt, at times, they'd pressure me to see how far they could 'come it' before I'd bite! Mum, who was the head of the household, was in her early forties. She kept herself and her four children very clean and had, at first sight, a very outgoing personality. Her home was well above average for the district and the kids were always well turned out in free school clothing supplied by the 'Education Department.' They all were getting free school dinners as well which helped. Every one of that household were nicely spoken and very, very polite, so much so that I began to wonder why they lived on Dodge City! I soon found out.

Within a month school attendance began to decline, mainly because of the middle boy (Harry) and Nancy, the eldest girl. Soon I was calling on the family nearly every day, first for one and then the other, but always the same two.

I already knew why there was no Mr J because on one of my first visits after being ushered into the house and sat down at the table to fill out the free dinner form and, after assuring Mrs J that her private business would be kept private ('I don't want those nosey bleeding neighbours knowing my business') I asked the question 'Is there a Mr J?'

Mrs J went all straight faced and solemn as she replied,

'He's a guest of Her Majesty!'

The penny didn't drop at first and she had to explain he was in the 'nick!' (prison)

Harry was about nine years. He had red hair and the hazel eyes that usually went with that hair colouring. He was seemingly the perfect child except for one major fault... Harry hated school even though his Headmistress, a maiden lady, doted on him. Let Harry be absent when the register was called and I'd be contacted post haste to fetch him in. His mother, knowing which side of the bread was buttered rarely, if ever, covered up for him, and she'd drag him out of the house and hand him over to me with the words,

'The bleeder's playing me up again!'

Once in my care Harry would settle down and I'd sit him on the saddle of my bike and push him to school some three quarters of a mile away. You can imagine how pushing a hefty nine-year-old that distance made my arms ache. Another service I performed for Harry was to scrounge football boots and kit outgrown by my scouts so he could play in the school team. Alas, the family's fortunes took a turn for the worse and the gear provided vanished, and no amount of questioning made it re-appear! I guessed it went to the highest bidder!

It was Monday morning, and I hated Monday mornings because Monday mornings follow Sunday evenings and Sunday evenings were 'working men's club' nights and this meant that having been taken to 'the club' on Sunday night most of the kids were too tired for school. So, for me, Monday morning was 'round them up, and get them in' time! I was up to my neck in visits when I received a panic call from Harry's headmistress...

'Harry's out again!'

Mrs J met me at the door, seemingly all upset and nervous.

'I've been expecting you,' she said, 'our Harry is ever so ill! I had to call the Doctor out to him in the night and he said he was going to call back, and if our Harry was no better he'd send him into hospital. I'm ever so worried Mr Boardman!'

What could I say other than I hoped Harry would soon be better and I'd inform the Headmistress. I then gave my best regards to Harry and said I'd call again the next day to see how he was getting on. I confess I felt rather upset for Harry as he was the sort of kid who, as it were, 'grew' on you... I liked him! I turned and went back up the path to return to my bike when a car came at speed along the road and stopped with a jerk and screech of brakes outside the house!

'Ah, I bet this is the doctor' I thought. 'Coming back, just as Mrs J said he would!' But no, for out of the car fell Vic, a fellow Boardman from the other side of the estate. Vic raced past me to get to the front door that had just closed behind me and said, 'J?'

'Yes,' I replied, wondering why Vic was involved in what I could only imagine was this emergency.

At Vic's pounding on the door, Mrs J opened the door again!

'Your Harry,' said Vic, 'he's not in school!'

I felt I had to interpose.

'No Vic,' I said, 'Harry's in bed, very ill!'

'Ill in bed, I'll be buggered,' said Vic, 'I've just caught the little bleeder down on the main road helping the milkman deliver the blasted milk!'

Ah well, we all have to learn, and I was learning fast!

Mrs J received her first warning from me of impending court action if things did not improve but had this episode taught her a lesson?! Had it hell! Within a few days I was back pounding on her front door! Bless her, Mrs J didn't ever bear a grudge!

At this point I should explain that to give a true reflection of conversations and emotions behind what was said I need to use the people's terminology, even the swear words, as swearing was part of everyday life and at times it added to it. Just like during my own childhood the word 'bleeding' was frequently used by parents but dare a child use it they would've been given a swift 'clout' round the ear!

It was time for the youngest J to be admitted to Infant School and proud mum dragged him off down the street telling all within earshot,

'I'm getting rid of the bleeder! I'll be able to do the housework at last without the little bleeder whining and getting under my bleeding feet!'

Duly presented and left in the charge of the teacher, mum departed 'to get my bleeding feet up!' But this wasn't for very long as ten minutes later a very angry Headmistress was banging at the front door holding tightly onto junior's hand! Apparently, he'd called his new teacher 'a rotten bleeder!'

Nancy J had the best alibi imaginable for not going to school and never hesitated in telling me she was 'under the school psychology department' for her attendance problems! It was the perfect unarguable excuse but why the whole family wasn't under the 'Head and Behaviour' department I will never know. Come to think of it, after a few months working Dodge City I could've done with professional help myself, as you will see.

To be fair, Nancy was a lovely girl but at the tender age of 14 years she was playing the system as hard as she could! It was 'my psychiatrist this and my psychologist that' however the day finally came when even mum's authority was challenged! I'd called to enquire about Nancy and to my surprise was invited into the kitchen where I was told,

'There ain't nothing wrong with our Nance! She won't get up and I want her out of the house!'

Now this really was a turn up for the books so I said,

'Is she in bed now?'

'Yes, and I've told her twenty times to get up, the idle little cow.'

'Right' I said and, standing at the foot of the stairs, I called out, 'Nancy, come down! I want to talk to you.'

Nancy appeared wearing a nightie and a most disgruntled look upon her face. Looking to her mother for support Nancy said,

'I can't come to school, I've got me periods on, ain't I!?'

But mum wasn't playing.

'Lying little bleeder' snapped mum, 'you finished this month's two weeks ago.'

This was my cue, an opening, a chink in Nancy's armour.

'Are you coming to school or not?' I asked, 'because if not then I will have no alternative...' and here I launched into threats of mum being taken to court for her non-attendance, Nancy being directed to the Juvenile court, blah, blah, blah, which was just talk really for the school psychologists would've blocked me doing that. In full flow I suddenly noticed that a man had come into the kitchen. He looked about seven feet tall, as big as a house, and rough with it. I knew at once who he was and at the same time realised I was in his house and there were no witnesses!

Without thinking I stuck out my hand and exclaimed,

'Mr J!'

He instinctively took my hand.

'Thank goodness you're out,' I said, realising at the same time why Mrs J was so keen to get Nancy off to school! You see they had a lot of making up to do!

'Your Nancy is sending your missus up the wall! She just won't go to school!'

'There's no need to tell her off like that,' he began but still holding tightly to his strong right hand I was already in full retreat.

'I'll leave you to sort your Nancy out then, and bloody good luck!'

The next day Mr J was waiting for me. This is it then I thought, that's me for a bloody nose, but no...

'They're all at school,' he said, 'and thank you for keeping them out of trouble with the authorities!'

As I beamed my thanks thinking, 'this Dad appreciates what I'm trying to do' Mr

J continued,

'You couldn't lend me a few quid till Friday could you!?'

Some seven years later, whilst working on another district, a pretty, well-spoken young woman smiled at me as I was on my rounds and asked,

'You don't recognise me, do you Mr Boardman?'

I laughed,

'How's Harry and your mam? Does that answer your question? And how are you, Nancy?'

We laughed about the old days and then as she turned to go she said,

'I fooled all the head shrinkers, didn't I! I even fooled the school doctors, but I never fooled you did I Mr Boardman? But I promise you this, when my own kids are old enough to go to school, go to school they will, and no messing!'

I do hope they did.

Janine:

Within a very short time of starting the job I realised I was able to tell simply by knocking at a door if anyone was at home without my waiting to see if the door was answered. As this developed I began to rely upon these premonitions, often with very little else to go on. Sometimes I felt such a sense of unease that my psyche would not be denied and even the hairs on the back of my neck would begin to prickle and stand on end, warning me that all was not well. Reviewing some of the tragic, heart rending cases I had to deal with allows me to say with confidence that there's another side to this life that one ignores at one's own or someone else's peril. Let me tell you about Janine.

Within two months of working with the children and parents of 'Dodge City' I knew my way around and was able to pinpoint the 'sore spots'. The visit I now held in my hand was not a regular. I'd found the absence form amongst others whilst setting up the night before and what puzzled me was that the form was clear of 'A's' which indicated perfect attendance apart from one absence mark for the next morning. In other words, she'd been marked as absent for a day that hadn't even begun! Did the school expect her to be absent the following morning then? Puzzling!

On my rounds the next morning I arrived at this particular house. Considering the state of the area in general this place was immaculate. The curtains were fresh and clean and instead of being filled with the usual junk, the front garden had tidy borders and a freshly cut pocket handkerchief lawn. In answer to my knock a most delightful 14-year-old girl came to the door. Her hair was jet black and her great blue eyes smiled as I started to explain who I was and why I'd called. Even as I was speaking I was wondering why her school had asked me to visit. Janine told me that her mother was at work and her father was in town on business, and she then gave me a perfectly legitimate reason for her absence from school and assured me she would be back in school the next morning. I was still puzzled as to why I'd been asked to visit for Janine had said she hadn't known she was going to be absent! As all seemed well I returned to my bike, all ready to go on my way after bidding her 'goodbye', but just before pushing off from the kerb something seemed to force my head around and I gazed back towards the house where Janine was now gazing out of the front room window. She smiled and raised her hand in farewell and at that exact moment I felt such a sense of unease that I stopped dead in my tracks and looked again for her at the window, but she'd gone.

For the rest of that day and through the night the feeling persisted, but with only that to go on I tried to shake it from my mind. I couldn't. The next morning, going right out of routine I went into Janine's school where I met the Headmistress coming along the corridor.

'Is Janine in school?' I asked.

The Headmistress, who appeared pre-occupied, replied in the affirmative.

'Thank goodness' I said, 'only for some reason I've been worried to death about her.' At this I recounted what I'd felt, finishing off with... 'and even the hairs on the back of my neck stood on end!' The Head listened attentively and when I'd finished my outpouring she said,

'Your premonitions or instincts or whatever you like to call them did not let you down, Mr Boardman. Janine's in my office now with the N.S.P.C.C Inspector and a woman police officer. It would seem that after you left the house yesterday morning her drunken pig of a father, if you can call a drunken pig like him a 'father,' came home that afternoon, beat her near unconscious and then tried, and we think succeeded, in raping her!' Here the Head looked very puzzled.

'We've been looking at Janine's register and she never ever loses time from school so how on earth did her absence form get put into your hands? Neither her form teacher nor the school secretary can recollect marking the child's form with an 'absent' mark!'

The McV family and 'them spots':

Honouring a promise I made when interviewed for this job, I enrolled at the local college of adult education. I was now 39 years of age and had three young children of my own, so the next three years were not going to be easy for me. I could've done what others in the past had done by enrolling and not seeing the course through or being washed out after the first year's exams, but that wasn't me and I was well aware you could not learn about people whilst sitting in a classroom! One week on my district was as good as spending a year reading about human behaviour, and I joke not! Oh yes... this was an evening course, once a week, and all studying was done in my own time. Three years of study later and having sat various tests and an exam, I was finally awarded my Certificate in Social Studies.

Working as I was on what was designated a 'problem area', I had more than my fair share of problems, compared that is to my fellow officers. Now don't get me wrong, for I'm not talking about mainly the poorer families, oh no, I'm talking about people who knew the system inside out and backwards. People with a degree of education and a lot of native cunning, so when I talk about 'problem area' if you're looking for someone to pity, well here I am. I had to deal with these buggers!

Nobody in the adult education college where I studied could've come up with the questions my lot asked, nor even the answers!

When problems did arise, it was never 'they' who were the cause of the problems, oh no, it was always 'them'. 'Them' being any representative of the local authority, be it the rent man, the rates man, the National Assistance man, or the Insurance man (fraudulent claims). In fact, even I was included coming as I did from 'The Education!' It was only my being approachable and to a degree, harmless (until they found out that if they didn't toe the line and get their children into school then I would prosecute) that kept them on side, but I was fair, and if they finished up facing me in the Magistrate or Juvenile Court, then they knew they only had themselves to blame! Excuses in plenty for non-attendance came my way! Many were predictable such as no shoes, no coat, waiting in for the television repair man (I noticed that rarely, if ever, did they lose time waiting in for the rent man), verminous head and the one I hated most of all – 'them spots'. 'Them spots' were evil looking small eruptions which developed to look rather like chicken pox. These grew and later opened up like craters on the moon. All the time me and 'them spots' had a nodding acquaintance, but I don't think they were diagnosed as being caused by an identifiable thing or virus, and certainly even the cleanest and most fastidious families got them.

One of my regular visits was to a family I shall refer to as the McV family. It was always a joy to go to this house. It was clean and tidy, and Dad was in regular work and would greet me like a long-lost brother if we met in the street. The

135

McV's had two lovely daughters, one was 14 and the other 15 years. They were always well turned out and again usually pleased to see me, although I have to confess neither girl was sold on school attendance. If they failed to attend regularly, knowing that mum was pretty ineffectual at enforcing discipline, then I would threaten them with the ultimate sanction of 'right, I'm going into town to fetch your dad out of work'. This always did the trick and they would be back in school with no ill feelings on either side... until the next time.

On this one occasion I had the older of the two girls to visit as she'd not honoured us with her presence at school for two days. Pedalling wearily up the slight slope leading to their house, feeling rather fragile for it had been one of 'those days' and things were not being helped by a mangy cur of a dog, one of dozens that seemed to run wild over the estate, trying to get a grip on my ankle whilst being goaded on by cries of encouragement from the queue at the local fish and chip shop I was passing. Then I realised that the girl I was on my way to see was not only in the said queue but was trying to draw my attention instead of hiding as she would've normally.

'Hey Mr Boardman,' she screeched, 'Me mam wants you!'

'Yes,' I hailed back, much to the queue's amusement, 'and so do a lot of other women!'

Mrs McV met me at the front door nearly jumping up and down with excitement and, dare I say, satisfaction, which told me she held a good hand and this time I'd be the loser! My worst fears were realised.

'It's them spots', she chortled. 'She's got them spots!'

At this my heart sank for if it were true that ruddy girl could be off school for weeks, if not months, and there wasn't a thing I could do about it. I went into the house closely followed by the older girl who by now had arrived home hugging the family's fish and chip dinner to her bosom. Putting the greasy parcel upon the table the girl, without being asked, turned her back to me and pulling her jumper up, said,

'It's them spots. Has me mam told you?'

'Yes,' I said but any further conversation was interrupted by Mrs McV who vocally and physically tried to point out the areas of concern on her daughter's fully exposed back. There were panic stations for a moment for only one tiny, pathetic, little blemish was to be seen. Suddenly, for me at least, the sun seemed to start to shine again, and I said,

'Oh dear, is that it then? So, when can we expect her back in school? This afternoon?'

However, Mrs McV was not prepared to concede victory so easily and red of face she grabbed her daughter and spun her around thus presenting the child's front to me and, yanking the girl's jumper up high, she exclaimed,

'What are these then, hey? What are these!?' she'd struck gold!

The girl certainly had spots on her front and so 'fair do's' it was game, set and match to the pair of them! I was ready to concede defeat but Mrs McV wanted to rub it in even more.

'She's got more spots just here' she said, pointing to the girl's bra, which was all the girl had on under the jumper, and with that Mrs McV tried to ease the bottom of the bra up to show me yet another small section of the spotty chest. With the bra fastened on tightly it wouldn't give and so red of face, and determined not to be done out of her moment of triumph, Mrs McV gave a God almighty heave! Suddenly, the whole of the bra shot right up and out fell two well developed breasts which, as I was leaning forward as directed by Mrs McV, nearly knocked me off my feet! Mother and daughter took one look at each other and the last I saw of them as I left the house was the pair of them disappearing through the door into the next room! It was the first time I'd seen any of the McV family lost for words!

Chapter 6: Mediation and the Art of Diplomacy

Generally speaking the more problems I identified on the district and the closer I worked with so many of the families, the more the Heads and their staff were also drawn in. Sensibly, one of the Heads said she would never ever allow a member of staff to visit a child's home lest the deplorable conditions to be found in so many of these homes might turn the teacher against the child and, in turn, teaching. I could understand this logic but at the same time so many school staff had no idea of the appalling home conditions in which their pupils lived. I was often asked to go and tell a mother or even a father that their child needed P.E kit or part of the standard school uniform when it was clear to me the parent or parents had hardly enough money left to feed their kids properly! This was often due to a mismanagement of income or because a goodly part of the family income had been frittered away in the pub or on the horses. I could've wept with frustration if the latter!

Another apparently insurmountable problem was the inability of so many of the parents to communicate with Headteachers and staff, and vice versa, with the consequence being that many minor problems developed into major ones. My ability to communicate at parental level though was a major advantage, and parents were soon coming to me for help and advice. In my experience most doorstep dialogue from the parent stemmed from frustration and, because of the respective school's response, often resulted in veiled threats and abuse. I could've been made a 'piggy in the middle' but no way was I going to let that happen! Frankly, if I'd given some of the messages to the parents from the school as they'd been given to me then many schools would've been burned to the ground in the small hours, but I always reworded the stronger and more inflammatory messages from school to parents, therefore:

'Go and tell that blasted woman that if she comes to my school again shouting her big mouth off at my staff, I'll get the police onto her,' became

'If you feel your kids are being victimised, my girl, send for me and I'll sort it out and I'll let you know what's been done!'

Or again...

'Tell Mrs so and so that her kid is stinking the blasted classroom out and it's about time she had a proper wash!' became

'Now that your girl's doing a lot of P.E she's sweating more than most of the girls in her class, probably because she's such an energetic kid, so could you let her have a good strip wash down before she comes to school as I know you can't afford to heat water every morning for a full bath!'

It worked. It always worked! Those parents might've been poor but daft they weren't!

I would spend much time and effort turning these early contacts to my advantage and thus, my bridge builder role was clearly working as more and more parents came to me with problems to be solved. Unfortunately, however, the best laid schemes of mice and men etc... Witness the following that started as a good idea and finished up as a God almighty cock up:

Living on the lower part of the estate was a family who regarded every representative of authority with the gravest suspicion and I knew what a major challenge it would be for me to ingratiate myself with them as a first step. Now let me say at once that educationally the children of the family presented no problems. They were clean, polite and went to school, but in the few times I met the parents I felt a reserve which I guess went way back, possibly to the parents' own school days. Someone, I guessed, had 'put their foot in it' and, if not handled correctly, I could get the backlash. Let me put it on record that I liked them, and gradually the barriers came down. In the beginning a knock on the door would be followed by a conversation through the half-closed door, and then later a voice, mum or dad, would call out 'come in Mr Boardman, the door isn't locked!' This was now a sure sign on the estate that someone was accepted.

I called on this day because the elder boy was absent from school which was unusual. Mum met me at the gate to tell me Alfie had broken his arm and he had to go to hospital in a week for a check-up but afterwards he'd be in school. I commiserated of course but never one to let the grass grow under my feet I suggested Alfie could go into school on the morrow and that as it was his writing arm involved he could sit and listen, and then at break time he could sit in the classroom so as not to risk further injury to the said arm. I finished with, 'after all, this last year is critical and he needs to pass his exams to get a good job!'

To my delight mum agreed and so I pressed on for, in my bridge builder role, I felt any contact with the Head and teachers could be another positive step forward. Why didn't I keep my big mouth shut?! I knew the Headmaster looked at the world in general with a biased and jaundiced eye, and in respect of that particular part of the estate I suspected he considered any pupil to be destined for 'borstal, prison or the colonies.' I had to learn the hard way!

'I wonder if you could do me a favour, mum? I won't be working the district near to your lad's school for two days so would you pop into school and tell the Headmaster about your lad's injury and what we've arranged about him sitting quietly in the classroom at break time?'

To my delight mum agreed, saying,

'I'm shopping down there this afternoon! You leave it to me Mr Boardman, I'll do just that! I'm glad to help!'

I could've cheered. I'd cracked it!

The next morning, I could hardly wait to enjoy the fruits of my craft and guile. I made the family house my first visit, savouring the thought of yet another barrier down but I might've known for, as soon as she opened the door I could see from her face it had all gone pear shaped.

'That was a lousy idea of yours,' she snapped.

'Why, whatever happened?' I replied.

'I went into school as you asked, and I have to say the secretary was very nice. She took me straight to the Headmaster's room where that old bugger was sitting writing at his desk. He looked up and said, 'Yes'? That was the ignorant sods way of greeting a lady visitor! Anyway, I told him my Alfie had broken his arm, but that bugger interrupted me and said, 'Alfie who, because with four hundred kids in my school I can't be expected to know who's here and who's away!' So I told him my lad was Alfie Jones! Do you know what the miserable old bugger said to that? He said, Oh, it's Alfie Jones is it? And he's broken his arm has he? Well, all I can say is knowing your son it's a pity it wasn't his blasted neck!'

With that mum turned to go back indoors but she then paused before saying,

'That Headmaster's a pig! Everyone around here says he's a pig!'

Silently I had to agree with her. Then she went on,

'Thanks for trying anyway. I know what you're trying to do for the estate but you're too nice to work for a pig like him!'

These weren't necessarily the words I would've used to describe the man, but it was clear to me I was in a 'no win' situation. My bridge would always have a span missing!

Travelling around the estate I was to see poverty aplenty, and if that's not a contradiction in terms then I don't know what is! However, I never closed my eyes to the fact that much of what we describe as poverty was, in fact, a mismanagement of income. At no time though did I need any reminder that whilst the parents might've been feckless it was the children who suffered. So often, cold, hungry and defenceless, they had no option but to be swept along, helpless, as the money that could've been used to their benefit, went into buying booze, cigarettes and bingo cards, and yet, I knew that the low wage I'd accepted to do this job, had it been a few shillings less, would've entitled my own three school age children to have free school dinners!

I visited one of the poorer families on the estate to renew the children's entitlement to free school meals. The wind blew cold that day and there was a nasty nip in the air. The filthy streets, strewn with litter and dog mess were quite deserted except for packs of near starving and abandoned dogs that roamed freely, snarling and going into attack mode against any resident who showed any fear. One of the District Nurses had reported dog bites as being one of the most frequent injuries in the area and as I swerved to miss the dogs who were trying to take a chunk out of my ankles, I cycled one handed whilst blowing first on one freezing hand and then the other. It was a wonder I didn't come a cropper.

At the first port of call I was greeted by a woman, so worn down and tired that I couldn't put an age to her. We'd never met, but before I could state my business I was invited in. This didn't exactly surprise me because any person passing through the estate was immediately identified by one of the various groups of women standing on most street corners, and at least one would've been visited previously by me. So, the new Boardman would've been pointed out to this mum. Even the old pensioners knew me by now and accepted me. Witness one old dear who seeing me pass by would regularly shout,

'You wait till I win spot the ball, Mr Boardman, cause when I do, me and you are going to Skeggy for a dirty weekend!'

My reply was always,

'Right young lady, but I want six weeks' notice so I can get myself built up on cod liver oil and malt!'

The natives loved a bit of banter!

I followed the mum into the house as invited and then into the main living room. The place stank! The hall and living room had no covering on the floor, just bare filthy boards, and what paper there might've been on the walls hung down in damp filthy strips. The door into the main room was hanging off its hinges, and the panels were splintered and broken. A small fire burned in the tiled, broken hearth, the fuel being a large piece of wood some three feet long which stuck out over what should've been the hearth. This I recognised as a length of the room's skirting board from under the window, the window of which was boarded over with plywood causing the room to be in semi darkness.

The room boasted one sagging armchair out of which hung most of the stuffing. Upon this lay a mite of around four months who, even at this early hour, was dirty and had matted hair. Was it a boy or a girl? In the middle of the room was a rickety wooden box being used as a table by four older children who were poorly dressed and shivering in the cold morning air. There they stood. Each child held in its hand a piece of very stale looking bread which in turn they were dipping into what looked like a basin of cold tea, probably to soften it. First one and then the other dipped. They didn't speak or laugh or push and prod each other as children normally do, and their shorn hair (cut to the bone as we used to say) told me that at some time recently they'd been lousy. This made gender identification difficult. The children turned to regard their visitor as I entered the room and my eyes met the gaze of each child in turn but locking onto just one. Was it a boy or girl? I couldn't tell but what I did know was it was as though I was looking into the eyes of the Christ child.

The most incongruous part of that visit was that poor mother, for all of the time

I was in her home she didn't stop apologising for the state of the house for, as she put it, 'I haven't had the time to tidy up yet.'

Before I left I made quite sure I'd left my mid-morning snack where it could easily be found.

Chapter 7: Post Probation and a Fully-Fledged EWO

On the other side of the estate was an older and, dare I say, more settled part of the area. Those in the know had assured me that this side, with the main road acting as a buffer, would give me very little trouble. This proved to be so, so far, and in fact I thoroughly enjoyed one little episode when the Headmistress of that side's Infant School asked me,

'Would you be so kind as to look after a class of five-year-olds as we have a member of staff away and I want to hold a meeting with a stand in teacher?'

What followed was one of the happier half hours on the district. With the Headmistress out of the way those tots and I had a ball! I remembered my own children's nursery rhymes and so we sang all of those, and when we ran out of those, as it was near Christmas we sang,

'Happy birthday dear Santa Claus' and following on from that 'Happy birthday dear Jesus' I think we sang 'Happy birthday Timmy Jones's dog' as well as his mutt was coming up to its first birthday! Certainly, when Miss came back to reclaim the class we were hoarse from singing.

Feeling on top of the world I again set off to do the few visits that needed doing on that 'better' area, and walked slap, bang, wallop, straight into it!

It came about in this way... one of the senior boys in the local school was doing an evening paper round and yet his mother was sending notes to the school claiming he was too ill to attend for lessons. What really got up my nose however was to receive through the youth employment officer a note to say that along with other kids, this lad was now doing a morning paper round as well! Obviously, if a child was too ill to attend school regularly then the said child wasn't fit enough to do one daily paper round, let alone two! I was explaining all of this to the mother but could see I wasn't getting through to her, for she kept saying,

'Well, it don't really matter because he leaves school this year and isn't learning anything anyway!'

Finally, I said,

'Take a tip from me, because unless your lad goes to school regularly I will have to call and see your husband to tell him what's going on and warn him of court action should things not improve. This could mean a hefty fine!'

At first she didn't react and then she went up in the air! She ranted, she raved, she told me to clear off out and then to come back! Next, she seemed to go hysterical or so it seemed, so I got out and returned half an hour later to see if she'd cooled down!

When I arrived I was met by a neighbour who greeted me with,

'You ain't half upset her, you have!'

I recounted back what I'd said to her, to which the neighbour told me,

'It's time somebody got behind her. Her old man don't know the boy hasn't been going to school.'

Now I freely admit to being a worrier, and have been all my life, and all the rest of that day I worried a lot for I was still in my probation period. The next afternoon I was in the office when the Chief Officer came to me and said,

'The Director's had a complaint about you and he wants a written statement as to how you've upset this parent.'

With that he dropped the letter of complaint in front of me. I read it.

Yes, I did say her husband would have to be visited if the boy didn't go to school regularly, and yes I did say prosecution could follow if the boy still failed to attend, but isn't that what I was supposed to tell mums whose husbands obviously don't know what's going on? Afterall the mother was the one complaining! I also bet her husband wasn't aware of this alleged incident! Well, I made the written statement and up it went to the Director. Ten minutes later the Chief came to me, laughing all over his face.

'The Director's read your report and says this new lad seems to be doing a grand job. This woman's to be sent an official warning letter backing up the Officer's verbal warning. That should do the trick!' (And it did)

Feeling a whole lot better I went back out onto the district feeling I must be extra careful even though I'd been exonerated.

At my very first call of the day a lady answered the door and, giving her my brightest smile, I introduced myself and explained how Sheila's Headmistress had asked me to call and enquire as to why she was absent from school that week.

The lady looked me up and down, then stood back, motioning to me come in. I was about to refuse, still with that previous incident in mind, when through the open door I could see into the living room where sat, I supposed, the young lady in question. I smiled and said hello to the girl who would've been about thirteen years old. She smiled and said 'hello' back.

The mother informed me that the girl 'hadn't been well,' whilst at the same time taking a bottle of what I presumed was medicine off the sideboard and pushing it at me. Instinctively I took the bottle but without even looking at the contents handed it back to mum saying,

'That's quite alright. I'm satisfied she's been unwell.'

With that I left the house and thought no more about it as I got on with my visits. The next bit takes some believing but I swear it's true, for when I went into the office the next day the Chief was waiting for me. Now in his time the Chief had rousted a few parents and yet I swear he had a look of admiration on his face as he said,

'We've had another letter of complaint about you!'

My mouth dropped open.

'Yes' he went on, 'This woman's saying you took her daughter's medicine off the sideboard, pored over it, checked every detail on the label and then, and only then, put it down again!'

I reached for my pen as we both said in unison... 'The Director wants a full report!' Another ten minutes passed with me sitting on tenterhooks and when the Chief came back, he was positively beaming!

'The Director said that as this child isn't a poor attendee we won't send mum a warning letter but what we will do is ask her to come into the office with her daughter and ask her to repeat these allegations to your face!'

The mother declined. Later, the Chief told me how the Director had said, 'by golly, this new chap isn't half doing a grand job up on the estate! Attendance is going up and up every week! It's about time some of them got a kick up the backside!'

The probationary period for the new officers was something like three months. I was made permanent in six weeks.

The months slipped by and now it was January which was marked with long spells of sleet and hail, even fog, and so no matter how derelict or unappetising a house might look, the climatic conditions would force me inside, especially when free school meals or clothing forms needed to be completed as neither of the two lovely girls in our office wanted soaking wet forms drying on the office radiators.

At the house I needed to visit today I could see from the dried dog faeces smeared on the front step just what the likely conditions inside would be. I was not to be disappointed. Inside, the sour, dirty, unwashed aroma, accompanied the lady of the house as she escorted me into what she referred to as the 'best room'.

The bare wooden floorboards were stained with dirt and there was a table in the middle of the room with one chair. Just one, with a missing back, upon which I was invited to seat myself while the lady went to fetch 'the books.' The first thing to catch my eye was the broken tiled fireplace which was so full of filth and debris that the aperture was completely blocked and spilling onto the floor. Old ash, tins, bits of discarded bread etc, you name it, it was there. Hang on though, were my eyes playing tricks on me? No! There was definitely something making the whole dirty mass to move! 'Oh my goodness' I inwardly exclaimed, 'it's a rat, a damned great rat!'

It wriggled out from the middle of the muck, sat up on its hind legs, looked me over and as calm as you like, walked around the side of the chimney breast and finally vanished into a hole in the skirting board. Very slowly I eased myself off the chair and tiptoed out of the room into the hall where I met the lady of the house coming back with her arms laden with the family's social security books.

'Missus' I whispered, 'did you know you have a darned great rat living in your best room fireplace?'

'Oh yes,' she replied, 'the children feed it. It's a sort of a pet!'

I learned very quickly it was not a good idea to eat a hearty breakfast on the district because there would be several households that needed a really early visit to make sure they were up and getting the kiddies ready for school! Alarm clocks were low on the list of items needed for running well ordered households! The smells and odours from so many of these first call houses could be so vile that any part digested breakfast would soon be brought back. Twice I was physically sick. I know it wasn't just me who had this reaction for other officers, before and after, reported the same. To be fair though, the many clean windows, polished door brasses and freshly scrubbed steps just went to show that living cheek by jowl with the hard cases lived numerous hard-working families who fought to maintain standards in a so often hostile environment.

More and more doors were now opening to me. The women in the street who'd formerly closed ranks and regarded me with the gravest suspicion as I rode by, now called out 'hello' and waved as I cycled past. One of my regular visits was to a family I'll call Mr & Mrs C. This family, so typical of many in the area, consisted of mam, dad and four children, with ages ranging from about seven to fifteen years, the oldest child being a girl. Mam and dad were rarely at home during the day, preferring to do the 'town shuffle!' I'll explain: Early in the morning they would catch a bus to the town centre and wander aimlessly about looking into shop windows, never seeming to purchase anything but breaking off mid-morning to have a cuppa in 'Woolies.' (Woolworths)

Now the eldest, Sophie, knowing her parents' routine, had a routine all of her own! As soon as the parents were safely on the bus, 'Soph', who'd been observing their departure from the bushes of the local park, would nip out and into the house, and in the afternoon would leave there just before ma and pa were due home.

I was on to her routine very quickly and would visit almost daily, but would Sophie answer the door? Would she hell, which meant that at least twice a week I had to pedal some six miles on a round trip to do night visits. This would stop her little game for a day or two as her parents didn't want trouble from the Local Authority (me) as the next child down from Sophie, a boy, had already developed a taste for arson having tried to burn down the local pub! He would be my first court case!

On this particular day I was biking past Sophie's house when I saw the curtains twitch, and so thinking to save myself another night visit I parked my bike and walked up to the front door which, before I could hammer upon it, swung open and revealed Sophie with a big welcoming smile all over her heavily made up face.

'I've been waiting for you' she simpered, 'do you like how I've done me 'air?'

'Lovely' I said, 'and I see you've washed your face as well, Soph! Does your mam know you've been putting her make up on? If not girl, you aren't half for it when she gets home! You must've used half the jar you've put it on that thick!'

(Which she had for I could clearly see the tide mark on her neck where the make-up finished!

'Ain't you coming in?' asked Sophie.

'Is your mam in?' I countered.

'No' she replied, 'come in!'

'Is your dad in?' was my next question.

'No' came the reply, 'come in!'

I persevered 'Is anybody in then?'

'No' hissed our potential Mati Hari, smoothing down her mam's best frock over her hips and pushing her chest out towards me. 'Come in!!!!!'

I didn't wait to find out if the great seduction scene was an act or not, I was off down the path at a rate of knots!

As I came out the front gate a woman, who lived across the road and was proving to be a right pain in the arse, beckoned me over.

'It's our poor Brian's ears' she said, 'I've been to the Doctors and he says our Brian's not fit to go to school, but the Doctor don't give medical notes and he says if the Boardman don't believe you then I'm to show you our Brian's medicine.'

Now, this was an old dodge because when attendance was in dispute I would have to write a memo to the school's medical officer who would then enquire directly to the family GP so as to get to the truth of it. The answer would usually be a highly indignant GP replying along the lines of... 'the lying buggers, I never said any such thing, and in any case, I haven't seen any of this lot for months!'

With all of this said a filthy bottle was pushed under my nose, so old, that I swear the green mould on the top of the contents was nearly its own age produced penicillin! An attempt had been made to rub out the writing on the label of the said bottle but in vain, for through the dirt could plainly be seen, 'for the relief of period pains.'

'Nasty' I said, 'very nasty! Not only is your Brian aching at both ends but he's changing bloody sex as well! Get him back into school and don't try it on with me again!' She fled!

A new term and Albert:

It was 'in with the new' time. This was the few days before the school year really got into its stride and we were making the infant classes up with whatever children in the area needed school places.

The Infant Heads (and I was servicing four infant schools at the time) would call me in and tell me to spread the word on the district that 'any child who'd reached the magic age of four years (sometimes even younger) would be considered for a nursery place.'

Children aged five years of course had to attend school regularly and it was virtually unknown for anyone servicing this district to have any unregistered five year olds. The form was that as soon as a child was born the mother would be worrying the guts out of Heads to take the little darlings in but once 'IN' there came a complete reversal of attitude and from then on I'd spend most of my time trying to get them to attend regularly.

The Headmistress of the infant school which catered for the part of the estate that gave me the worst problems was an absolute darling. Sitting on an easy chair in her study, all big & tweedy, legs splayed apart and not giving a dam about decorum, all beams & smiles, she would happily warble,

'I've got plenty of room, Mr Boardman! Get the little darlings in! Four year olds get priority and any room left goes to the younger ones. First come, first served!'

Armed with this command my routine hardly ever varied. I knew that once word got out that 'her at the school's got some room' those mums with children in the intake range, who'd likely got another baby on the way, would be only too keen to get rid of the older children. Therefore, I would simply stop one or two mums in the street and tell them the good news. 'And don't forget to tell all your friends' I would add! You can bet your life that before I got my leg over the saddle of my bike mums would be pouring from their homes dragging screaming kids who'd be bawling,

'I don't wanna go schooling!'

All hell would break loose, just as though I'd taken a stick and stirred up an ant's nest!

Having started the ball rolling, for the next day or so I made darned sure to be working on the other side of the estate! You see, I'd quickly learned that for sure some of those mums desperate to get their kids into school would be trying to con the Head that their obviously below school age child was in fact older than stated on the birth certificate and I'd be drawn in to mediate. Bugger that for a lark!

One child who was a 'compulsory' but didn't turn up, was Albert. His not turning up surprised me not at all. This was some boy! He and I had already met for riding past a house one day I realised that someone had just thrown a brick end at me. Fortunately, it missed me but had hit my wheel, breaking a spoke and knocking several others out of line. There was no doubt in my mind the thrower was that red faced, snotty nosed, raggedy arsed little so and so who, having armed himself with yet another missile, now stood with arm back ready to let fly with a brick just in case I wanted to lodge a complaint, which I certainly did not! I always stayed clear of dogs and aggressive children! Of the two, I considered dogs less lethal as they didn't kick! After that initial introduction, and for all other subsequent times my path crossed Albert's, I chickened out! Today though was another matter and there was no dodging the issue! 'Miss' wanted Albert in school and so I had to be very brave and act like a big boy!!

I set off to Albert's house and upon arrival scouted the vicinity to check that 'boyo' wasn't waiting for me with a brick end in his fist. Satisfied, and with the first obstacle so easily overcome, I approached the second. I crept up the path to the front door and knocked, ready to take flight should I hear the sound of Albert dragging a chair down the uncarpeted passage to stand on (or throw at me) whilst he opened the door. I was a lucky man that day for it was Albert's dad who opened the door. A thin, harassed looking, weedy, unshaven man with a Woodbine stuck in the corner of his mouth. In other words, about par for the course. Dad recognised me and his face lit up.

'Have you come for him? He asked and then casting a haunted look behind himself he whispered, 'He don't want to come you know!'

'Oh come now,' I replied. 'Who's the boss in this house. You or Albert!?'

I needn't have asked. The furtive, frightened glance he gave over his shoulder gave me the answer.

'Where is he?' I bluffed, praying that dad didn't say 'coming up the path behind you!'

'His mam's took him shopping with Jack,' he said, reminding me that in this household 'Jack' was the lodger (and if neighbourhood gossip was believed, more besides)

I explained to dad that now Albert was five years old he had to go to school and, message delivered I began to leave without loss of face. I wanted to be well clear when 'boy wonder' was told his time was up and he had to go to school. I didn't want my bike knocking to pieces. I then realised I had to ask the 64 dollar question!

'Is your Albert toilet trained yet? Only if he's not it may delay him getting into school!'

I thought dad might throw a fit at the thought of having his pride and joy at home one moment longer than he should.

'Toilet trained!' he warbled. 'Is he toilet trained? Of course he's toilet trained! Why, when he wants to do his 'bob' he goes to the kitchen sink and stands on a box to reach the bowl. Then he climbs down, puts the bowl on the floor and takes his trousers down. He then sits on the bowl and does his 'pee' and 'bob'. When he's finished he pulls his trousers up, climbs back on the box and empties his 'pee' and 'bob' into the sink for us to wash down. Is he toilet trained? Of course he's toilet trained!'

I turned to go making a mental note for the Head, 'Yes he's toilet trained but you'll need to wipe his bum!'

Turning back towards dad again I said,

'You may need to see your doctor to get his advice about Albert going to school. Tranquillisers might help!'

Dad looked thoughtful before asking,

'Do you think he needs them?'

'Who, Albert?' was my reply, 'I was thinking more for you!'

Mrs B and Trixie:

Mrs B was a mum I visited on a fairly regular basis. It wasn't that her children missed a lot of school it was just she had 'fits & starts' when she couldn't bear to see them leave to go to school, and so like a miser she would gather her little brood around her protectively and bolt the door against me! Me! The evil ogre she felt was taking her precious treasures away from her!

Of course, when her brood, one after the other, moved from the 'stay at home under five' stage to 'got to go to school because you're an infant' age, I really went through it, for at that time I'm sure she really did hate me! (and she told me so on so many occasions)

Mrs B's husband was in the Army and often worked away from home. I'd been chasing like mad to get her kids into school and threatened that if she didn't cooperate I was going to visit the Army Barracks and ask them to contact her husband. Give Mrs B her due she knew all the moves and thinking she'd 'get in first' she visited the local Barracks to give her version of the story. I found this to be so when my office phone rang and a voice at the end of the line introduced himself as Lieutenant Colonel Smythe Brown of the 23rd Regiment of Cavalry, dismounted, D.F.C., M.C and bar with the British Forces in Bratislava (or words to that effect) who wished to speak with me about a matter concerning one of his men. Apparently, I'd been harassing the wife about the non-attendance at school of his children! That did it!

'Oh really,' I replied, 'Well, this is ex galley cum cabin boy Norman Boardman, ex Merchant Navy 1939 – 45, War Medal and Star Member of the National Union of Seamen who respectfully wishes to inform you that 'No' Way' would I ever 'harass' Mrs B or any other mother I'm required to visit!'

For a split second there was a stunned silence followed by laughter!

'I suppose I asked for that!' he said.

With balance restored we had a nice little chat and he promised to help!

Now I was back at Mrs B's house and the subject of discussion was her eldest girl 'Trixie' who was just under 16 years. This time Trixie was pregnant and mum wanted my advice.

'I want her to keep the child and Trixie wants to keep it as well, but that sh*t of a boyfriend who got her into this mess has told her she has to have an abortion, and he's even arranged for a local GP he knows to carry it out! Trixie is so under this man's influence she's prepared to have the abortion come what may.'

Now in those days abortion was illegal but back street abortionists thrived and could and would, for the right price, abort a foetus at whatever stage of a pregnancy.

'How many weeks is she?' I asked.

The reply stunned me! She was so far along that in my book this would've been murder! On top of that should the slightest thing go wrong, sepsis through dirty instruments for example, it could be murder on two counts! Mother and child!

'Why not go to the police?' I asked, 'they'll soon put a stop to this!'

Mum hesitated, 'Can't you go on my behalf? If she finds out it was me that 'shopped' him she'll never forgive me!'

'I can't, girl!' I said. 'The information must come from you. You know all the details!'

'But somebody might see me going into the police station!' was her next objection.

I knew I had to tie this up quickly before she panicked out!

'Look, I'll come around tomorrow morning. Should anyone ask just say I'm taking you to the school to discuss the children. I'll take you to the local police station where you'll be treated sympathetically and you can tell them what they need to know, otherwise Trixie's life could be on the line!'

The next morning, as planned, I picked Mrs B up and took her to the local 'nick' where I introduced her to the Duty Inspector. They disappeared upstairs whilst I waited downstairs and an hour later she was back home.

As for Trixie, she got rid of her bloke and had her baby. Never was a child so loved, although the new Grandma's screamed threats of, 'I'll cut your bleeding throat if you try to take this one off to your lousy school' didn't bode too well for the future!

The GP abortionist? Well it took our local constabulary a little time but they eventually 'nailed him' and he was 'struck off!'

Several years later after I'd left this district, a fellow officer came to me and these were his exact words:

'You know Mr Boardman, I always understood you were a really hard case when it came to dealing with school attendance problems but I've just been to see an old client of yours and she told me you're one of the kindest and most helpful men she's ever known, and that although you always told her kiddies 'you must go to school' you were never harsh with them or cross no matter how difficult they were.'

'Really?!' I said, 'and just who was it who had all those nice things to say about me?'

You've guessed it, it was Mrs B.

'Have you got Trixie's little one into school yet?' I asked innocently.

Honestly, I never ever expected to hear a public servant use such filthy language!!!

Chapter 8: Goodbye to Dodge City

The hard work I was putting in was paying off and was reflected in the figures of attendance from each Officer's district published monthly. Each month I was over the 90% mark, this on a district where excuses including no shoes, no trousers, septic spots and dog bites requiring visits to the Infirmary were all part of everyday life.

My relations with the senior school Head however was fast reaching rock bottom. He'd already tried to drop me in the mire by sending a list of names to my boss of all the kids he claimed were out of school for no good reason but what got up my nose was instead of asking me to pop in whilst I was in the school (three times a week) to explain what was happening, he'd gone to the school governors' meeting and complained to them without giving me a chance to explain or defend myself.

My boss read out the names sent to him one at a time and as he did so I told him the up to date position:

Name 1 – court next week

Name 2 – under school psychological service

Name 3 – fully covered by a medical certificate

Name 4 – excluded by school nurse

Name 5 – prosecution brief being processed

It went on just like this. The boss finally threw the list down on his desk and said, 'You're completely exonerated. The man's a fool!'

Unfortunately, 'the man' didn't give up so easily because within a week he'd sent for me and said,

'You're going to prosecute young Brown!'

'Really?' I replied. 'On what grounds?'

He told me the story. The Head and his Deputy had been passing through the local park when they saw young Brown coming through the swing yard. As it was school time the Head and his Deputy had shouted at the boy to 'STOP.' The boy had set off like a hare with our heroes in hot pursuit but without a celluloid cat in hells chance of catching him!

Up hill and down dale they sped, finally arriving at Brown's home in time to see him dash inside whilst slamming the door behind him. The Head and Deputy had then taken it in turns at shouting through the letter box, ordering the boy to 'open this door!' The child had refused.

By this time the neighbours were out and cries of, 'leave the kid alone' and 'bullying bleeders' rent the air, and so with the crowd getting more and more hostile the pair had departed with a final, 'wait till we get you in school tomorrow! It'll be the caning of the century!' (or words to that effect!)

Now I was being told by the Head that he wanted the boy and his parents prosecuted as soon as possible!

'We're not going to be shown up as that boy was fit enough to outrun us yesterday, so there's nothing wrong with him! Just get on with it and 'do' them!'

Ahhh, I thought! Now we've come to the crux of it. Justice flies out of the window when Sir's made himself look a prat!

Outside the office I mentally cancelled the appointments for that evening. No way was I going to threaten anyone with court until I'd tipped dad off that his son was out of school without a seemingly good reason. An evening visit of around 8 miles by push bike was called for and that night found me knocking on the Brown's door with an awful gut feeling of apprehension. There was no way of telling what sort of reception I'd get. Father didn't know me and if sufficiently incensed over the incident, it might just be me who got a punch on the nose!

I'd met Mrs Brown before and liked her. She went out to work, as did Mr Brown, and her home was clean and comfortable. Mrs Brown was alone in the house as far as I could see. I was asked inside where I sat down and began telling her what had been recounted by the Head but before I could ask when Mr Brown would be home as I needed to talk to him, Mrs Brown went to the sideboard and took up a piece of paper which was lying there. Still in the middle of my sentence I changed tack. I'd guessed what that paper was.

'Is that a medical certificate? Does it explain why your lad seemed in such good shape when the Head chased him, and why didn't he save us all a lot of trouble by stopping and showing the sicknote to the Head and his stooge?'

It was indeed a sicknote and all was revealed when I saw it. It put the lad on the sick for a fortnight with NERVES. Thus, the boy's full mobility was explained

167

PLUS his fear of the adults who chased him! For myself I didn't believe a word of it, but you can't argue with sicknotes!

'We're going to crucify that bleeding Headmaster!' Mrs Brown told me.

'As far as I'm concerned you can throw the book at him,' was my response. I didn't like what I'd been told about the incident in the first place and this was the clincher!

'I'm sorry to have bothered you. I was going to ask to meet your husband but he doesn't seem to be in. I'm sorry your kid was frightened and thank you for speaking to me!'

As I stood up to go the kitchen door opened and it didn't need any inspired guessing on my part to know it was Mr Brown who stood there. He'd obviously been listening all the time from within the kitchen and I reckon that had I handled the interview any differently I'd have got that punch on the nose, and who would've blamed him! Certainly not me!

'I think we need satisfaction over this,' said dad, 'but not from you. You did it the right and proper way and I thank you for it. Now it's up to him!'

I persuaded them to let me handle things from then on, that way it was better for the boy. Afterall, he had to go back to school at some time!

I think the Browns would've enjoyed seeing the look on the Head's face when I slapped that sicknote on his desk diagnosing NERVES, especially when I rubbed it in a little with,

'You didn't help his nerves much, hounding him through the streets like that! In future leave the home visits to me, will you?! Oh yes, that certificate; Just suppose the mother, after being told the kid had played 'hooky' and had been seen & chased by the Head who was known to be hot on prosecutions, had gone to the doctor and told him her lad wasn't eating or sleeping, and when he does finally get off has awful nightmares so I want to take him to the seaside for a rest! Could you give me a cover note for the school?! I'm not saying that's what she did, mind you, but just suppose!'

Fourteen months after I started work on Dodge City I was in the office catching up on my paperwork when the boss came up and asked me to accompany him to his office. He closed a drawer to the right of his desk as he sat down. Inwardly I smiled for it was a well-known fact that when things were slack he would pull open the drawer in which he kept a library book and have a quiet read.

'Sit down' said this predominately grey man: grey hair, grey suit, grey eyes and grey complexion. 'I want to talk to you about a change of district and the potato harvest.'

'Crikey, he's flipped!' I thought!

'First things first then,' he began. 'How do you feel about taking on Centre Point as your district?'

'That's it then' I thought. That senior school's Head has finally put the bung in for me!'

But the boss went on......

'I realise I'm swinging this onto you out of the blue as it were, but Mr Naylor is leaving and I must have an officer on that district I can rely on 100%.'

I felt I had to ask the question.

'Why me? Aren't you satisfied with my work on Dodge City?'

My mind was soon put at rest.

'I assure you the Director is more than satisfied with your work, however, as you know we have a compliment of twenty officers out there, each of whom I've asked if they would be willing to go and work on that district (Centre Point) and each in turn has refused.'

At the back of my mind I was wondering, Potato harvest? What does a change of district have to do with a potato harvest? It rather threw me at first and then I thought, 'what the heck!'

'Right,' I said, 'I'll work the Centre Point district!'

Never did I realise that a whole new world was to open before me that would change even my basic thinking before I was done!

To say the boss was surprised (and pleased) was an understatement. He never dreamed he could unload the district so easily. To be truthful I had no illusions about what I was letting myself in for but weighed against everything else was one simple fact: I was going to save myself an eight mile round trip on a 'pushbike' each day cycling to Dodge City. Add to this the district mileage plus travel from home to office, and then doing it all again for evening and weekend visits, then you'll realise that a move to an area only one mile from my home had definite advantages. Now for the potato harvest!

'I've been tipped off that due to the good weather the local farmers are ready to start lifting the potato crop and will be requiring casual labour in the fields. Now, can I suggest you try to find out where the lorries are going to pick up this casual labour because if you don't your current schools are going to look pretty empty. By the time you've dealt with that Mr Naylor will have left us and it will be time to take up duties on the new district. Good afternoon, Mr Boardman!'

For the rest of the potato picking week I rode up and down glaring at every lorry driver who might just be heading to a pick-up point. Day followed day and the patrol went on. Let me hear a car or lorry engine stop or start and I'd chase it like a man possessed. I didn't stand a dog's chance! It was hopeless! Anyone who in the normal course of the day could dodge the rent man, the Tally man, the Insurance man, the social investigators and the innumerable coppers who were trying to hand out summonses like free soap powder vouchers, were going to have no trouble dodging me! There was one consolation for me though. That blasted farmer who'd decimated my schools wouldn't have laughed so loud had he seen the tons of 'buckshee' spuds floating around the district for months after!!

All that remained for me to do was tidy up on the district before I left. The boss wasted no time in introducing me to the young fellow who was to take over from me and I was instructed to take him into the schools, introduce him and generally show him the ropes. Just over a year earlier I'd been left to get on with it by myself, sink or swim, and yet here I was, an instructor now!!!

I spent that last sad week making my farewells and I understand the idea was put forward to make a collection for me, but I let it be known 'No thank you!' Any collection from that lot would mean the intended recipient would be out of pocket and the fraud squad involved!!

On my last day I pedalled those dirty streets for one last time. I felt in need of being cheered up and wasn't to be disappointed for coming out of one of the houses that owed me pounds in wasted shoe leather for the times I'd walked up the path to hammer on the front door, were two CID officers with a uniformed police Sergeant. The Sergeant was holding tightly onto the scruff of the neck of two young brothers who lived at the address. The Sergeant was grinning broadly and his voice, I swear, was full of admiration for the miscreants as he said,

'Would you believe it! These two little buggers, no bigger than ten penn'oth of coppers (if you'll excuse the pun) broke into the local Working Men's Club! That's a laugh for a start because none of the buggers round here work anyway, then, having made unlawful entry they each drank 6 pints of 'mine unknown hosts' best ale! Each! We know that because they used a clean glass for each pint! When we arrived, this one (and here he shook the lad in his right hand till his teeth chattered) was bashing the Club safe with a 'jemmy!' Now aint his old man got a lot of explaining to do as to why he keeps a 'jemmy' in the coal house! This other sod had some three tables stacked one on top of the other with him on top trying to unscrew the Club 'telly' from the wall! If we hadn't got there when we did the whole lot would've likely fallen and killed the little sod!'

With that the Sergeant, still chuckling with laughter, swung open the doors of the police van and invited the culprits to 'take a seat please, gentlemen', adding 'if you try to take anything else that aint screwed down, I'll have you!'

Just before closing the doors and locking them safely in the Sergeant yelled,

'And if that beer you drank makes you sick all over my nice clean van, you'll be cleaning the bugger up!'

The van then drove off with two excited little boys waving frantically at me out of the rear windows, and as they pulled away one of the little darlings mouthed at me,

'Tell my teacher to get f*cked!'

As the van turned out of the street their father, who must have hidden himself away so as not to go with them (I suspect he needed time to dream up a good excuse for that 'jemmy') came sidling up to me and began explaining he was sure it was all a terrible mistake!

Leaving, after first checking the real wheel of my bike was still attached, I again set off, passing a gang of Council Workmen who were engaged in replacing the rear and side fences to the houses. A job I likened to painting the Forth Bridge. This time they were replacing the wooden palings and posts with concrete after finally acknowledging that anything wooden erected by the Council would soon be taken down, sawn up and used for firewood by the tenant, sometimes even when the workmen were still in the street!

The Foreman Chargehand, who knew me well and loved to shout out helpful comments such as, 'Six of the kids just ran up there!' or 'You're wasting your time trying to get this lot into school!' now informed me,

'They won't be able to tear this down for firewood!'

I just couldn't resist it and hollered back,

'I reckon you're about right on that point, but I bet anything you like those concrete panels will be ideal for converting into garden or allotment sheds! They'd easily fetch a fiver apiece!'

The Foreman burst out laughing!

'You're a card, you are! Sell them for a fiver apiece as garden shed panels! You must be jok......'

His voice tapered off and a look of horror crossed his face! His mates who'd been sharing the joke weren't laughing anymore either!

'They wouldn't; they couldn't!'

The Foreman began to sound hysterical.

'They bloody well would you know!' and with that he dropped everything and dashed off to ring the department to tell them, 'concrete panels aint the answer to the thieving!'

As he disappeared up the street local residents who'd heard my remark (said in jest I might add) came creeping from their homes, tape measures in hand and thoughtful looks in their eye as they felt to see how firmly the concrete support posts were set in the ground!

I only went into the senior school that last day. I couldn't bear to go and see the little ones one last time, for I knew most of them almost as well as I knew my own children. To see a class of twenty or thirty tots, all shiny eyed and trusting, warmly wrapped up, walking along holding hands in pairs, little girls and boys mixed. To see the simple joy and wonder in those little faces as various things were pointed out to them by the teacher; a blackbird singing it's heart out, daffodils in a front garden just poking through the ground, and two dogs (just poking)! Seriously, a child's face is the happiest yet saddest sight on God's earth. I couldn't face them.

As I entered the senior school for the last time the Head was nowhere to be seen so I set off on my own down the long corridor which smelled, as all senior school corridors do, of woodwork permeated with the scent of sweaty plimsoles and musty polish.

The bells started to ring indicating the time for class changeover. As doors burst open I was nearly felled in the stampede of shouting and chattering kids of all ages from eleven years up. Noisy as they were the noisiest person was the young teacher who 'out shouted' them with threats of what he had in store for them if they didn't 'shut up!'

My mind went back to the early days when a mother on the district was recounting a long list of complaints against her son's teacher! Mr Timberknob said this, and Mr Timberknob did that, and Mr Timberknob would get a mouthful if she came up to the school, Blah, Blah, Blah!'

Her son was in 2c and I'd never met the teacher in question so when I finally collared the man I told him of the mother's complaints, finishing with,

'Is there any truth in the allegations, Mr Timberknob?' to which he replied, 'Actually.my name's Woodcock!'

The district grapevine had been working well for all of a sudden I was surrounded by kids I'd chased up hill and down dale! Big 'uns, little 'uns, thin 'uns and fat 'uns and, counting among them was dear Sophie!

'Please Sir, is it true you're leaving us, Sir? Will you be coming back to us, Sir? And, best of all, 'You aint got the sack have you, Sir?'

From the back, a voice (unidentified)

'Sophie loves you, Sir!' (the highest accolade!)

All of a sudden I didn't want to leave them. Finally, from various pockets and satchels appeared grubby bits of paper which were shoved at me.

'Give us your autograph, Sir!'

'Lens your pen, Doris!' (I think Doris was in the English Exam class)

'Will you sign this for us, Sir?'

I felt like a film star and was just about to comply with my usual flourish, hoping I could still spell 'sincerely,' when a doom-laden voice hissed in my ear....

'Are you out of your mind, man! Don't write, print or sign your bloody name otherwise this lot will be forging your signature on every document going!'

It was the Head. I echoed that Foreman cementing in concrete fence panels,

'They wouldn't, they couldn't.....THEY BLOODY WOULD YOU KNOW!'

Chapter 9: Centre Point District

It was my first day on the new district as an Education Welfare Officer (EWO) but certainly not otherwise. I knew it well for apart from the years I was away at sea, I had always lived near to, or on, this district.

The Centre Point was, and still is, one of those inner-city areas that today are the 'IN' for those with theories to advance, axes to grind and empires to build, especially if someone else has done all the spade work, and God knows in the coming years I was to do plenty of that. Thank goodness the politically indoctrinated and motivated person in the faded and tatty jeans, loud check shirt, seemingly unwashed, often unshaven, had still to put in an appearance, and it was relatively calm and peaceful, but that wasn't to last for long.

With my stock in trade eraser, pencil and saddle bag full census cards I was soon in the thick of things and wondering just what the hell I'd let myself in for! Every visit threw up new surprises, not to say shocks! The officer leaving the area had already suggested I visit one difficult family whilst in his company and as I wasn't known I'd be introduced as his very mean & nasty senior officer who wanted to know why the heck the kids weren't attending school regularly! In the past he'd had a lot of absenteeism from them. I didn't go along with the mean & nasty bit, that wasn't my style, but I would play along with the rest of the farce (which it quickly became!)

The house was very neat from the outside and the woman who came to the door was very smart and business like. My colleague introduced me as 'the senior district supervisor' and the ball fell into my court.

'I wonder Mrs T, could you tell me why your child is again absent from school?'

Without a word the dear lady turned her back on us and went into the house, leaving the door ajar. We looked at each other and my chum whispered,

'If she hasn't got a medical note this time, I'm going to threaten to nick her!'

At that point the lady returned and without a word spoken handed me one of those small ice cream tubs with a lid on the top. I took it wondering, what the Dickens!?

The lady motioned for me to open it up! 'Strawberry or Vanilla' I thought! WRONG!

Inside, leering up at me was a small stool; excrement! A sample to be collected by the health department – suspected bowel infestation!

Although the new arrivals from the West Indies, India and Pakistan were many, the Ugandan Asian crisis and 'out of control' immigration was still some 5 years away. When I arrived to take over (singlehandedly) the responsibility for school attendance, the area had so many children from these new arrivals they had to be transported by bus to schools in the outer city in order to accommodate them all, and the old Children's Department was still going strong. The social services of today just didn't exist.

Most properties dated back to the late Victorian/ Edwardian era and many of those earlier streets and yards were soon to be demolished so a big new estate of

179

high-rise flats and maisonettes could be built. As it turned out this meant that within ten years a modern slum stood in its place! The remaining district was about half and half: half terraced style back to back houses with shared entry and the rest were three storey high houses with small gardens front and rear. The bigger houses were ideal for multi occupancy and converted into flats for the tide of new immigrant families pouring in from abroad.

With such a mixture of people and policy from Central Government, the situation could in no way be described as 'stable.' There was in a constant state of flux with new arrivals that could, 'moving on,' whilst others 'moved about.'

I arrived on the district to find problems aplenty: drugs, prostitution, crime and violence but no, and I repeat, NO racism or race discrimination! The Empire Builders who would later jump onto that particular bandwagon were still hiding under the skirting boards!

At first the different racial and religious groups had little or no contact with each other. This wasn't deliberate and there was no antagonism or friction between the groups, in fact one only had to talk to the new arrivals to hear them say so many times that having arrived in a strange country burdened down with children and luggage, they were helped by white people to wherever they wanted to go!

'Yes' said one West Indian mother, 'White people were lovely to us!'

I actually remember a black youth giving me a load of mouth along the lines of 'You whites never wanted us blacks. All of you are racists!' Unfortunately for him a passing elderly black lady overheard what he'd said and boy, did she settle on him! As near as I can remember it was along the lines of, 'too many single black men came in the beginning and the white girls went daft for them. Then the black pimps crawled out of the woodwork and had a field day. From then on it was downhill all the way!'

The black lady then came out with something that had I dared to say publicly would have got me hung, drawn and quartered, for she said,

'The only ambition this boy's got (indicating her countryman) is flash clothes, a big car, plenty of spending money with free holidays in the West Indies and a stable of young 'Tarts on the Game' to earn it all for him!'

The Indian and Pakistani families got on with the serious business of securing work. They clung together as families and helped each other, clubbing together to buy communal houses that were intended as lodgings for their own people until they too got jobs and were able to buy.

The Banks and lending agencies had a field day and I well remember taking a free school meals application from a chap whose outgoings plus mortgage repayments exceeded his total income. Already the big boys were having a field day leaving the poor old tax and rate payer to stand the cost of the free school meals and clothing etc.

I met my senior Headmaster for the first time but due to my unhappy experience with the Head on my last district, I was wary to say the least. I needn't have worried. This one was top drawer although I must admit to begin with our first meeting didn't go quite as I'd planned. It happened in this way.

If you remember, prior to going into Local Government work, I'd been employed in private industry. Well, even then the writing was on the wall that a slump was coming and the probability was that a lot of people would be out of work. Alongside this, I had said many times that rightly or wrongly it was pointless advocating birth control if the doors were going to be opened wide to millions of people coming from countries where birth control was not practised! In other words, moving their overpopulation to a tiny little island already bursting at the seam. I contend this as common sense and not racist.

So at our first meeting the Head and I talked, during which time he put the question to me,

'How do you feel about immigrants and immigration?'

It was a question I had no intention of ducking and I answered thus,

'I cannot find it in my heart to blame any man for trying to get a better standard of living for his wife and kids, and I say this as a man who's been to India and seen the poverty first hand. However, I query the wisdom of allowing thousands of people who are so completely different to us, to come pouring in with virtually no controls, and if you think Headmaster that I'm echoing Enoch Powell's thinking, forget it! I was saying this long before he was!'

The Head rocked back on his heels at this but before he could comment on my words I went on,

'However, whilst they're here they will get the same courtesy, respect and help I'd extend to my own people. In conclusion, anyone who tries to pick on them or their kids will soon get the sharp edge of my tongue!'

'Welcome!' said my new boss, 'I think we're going to get on just fine!'

And from that day we did!)

Chapter 10: 'Working' Women

I was soon to find out how many prostitutes could be found on the area and how many had young children whose welfare was now down to me. Most of these mothers were forced to work all hours by their pimps and their insatiable appetite for more and more money resulted in rows and upsets. If this wasn't forthcoming the mother would then have the living daylights punched and kicked out of her, often in the street or with the infant looking on. This went some way in explaining why we had so many disturbed children on our hands. Add to this that so many of the little ones were keeping late, very late hours due to the nocturnal working hours of their mothers, Blues parties and drunken brawls, and it's not hard to understand why so many were late for school or practically falling asleep at their desk.

All of us in the schools were most concerned. We knew what the children were observing in their ordinary day to day living and how this was affecting them adversely. For example, we found from listening to the little ones, some of them as young as 5 years old, that they could quote the going rate not only for normal sex but also for perverted practices. If you find this difficult to believe then remember that any mother/ prostitute lived in just one room; eating sleeping and 'doing business.' The children were just told to 'turn your face to the wall!

One 11 year old girl had to be forcibly restrained from dashing around the playground at breaktime whilst holding up her skirt with her knickers pulled down to just above her knees. As she ran she was pointing down and shouting,

'This is where you get f*cked!'

Another girl, after watching her mother perform for clients, had her own little breaktime racket going. Cramming as many boys as she could into the cloakroom she'd strip off and in return for their dinner money would allow them to inspect what she called her 'money box.' This racket was spotted when the school dinner takings fell sharply and continued to fall. The Headmaster called a special assembly and warned the boys thus,

'From now on I'll have the hide off any boy who doesn't run a mile if a certain girl so much as takes her gloves off in front of him, and I shall require a note signed by your parents for any dinner cancellations!'

A nursery child became very upset in class one day and even the Headmistress wasn't able to pacify him. As I couldn't be contacted the Head took the child home. He didn't live very far from the school and the pair of them soon arrived at the child's front door. The mother answered, obviously straight from bed even though it was nearly midday. At first the mother tried to keep the Head on the doorstep but when it was made clear the child's unsettled behaviour needed explaining the mother had no option but to allow the Head inside. The property was a six roomed terraced house Let off into bedsits, with a shared kitchen and toilet. No better or worse than similar houses in the street. The little procession passed through the front room which was occupied by a young woman who was fast asleep on the divan bed, and on into the living room at the back of the property. This room was sparsely furnished with a stool, cupboard and divan bed as per the front room, but clean, and if anything, over warm.

During the conversation the mother freely confided she was 'on the game' and this was where it all happened. Puzzled, the Head asked whether this was the only room, and when answered in the affirmative she was very puzzled indeed.

'Now my dear, if you only have this one room to live in, and if you also have to entertain your gentleman friends here as well, what do you do with your little boy whilst you're......entertaining?'

Showing no shame or remorse the mother replied that he had to stand in the corner facing the wall with his hands over his eyes!

When the Head related this to me, I couldn't trust myself to speak. One thing I was sure of though was another little mite's mind was scarred forever.

For those first three months I concentrated on the prostitute mothers of all the young children in my charge. I cajoled, threatened and pleaded, and when all else failed I used the sanction open to me. I banged the 'couldn't care less' mother's into court! To be fair though these young mothers, many of them little more than children themselves, listened to me. I explained to them just what I felt was going on in their children's minds and how this was reflecting back in the child's attitude to school, to the teachers and society in general in an adverse way. I would usually go on to say that whilst I understood the problems of their business life in relation to their children's ability to function at school, I was only prepared to meet them half way and it was up to them to get the children attending school regularly and on time. I succeeded in 95% of my worst cases. I was now left with the 'I don't care, so there' residue and with these few I had no hesitation in banging them into court!

The first of these was a hard faced brassy one! As usual her little boy was a grand little chap who loved school but due to his continual lateness he was never going to settle. I took her to the Magistrates' Court where she tried to make me out a liar by claiming I'd been given a medical note to cover the child's poor attendance. She was shot down in flames when I contended that one sicknote, which I'd never received anyway, didn't cover 3 months of poor attendance, and as most of the absences were by reason of excessive lateness, a sicknote (if supplied) wouldn't have qualified anyway! Case proven! She was fined £10 which at the going rate of £2 for a 'short time' meant 5 'jumps' as it were, on the house! I bet her pimp wasn't very pleased about that. Not long after she moved some 25 miles away which didn't surprise me as a vice ring had moved in.

On the question of the pimps, never ever did they bother me even though I must've cost them a lot of money in my time. Anyway, it worked. Don't ask me how, but it did! From the early days until I left the district some 18 years later those early problems, mainly confined to and peculiar to the children of prostitute mothers, rarely recurred. Perhaps much of the thanks should go to the Heads and teaching staff who made it clear to the kids that they didn't care how their mother made a living or how their parents conducted their lives. When the children were in school they were just another child with problems amongst many with similar problems.

It was very difficult to understand why so many of the young, 'good time girls' who turned up on the district, being obviously from good homes and with above average intelligence, could allow themselves to be caught up in the round of

'Blues Parties,' vice and drugs which led them into prostituting themselves for the pimps and other 'hangers on.' From then on their degradation was inevitable.

One young married woman, who was quite alone and unescorted, went into the 'seediest' pub on the district for a drink. Whilst there she was approached several times by pimps who, with no hesitation asked, 'you going to work for me, Honey?' It wasn't really a question but a statement. She was also asked what her charges were for sexual favours. When I asked her whether she got out of the place fast she replied, 'No, why should I?'

To my mind if she didn't know the answer herself, then I couldn't be bothered to tell her!

I remember one young mum very well indeed: Had my son brought her home and introduced her to me as his 'intended' I wouldn't, on first impressions, have been anything other than pleased, but I knew she was playing right on the edge of trouble, BIG TIME! At first I wasn't too concerned but I did keep a watching 'brief.' Her flat was cosy and clean, she didn't swear or flaunt herself, and at no time did I see her pimp boyfriend 'streeting' her. In fact, not to put too fine a point on things, this girl had CLASS. Then it all started to go wrong. The child's Headmistress reported that the little girl was becoming very disturbed and unhappy, was stammering and 'drawing' into herself. I needed to intervene and had my 'IN' when the child missed school.

Mum, by this time, had moved house (a bad sign) but she came to the door in answer to my knock. At first she was all smiles and invited me in, but the smile vanished when I asked why her little girl was absent from school and becoming so upset for no apparent reason. I thought we were alone in the house but as we talked the door to the stairs burst open and a man who I knew well by sight, he being a pimp, fell into the room. He was either very drunk or 'high.' Startled by his entrance I blurted out,

'What the bloody hell's your game?!'

She answered for him, shamefaced I thought,

'He's a friend.'

Her friend, now lying at my feet and unable to get up, leered up at me whilst the terrified little girl clung to my leg. The mother helped the man to his feet as best she could and guided him through to the front door. When she came back I flipped and without mincing my words I told her just what I thought of her, her lousy so called 'friends', and how I anticipated she would end up, before finally telling her,

'Lady, I'll tell you now. You can go to hell any bloody way you want but no way are you taking this little mite with you!'

At that I picked the child up and gave her a reassuring cuddle. (not something I'd be allowed to do nowadays)

'The next time I pick her up' I went on, 'it will be to hand her over into Care because I'll have satisfied myself that you're not a fit person to have control of her!'

Not trusting myself to say anymore, I left.

That afternoon I went into the school to see if the child was 'In'. She wasn't, so back to the house I went. It was empty. The neighbours couldn't help. She and the child were gone. I prayed it wasn't down to the canal. Afterall, I hadn't minced my words.

Later, whilst in the office, I was called to the phone. An obviously well-educated voice introduced himself as the young woman's father/ the child's grandfather. He was ringing to let me know his daughter and the child had returned to their home and would remain there. I told him that I only had his word on that so he asked me to ring a certain firm of solicitors to check the truth of what he was telling me. I did, and it was true. I then rang him back. The man thanked me for talking some sense into his daughter and added,

'She respects you!'

Two years after this episode I was walking through town. I'd just spent three hours in a dingy court waiting room waiting for a case to come up which was subsequently adjourned without my being heard. Fed up to the teeth I noticed that one of two ladies coming towards me seemed familiar. They were obviously mother and daughter, beautifully dressed and proud & erect of bearing. They positively sailed towards me, laden down with parcels. The scent of perfume wafted into my nostrils and in the split moment we drew level the younger woman's eyes met mine. I felt she wanted me to acknowledge her, for recognition was there, but sleeping dogs must lie. A slight flush spread across her face and she looked away. As to my own face I kept it absolutely straight as I looked through her and saw only a vulnerable and frightened child, little more than a baby, and so we passed as total strangers.

Ada:

In all the years of going into the homes of prostitutes to chase their kiddies into school I can only think of one who married in with the traditional picture of what a prostitute is supposed to look like, and that was 'Big Ada'.

Ada was a whore and she didn't give a damn who knew it. She was a dyed blonde, with bulging blue eyes, and a bulging body to match which could be seen through the loose kimono she was invariably wearing whenever I called on her. I suspect this was her working uniform.

Ada had the greatest difficulty in getting out of bed in the morning. Give her, her due though, she did try, usually without success, to get the two kiddies off to school on time in the morning. Both children were mixed race, one 10 and the other 8 years of age. If the kids were missing from school then round to Ada's I would go. One or both children would meet me at the door, invite me in and then standing at the bottom of the stairs, would shout up,

'Mam, it's Mr Boardman!'

I never worried about going to that house in the daytime for unlike many others, Ada was, dare I say, self-employed, and only 'put it up for sale' in the evening. Given time, Ada would appear, eyes matted up with sleep and still with last night's lipstick and mascara spread over her face, full of apologies for taking up so much of my time. As we spoke she was constantly on the move, pulling her kimono across her ample bosom and groping on the shelf for a smoke amidst the clutter of ashtrays, loose coins and condom packets, already opened for the coming nights action. The couch where it all happened was in easy reach of the shelf so all Ada or the client needed to do was reach up and it was all systems 'Go!'

Ada loved to talk, and I was a good listener. She was a mine of information without any prompting from me. Many times it was Ada who alerted me to the fact that this or that schoolgirl was going wrong, not I hasten to add because she had a social conscience, but because these amateurs could undercut her on price and she feared VD which she always referred to as 'the pox.'

What Ada had to say opened my eyes and broadened my own education in areas which, until then, were only surmise, containing as they did, in near monologue form, such snippets as:

'A lot of people think that black men have bigger pricks than white men, but that's a load of bollocks! The only difference between black and white men is black men move differently, and I should know! I've been f*cked by both more times than you've had hot dinners. In fact some white men have enormous pricks!'

On another occasion she came out with this gem, and you must tell me what this has to do with my initial question of, 'do you want to apply for free school dinners for the kids, Ada?'

Ada replied with,

'A lot of men are kinky! If all the men who've been through me had wanted straight sex, my fanny would've been worn out by now!'

I never asked questions or pried into Ada's private life and I believe that's why she was so open with me if I did need information urgently, otherwise I never spoke about much else other than the kids' school attendance and related matters. Perhaps deep down Ada wanted to shock me. Failing that I think the psychologists would've had a field day with her.

One day Ada sent for me. This was so out of character I was aware at once something was very wrong. Her 'umming & ahhhing' confirmed this. Eventually though, she came to the point.

'I'm getting out Mr Boardman. The kids are noticing.'

'How do you mean?' I asked but was aware the older child, a 10 year old girl, had come home from the park recently with semen down the front of her dress after sitting on a man's knee in the park.

Ada called out to the younger child, a boy,

'You tell Mr Boardman what that boy at your school did with your sister!'

Without turning a hair, he told me how the girl had been taken into the toilet block where the boy had taken her pants down. He then took out his 'wee wee' and put it into her 'wee wee.' Now, what can you say to that!?

'Ada, I've got to report this!' I said, and did, but I might as well have saved the 'Biro.' By the next day they were gone! Five years later I heard through the grapevine that Ada was 'inside' and the children in Care, the girl having 'gone on the game' before she was 14 years.

Stella and Apple Mary:

Over the years a private Housing Association had become most active on the district. The general idea was they'd buy up the older, more run-down properties that nobody wanted due to neglect by the previous owners or tenants and with help from various government agencies the years of neglect would, or should in theory anyway, be put to rights. Walls were stripped of plaster right down to the bare brick then replastered after damp proofing work had been carried out. Total rewiring was undertaken, back bedrooms were converted into bathrooms with inside toilets, kitchens were extended and new units installed, new internal and external doors were fitted and the roof refelted and slated. The homes, for that was what they'd reverted to, were then Let to lower income families and some went to 'problem' families. Until they were fully occupied though the local prostitutes would get their pimps to kick in the front doors so they could conduct their' business' on the nice fresh floorboards.

Unfortunately, alongside the genuine tradespeople were a number of 'cowboys' who moved in to make a lot of money for the minimum outlay or effort, tools and materials.

I needed to call at a newly renovated house to ask after a child and was invited in by mum. I was sitting facing a window through which the morning sun beamed with a blinding intensity, even so, I could see enough of the inner wall to cause me to come out with,

'Please don't think me rude missus, but what on earth decided you to paint the wall such a lousy looking green colour? It doesn't match the other three walls at all!'

The mother burst out laughing and with a 'no, I'm not at all offended,' she drew the flat of her hand across the surface of the offending wall.

'Look,' she said, and held out her palm for my inspection. The whole of her hand was green. 'It's mould! It's growing on the wall and has been since the wall was replastered!'

And so it proved to be. I shuddered to think what would happen if any of that muck got into the family's system!

Into one of the better renovated homes moved one of my prize beauty's. Stella! A right pain in the backside if ever I met one! A one parent family because the 'old man' had done the only sensible thing in his life when he left her to it and cleared off! She was cunning though, fringing on the vice game but give her her due, she was plausible, very plausible, she must've been because with a record of never paying any rent she not only got the tenancy of one of these better homes but the association who owned it, a charity, furnished it from top to bottom! If only they'd spoken to me first! I could've put the bung in for her and saved them thousands of pounds!

Stella had chummed up with another of the good time girls, the one nicknamed

'Apple Mary.' The two of them lived the life of 'Riley' and robbed the state rotten. My concern was the kids though: Mary had two, as did Stella who had a boy of 11 years and a girl of 10 years. It was Stella's daughter who finally brought everything to a head when she confided to her teacher that she shared a bed with her brother and it was he who was giving her 'love bites' on her neck!

The first split had already appeared in Stella and Mary's friendship as Mary's boyfriend made a habit of climbing out of her bed in the morning and getting in with Stella. What really upset Mary though was not so much him sharing Stella's bed and body but after the fun and games the pair of them would lie in bed and expect Mary to take them morning tea! Too much, too much! Mary moved out taking her most decidedly knackered looking boyfriend with her, though she still kept in touch for moral (or immoral) support!

Even the kids at school had spotted the love bites on Stella's daughter's neck and the poor girl was taking a lot of 'stick!' Don't let's forget the child was only 10 years!

I began to put my evidence together. Calling at the house one day I was surprised to see Apple Mary, who opened the door to me. Feigning pleasure at seeing her again I went into my usual routine and made a fuss of her, telling her how much we'd all missed her. Mary told me she was back living with Stella but just to help out during a dire emergency. Eyes big and round and all agog I asked,

'Why, whatever's the matter me duck?'

Mary then went on to explain how an irate coloured gentleman had given Stella a 'good hiding,' although the language she used was a lot more 'fruity.'

'Whatever is this country coming to,' I exclaimed, before pushing past her and into the living room which, in farmyard parlance, resembled a 'pig sty', and there, lo and behold, sat Stella nursing an absolute dream of a black eye!

'Oh dear, whatever's the matter?' I asked.

'I've bin beat up by a punter,' she stated, gingerly touching the bruising.

'But why aren't the children at school? Have they been hurt too?' was my next question.

'Oh no,' reassured Stella, 'but they're upset and I daren't send them to school!'

I eventually left the house cheering inwardly for I knew Stella's 'big mouth' had won any Court case I'd intended to present, hands down. Her words, when I repeated them to the Juvenile Bench, would cause quite a sensation and the case was mine! The verdict? Supervision, both children to the Probation Service.

School attendance improved dramatically after that. They had a Probation Officer who wouldn't be messed around, and they knew it!

A while later I had cause to call at the house; the family having recently vacated. A very well dressed, business type gentleman opened the by now filthy front door to me and in silence regarded me with suspicion until I identified myself. Satisfied I wasn't 'a punter' wanting to get 'his tubes blown' (I think that's the expression used back then) he invited me in.

'I've got a pretty good idea what sort of mess I'm about to see,' I told him, 'as I've been coming to this house for months and watched it being turned into a tip!

Don't you people ever visit to see what these people are doing to your Homes?'

All the furniture, new only six months ago, was now gone, having been flogged, bartered or exchanged for commodities like 'fags' and 'booze.' The only things remaining were filth and stench.

I was led upstairs to the front bedroom. This contained a double bed and commode chair. The mattress on the bed was stained with blood, urine and excrement, and what I took to be other bodily fluids deemed to be a hazard of a prostitute's trade! It was the commode chair that took pride of place though as it was overflowing with urine and faeces and at least two used sanitary towels. With Stella, having 'flitted' at least two weeks previously the stench was unimaginable.

The man from the Housing Association merely stated that all this would 'have to be burnt.'

Moving into the bathroom, new and unused just a few months ago, the wash basin was broken and stained as was the toilet pan. This too was full of excrement which had found its own level by oozing onto the floor. An old cardboard box contained a vast quantity of used sanitary towels which led me to wonder whether Stella had gone into the 'abortion business' herself, along with used condoms and various other items which didn't merit closer inspection by me or anyone else!

I couldn't go into the back bedroom as it was in the process of being 'stoved' but I could see in the back yard another man from the Housing Association who was burning items from the house on a huge bonfire as fast as they could be carried out.

Twelve years later I was invited to a case conference on Stella and her brood. This had been generated as she owed over a thousand pounds in rent arrears to the Council, and she and her family were such a bloody nuisance that the neighbours had petitioned the Council to get her out.

The Council decided, in spite of my protests, to scrub the arrears! Not only that but she was given another council house on one of the better and more settled council estates and the house she was to occupy was next to a little block of the only few privately owned houses in the area! What on earth do you make of that!?

Chapter 11: Pressures on the Schools

By now I was known and accepted by Headteachers and school staff alike, who never spared me. I'd been very wary of two Heads initially, one because he seemed such a cold sort of fish. However, when the nasty stuff hit the fan and boundary lines had to be crossed, he was proven to have a heart of gold. No child in his school was allowed to miss out on a school trip no matter how poor or troublesome that child may have been. Time and time again he put his hand in his own pocket to provide the wherewithal so all the kids could be accommodated on trips to the coast or London. That made him an Ace with me! The other Head, because of my unhappy experiences with my previous district Senior Head, I was very wary of until time proved he was OK. His secretary told me some three months after joining the school, that her boss had confided to her how he hadn't thought they'd be able to replace the quality of the previous Boardman, but this one was far better!

This Head could spot a truant just by looking at the registers. He would sit on a chair and slide a finger down the list of names. He had enormous hands. His finger would stop moving and he would say,

'Chase this one!'

More often than not the boy would be a first time absentee. Others in the same class would have a far worse attendance record but if I queried this, he'd say,

'No, chase this one. The others are genuine.'

Invariably, the Head would be right for when I arrived on the doorstep I'd be told,

'Not in school today, mister? Well, he should be!'

It was my good luck to have, in my opinion, the best Heads in the city for they were prepared to be involved in the whole life of the community. The classrooms were tightly packed wall to wall, with desks and chairs crammed in to accommodate the new arrivals who poured in. Playground space was given over to mobile classrooms, and even empty houses nearby were being taken over and used as English language annexes. We were so overloaded that scores of children we were unable to accommodate were being bussed to outlying schools, but still I was expected to cope single handed! Lest I be accused of self-pity, let me say at once that if any credit is to be paid to anyone for the absorption of these new arrivals then the credit must go to those who truly deserved it: the tireless Heads and staff on my district who never spared themselves, or me, to make it gel. It truly was service over and above the call of duty!

It seems scandalous to me that after all the hard work and extra work done by us in the early days, often without any acknowledgement, let alone asked for or given, that so many have crept in today, like scavenging vultures to feed off what was a very healthy body indeed, and to carve empires, exceedingly lucrative empires, out of and on the foundations we pioneers put there. As a very bitter and disillusioned Head said to me much later when scanning the latest list of senior community and race relations posts, stipulating: must speak one Asian language,

'Where were this lot 15 years ago when the flood gates opened and we had to cope on empty promises and damn all else?!'

One of the district prostitutes, a girl of limited sexual appeal and exceedingly low intelligence, was enjoying a bigger measure of success and gaining repeat business from clients in spite of a huge number of better endowed sisters of the night. The other girls, and I use the word 'girls' advisedly, were equally bemused and upset because they were losing many regulars to her, the opposition! Their pimps didn't go very much on it either, especially as the lady in question was such a wreck that none of them had thought to 'sign her up!'

The answer finally emerged. As a young girl the lady in question's father had been sleeping with her and had initiated her into 'matrimonial joys' whatever they are! This had become common knowledge on the streets and believe it or not, had proven to be a bit of a 'turn on' for the clients who were not getting on very well with the wife. The client, at a critical stage of the sexual proceedings would ask whether it was true her daddy used to 'do it to you?' (or words to that effect) She would answer in the affirmative adding a few lurid details, both real and imaginary. This was sufficient to bring the proceedings to a satisfactory conclusion for those involved or, to put it in the way the lady was alleged to have confided to one of her chums,

'My old man's incest brings the buggers off faster than tickling them under the balls with me vibrator!'

With so many distractions of a sexual nature around, much of the advice given to the schools' senior girls was direct and to the point, and it needed to be as most had been approached at some time or another by men on the make. One day

I overheard this conversation between a girl and a senior mistress. The teacher in question was an elderly lady, a typical school ma'am with many years' experience behind her: grey haired and motherly to those who needed mothering. She was talking to a very forward young miss who was mature for her years, cheeky, and not averse to chatting up any male, whether caretaker, teacher or Boardman! However, it was her activities 'out of school' that were causing the most concern.

As I passed I heard Miss say,

'If you don't learn to keep your drawers up around your waist and your knees together Madam, you'll get pregnant!'

Those few words put everything into perspective and highlighted the pitfalls of boy/ girl relationships far better than all the sex education lessons given in the homes and schools today. I'll go further and wager those few to the point words will be remembered when all else is forgotten!

Chapter 12: Immigration and Visitors From Afar

Those first new arrivals from India didn't carry much weight and the children had such thin, stick like arms and legs mainly due to the rotten diet which was totally unsuitable to our climate so one of my first jobs was to try and persuade the parents to move away from their traditional foods and get more protein into the kids. I could've wept on finding that many were fasting or abstaining from foods on religious grounds that would've built them up. One little girl who was fainting at school from hunger was fasting on the orders of a priest and yet the priest's gut considerably overhung his belt!

Within the family and the caste system Asian families were very close but outside these there was very little mixing. No way would a Muslim willingly have anything to do with a Hindu and vice versa, and then one day to my absolute amazement it dawned on me that the white man, representative of the old colonial order that the 'stirrers' went on about so much, was the common ground on which all the races and religions were meeting simply by getting the kids into school. I was the spot of soft soap that helped the oil and the water to mix.

Not the least of my problems was communication. I had so many non-English speakers with more arriving every day and these I had to record for medical checks before being allowed into schools in the City. Each of my Census cards had to carry the name of every household member and if multi-occupied, as so often they were, every member of every separate household within the house. After knocking on the door I would invariably be ushered inside by an Asian father whilst mother was kept in the background, never speaking and very rarely smiling at me as I tried to draw her into the form filling conversation. Inside the home were smells foreign to me, cloves, curry and spices, and many times I was sorely tempted to ask father not to breathe all over me as the aroma of some of the bean like peas he chewed nearly knocked me out! However, let me say at once that not one home I entered was dirty or offensive in any way. It was basic hygiene that let them down at times with filthy drains, and spitting on their own doorstep the norm, yet with so many of them having small children and babies how on earth did they avoid the smell of excrement that was so prevalent in some of the homes of their white counterparts!

Often, on entering Asian homes, I would find myself in a heavily draped and curtained front room with most of the daylight excluded, whilst on a divan would be the sleeping form of a male with a blanket covering his face to exclude any remaining light or noise that junior members of the household might make. Most certainly a night shift worker. The only other item in the room as often as not would be a wardrobe, very battered and old, on top of which would be kept the family papers. At father's command a chair would be quickly brought into the room and as I sat down the room would fill up as though by ghosts: women in a sari or heavily veiled, plus children. All of them would then gaze at me as though I were a visitor from another world.

The head of that household would reach up or stand on a chair to bring down a suitcase from the top of the wardrobe and a search would be made for papers, birth certificates and passports. Always at some time in the proceedings father would begin to chatter to his wife and all the kids would join in, with arms waving. They were the most disorganised people I ever met, but nice with it. Passports would eventually be located, pored over and then thrust at me. The head of the household grabbed, pushed and shoved out of the way, though very gently, the shy little boys and girls, all shades of brown, who now came to see me. Fingers pushed into their mouths, smiling back in response to my smile as I leaned forward to touch their cheeks with my finger tips to communicate a greeting of 'hello.' I was offered tea, and at first refused, but they looked so downcast at my refusal that I relented, not wishing to offend or hurt their feelings. Many called me 'Sahib', using the proper pronunciation of 'SAB', and I guessed it was a feather in the cap if the school sahib took tea with them. The tea tasted very different to the tea I was used to, and at father's prodding mum would shyly show me how they made it. In between socialising and setting the family at ease I would be writing furiously on my Census card: Family name, father's name, mum's name, children's names, ages, gender, spoken language, any physical abnormalities. The list seemed to go on and on. Straight afterwards I would be asked about free school dinners for the children and warm clothing, all supplied at the tax and rate payers' expense. More forms to be filled out. It seemed to go on and on and I was having to do the lot! There were no home/ school liaison officers back in those days.

In one Asian household I visited I listed 35 children. Then there were the adults! Today the authorities tend to shy away from asking the questions I asked for fear of upsetting the race relations industry.

I confess I enjoyed the challenges presented and was hard put to understand my fellow officers' reluctance to take on this district when it was offered. My thinking was always along the lines that people, all people, are pretty much the same no matter where they come from, and so I thought that if I couldn't get these people to accept me then I might as well pack the job in! I had to make the breakthrough very quickly if I wanted to succeed and make it with my English for I didn't speak any of the languages I was now finding being used on the doorsteps. With only English to fall back on I began to gain the trust and confidence of all, or nearly all, and was accepted as a friend and councillor.

Only the Heads and staff in my schools seemed to understand the problems being thrown up. I don't think the top people in the council chambers understood or even cared just how much work I was getting through in a day. At times I felt as though I was being carried along on a tidal wave of new entrants into this country, and I reckon it was about two months before I felt my feet touch the ground and I began to function in a positive way.

Winter was now here and, forgive the pun, but I was snowed under with visits. I 'streeted' up and found I had to make 130 visits. To fit them all in I left home at 8am and was still trudging around in deep snow at 3:30pm having had not a bite to eat or hot drink. I still had to go home, have some lunch, dash into town to the office and get my paperwork done. It didn't help on arrival to see so many of my fellow officers lounging around smoking and socialising whilst I was working flat out to clear my desk. No wonder the boss had no joy in getting a volunteer other than this prize mug to take the district on, but I loved the job and the contacts I was making! It was fascinating trying to communicate with so many non-English speakers even though trying to communicate with a non-English speaker could and often did take ten times longer than talking to someone who could understand me. When asked, as I often was, 'well, just how did you get them to understand if they spoke no English, and you had no Urdu or Hindi?' My answer, tongue in cheek, was always the same, 'I just shouted a bit louder!' And yet the truth was that should difficulties occur I would proceed thus:

When the door was opened to me and it was apparent language was going to be a problem, I would simply put my hand to my chest and say, 'school' – the one word that seemed to be understood by all non-English speakers. I would be invited in but should the word 'school' not be understood I'd stand on the doorstep and call out to Asians in the street, 'Speak English?' until someone came over who did. Usually though 'school' was enough.

The routine went like this: The door would open and the Asian lady or gentleman were greeted with, 'school'. They would smile, nod their heads and repeat 'school'. Pointing at them I would then say, 'You Mr Patel/ Singh or whatever the name might be on my bit of paper. To another affirmative nod I would then say the name of the child for which I was visiting. With this understood I was practically home and dry except for why the named child was 'no school'. The 'no school' was heavily stressed. At this father, mum, little brothers, sisters, aunts and uncles, friends and neighbours, even passing strangers who'd stopped to find out what was going on, would shout seemingly in unison, 'sick, very sick.' Ok, now we had it or so it would seem, however, I now had to find out the type of illness, so off I'd go again! I'd put my hand to my head and say, 'sick here?' (is it a headache?) Depending on the response I would move my hand slowly down my body whilst at each stage putting the question, 'sick here?' until I got a positive response. If I reached my throat and got an affirmative nod I could safely put, 'throat trouble,' and so on. It was only after reaching my navel and still getting a negative response that I'd begin to worry. How on earth would I indicate circumcision, period pains or undescended testicles!!!

One of my fellow officers came to me with a problem. The first Indian family had moved onto his district and he was worried in case he wasn't able to be understood when he visited. Dear old Ben, who wasn't known for having the sweetest of temperaments, listened whilst I explained. He wanted no 'slip ups' as the boy concerned was known to be playing 'hooky'. Calling at the boy's home Ben hammered on the door which was opened by a Sikh man wearing traditional robes and a turban. His heavy beard was covered by a mesh net and he was wearing ornate and beaded slippers. Without giving the poor bloke a chance to speak, Ben let fly with,

'Good morning. You Mr Singh? Your son Jagdish Singh? Jagdish Singh your son not go to school!'

Here, Ben bashed himself on his chest so hard he couldn't get out the words, 'me school,' for coughing! Somehow, he continued with,

'Jagdish Singh your son very naughty boy. No go to school. You his daddy; you get Jagdish back into school or plenty, plenty trouble. You savvy??'

At this point dear old Ben who'd stopped to draw breath was waiting for a reaction, any reaction, but the one he got, for in the broadest Birmingham accent you could cut with a knife the father, who up to then had stood through it all with his mouth wide open (old Ben had that effect on me sometimes) sort of gulped, shook his head and in perfect English said,

'Why the little bugger. Wait till he comes home. I won't 'arf tan his bloody arse for him!'

Exit Ben, absolutely shattered. I swear he thought it was all my fault!

In a general way I spoke about Indians and Asians but I never forgot that these generalisations covered many people of a very large continent worshipping in many different ways. Probably the most important difference was in the religion they followed, and when that religion tolerated no slackness of standards in its followers, then be doubly careful! I found this out to my cost when right at the beginning some parents, out of a sense of misplaced modesty, objected to their daughters changing for PE even though the school in question was an all girls' establishment. The priest was a fanatic on Islamic Law. I'd never met the bloke and wasn't aware such strong feelings were held until I, like Mohammed, was expected to move the mountain! I was with one girl's father and because he had no English, I was using an interpreter. One drawback to this I'd already found was if you didn't watch it the interpreter would take over, and so I was constantly checking him without knowing just how accurately my words were being translated. Trying to persuade the father to allow his daughter to use clothes other than normal dress for doing PE I stressed the hygiene implications as well as the benefit of doing exercise,

'Exercise strengthens the limbs and bodies' I waffled. 'In our country even pregnant women wear shorts and do these exercises!'

It had to happen I suppose! That idiot of a translator, full of his own importance at being asked to do the job, screwed it up completely and what came out was,

'We want your daughter to do PE when she is pregnant!'

It was a close call for a few minutes, in fact I thought I'd been the cause of England's first 'Holy War!' Fortunately, wiser council prevailed. These were the early days and people were more prepared to listen. I'd made my first break through and the girls changed for PE.

Chapter 13: A Year in and the Cane

In the first year of working on the district the severest problem came from the white section of the community. Looking back over those early days I can't remember any acute problems arising or developing from the new immigrants who in the main came to school and behaved.

My school Heads were sympathetic and tolerant but no way would they accept bad behaviour, bad social habits or intolerance from any child, be they black, brown or white. In those days every Head had within a cupboard in his study the means of enforcing discipline if all else failed, and few of them hesitated to use the ultimate sanction open to them. The cane. Hand on heart, although we were dealing with boys and girls, some of them sixteen and big with it, I can't remember even one child we couldn't cope with. Today the cane is gone and the sanction used is exclusion. Children, some of them under ten years of age, are being turned out of the schools and onto the streets under the exclusion or suspension rule. Where for goodness sake is the sense of taking or removing a child out of the protected and benign environment of the school and turning him or her out onto the street thus making more problems for the forces of law & order, and eventually society in general?!

New arrivals from Scotland:

It was my 'pick up' day and I went into my Senior Boys' school secretary's office to collect those visits which had to be done. The school building was old Victorian, gloomy & forbidding from the outside but inside clean, friendly and warm.

The boys (and I always thought of them as 'my boys') were a mixture of races who shared a disciplined and caring friendliness. They were chatty but never cheeky to me, and this friendly approach was extended to any visitor to their school, whatever their business. Without being asked these boys would go up to any stranger wandering lost within the building and, after asking who it was the visitor had come to see, would escort them to their destination. Now, if this sounds normal for a school in England then just remember that most of these boys only a year or so previously, were living in Bombay, Calcutta or even on the plains of the Punjab. Quite simply they were maintaining the traditions of courtesy and public service for which the school had been noted for over many generations.

As I walked through the musty smelling hall that cleaning never seemed to sweeten any, I was greeted as an old friend by the lads changing classes. I boast that every lad in the school knew me. It was all smiles and cries of,

'Have you caught any skivers today, Sir?' or 'Baljit's dodging maths, Sir!'

Ignore the skin colour and these were just your everyday school children.

My conversation with the secretary was interrupted by the Head sticking his head around the door.

'Can you come up please?' he asked.

Dutifully, I went up to his room where I was invited to be seated and have a smoke. The boss was grinning all over his face.

'Boy, have I got two beauties for you today!' he chortled, 'and if I'm any judge of character these'll have you run off your feet and tearing your hair out in handfuls because I'm 100% certain that the whole ruddy family's trouble with a capital T!'

It appeared that the new admissions were Scottish and newly arrived in the City. School was the second port of call with the first being the pub, judging by the state of the father when he brought his sons in. Just before they left, with orders to begin attendance the next day, the father had asked,

'Do you use the leather strap here?'

'No' the Head had replied, 'but I do use this' and going to the cupboard he'd taken out the cane.

'Good!' he'd chortled, 'these beggers of mine could stand some discipline to keep them in line!'

With that the tribe departed, led by father, but only after he'd glanced regretfully at his empty cup that had once held milky coffee, then a second appealing glance at the Head to see if another free smoke was forthcoming.

'I explained the school rules to them' the Head declared 'but seeing who they were and what they were I modified things slightly by making the first rule to be, RULES SHALL NOT BE BROKEN!'

Within a week, as predicted, I was a regular visitor to the family!

Besides mother, father and the two school age boys there were two older brothers of 18 and 20 years respectively. I got on fine with them, especially after comparing notes and finding a ship I'd served on during my Merchant Navy days had been built quite close to their former home address up in Scotland. Unfortunately, I couldn't win with the younger ones as the truancy, which seemed to be the norm in the family long before I met them, was too ingrained.

I was soon to find out that all of them were on speaking terms with most of the local constabulary! That is to say the 'Bobby' would declare, 'You're nicked' and our friends would reply, 'It wasn't me officer!' To be fair though, I found them to be very likeable rogues!

The visit I made to them that sticks out a mile was when I called at their house to enquire into the latest round of absences. The day was hot and humid but never the less they had a fire going in the living room hearth that looked fit to set the chimney on fire it was roaring so! The fire had in front of it a dustbin lid to make it 'draw' properly and this had achieved its purpose. Unfortunately, no-one had bothered to remove the lid and so the fire was blazing away as though on a fixed draught. What I could see of the old-fashioned fire range was covered in white, burnt on, blobs of spit. Hankies were not used in this household and so the family would 'hawk up' and spit onto the open fire. (or try to) Sadly, most of the time they missed!

Father was lounging back in the only chair the room boasted and I spotted at once that the wooden arms of the said chair were what was keeping the fire going! Mother was in her customary place, that is half in and half out of the kitchen door, although goodness knows why she should choose that particular spot for she never, so far as I was aware, did any cooking or even cleaning. It did cross my mind once that she stood on that spot in case she had to make a 'quick getaway' but I dismissed that as being 'too unkind.'

Father waved his arms around and told me the two younger boys were at school. I then told him they weren't!

'Ain't I got enough troubles?' he griped in a heavy Scottish brogue. 'The two big lads are 'doon' at the nick helping police with their enquiries!'

'How very public spirited of them both,' I said. 'Is it a sort of neighbourhood watch?'

At this the father started to make all sorts of scurrilous and slanderous statements about our local gendarmerie of which 'fooking pigs' and lousy bastids' were the least offensive! Red faced and by now foaming at the mouth, father told me the whole sordid story!

The night before, a local tobacconist had been 'turned over' and the two older boys had been picked out as chief suspects. Now, at this early stage and with only the father's description of events to go on, I was simply an interested onlooker as it were and not prepared even to consider whether his lads had been involved. Father was still holding forth however and 'rabbiting' on about police harassment of decent, hard-working, Christian people, which threw me somewhat until I realised he meant HIS family and he wasn't bringing outsiders into his story! In the middle of this diatribe he paused, climbed onto the table which stood in the middle of the room and reaching up and into the dusty, electric light bowl, left I suspect by successive tenants from the day the house was built it was so filthy, he extracted three 2oz tins of Golden Virginian tobacco, selected one that had already been opened and, after replacing the two unopened tins, proceeded to roll himself a smoke using a cigarette paper from a pack....also new, which emerged from the same place. Puffing away contentedly the makings were then replaced in the light bowl. Stepping down, our Hero looked up to survey the light bowl from all angles to make sure nothing could be seen through all the muck and debris therein. It was then I began to wonder for, as I'm sure you'd agree, that was just a damn funny, not to say inconvenient place, to keep one's smokes!! Why not in the pocket I asked myself?

Still sending up clouds of Golden Virginia smoke, father then began to describe the scene of the night before when the forces of law and order came to arrest those 'poor bairns of mine,' and yet wasn't it only the day before he was describing them as 'those shiftless, bone idle, tight fisted sods who won't buy their father a dram!

So determined were the police to get his sons for 'the job', he said, as one 'tec' was questioning the boys, another was dribbling sawdust from the crates in which the 'baccy' had been packed into their trouser turn ups!

'In all my years', confessed father, 'and I admit I've been in trouble with the police a few times myself' (at this point mother almost choked on her tea) 'but I've never known anything so unethical! It's dirty and it's......' and here he pondered a moment for another word but 'unethical' was the only word he could think of, and he'd already used that one! What he said next left me speechless!

'OK. My boys did do the break in, but to get a conviction like that, why, it's unethical!'

The art of truancy (or not):

Within a few months on the district I was to see the cane being used on senior boys although I hasten to add it was only used as a last resort or if the matter under review was serious enough to merit its use. So far as truancy was concerned the cane was used only after fair warning that the culprit must mend his ways, 'or else!' Should this fail, then, and only then, was the cupboard opened and that subject of so much controversy and the punishment book emerge into the light of day.

If I caught a boy playing 'hooky' I would escort him back to school then try to find out if the truancy was a 'one off.' The boy was then warned and without taking any further action I would send him to his classroom with instructions to tell the teacher that 'Mr Boardman has sent me to you and he will discuss it later with you, Sir!' The teachers knew the way I worked and were happy to leave the 'sorting it out' to me. If the truancy was repeated the boy was caned. They were only allowed one chance, and yet I cannot recall a boy being caned above once or twice for this reason:

The only time a boy was caned for a first offence of truancy was if I identified him in the street and he ran away. This was agreed by the Head and myself in the early days at my request for there was 'no way' I intended to be shown up by chasing all over the city after kids on the skive from school. Every boy, and I include those who would never think of playing truant, knew the drill. Whenever I said, 'stand still, son, you're caught,' as a rule they did just that! Of course we all had the occasional 'runner'; the clown who thought I was too far away to make a positive identification and relied on the bare faced, 'Please Sir, it wasn't me, Sir!' to get him off the hook! In these cases I always visited the parents straight away, even fetching father out of work if need be! Once 'fibber boy's' truancy was confirmed then, 'Hard Luck, Mate' for we had another rule for liars and runners, which was 'they get double!'

I was passing the local Spinney Hill Park soon after the registration bell would've been sounded in school when I heard screams (Girls) and shouts (Boys). Some kids were having a whale of a time! Peering over the hedge I saw a small group of 15 year olds of both sexes dashing in and out of the bushes halfway down the slope. They were having a ball! As I watched I saw the hands of one of the boys shoot up the skirt of a girl which triggered yet another of those screams girls love to emit when they're trying to get the boys to 'try harder!' I knew there was no mistake on this score because the girl in question was trying to grab the boy's 'goolies!' This had gone far enough and so slowly I moved towards the crowd. Keeping the trees between us I got close then announced my presence with,

'According to my watch the registration bell went half an hour ago!'

The kids spun round open mouthed and I saw that close to, none of the boys were smaller than me, in fact two of them, West Indians, positively towered over me (and I was 6foot). Fortunately, I saw that two of the tallest were my boys, and they knew me, otherwise they could've 'had a go' claiming I was 'a peeper!' (peeping Tom) To their credit they stood absolutely still. In those days kids still wore a full uniform and when the girls went to unearth theirs from the pile of gear on the grass I realised the girls were mine too! I ordered the girls back to school, telling them I would check later they were 'IN' and escorted my three male 'skallywags' back to their school personally and we chatted quite easily on the way in. On arrival the lower hall and staircase was clear otherwise they would've taken some ragging from the other kids, and up we went to the Head's room. In we trooped when invited! To his enquiring raised eyebrow I began to recount the details, ending with,

'As the others involved were girls, and the language was pretty fierce, I brought them straight to you, Sir! However, I think it should go on record that the girls were more than willing and the boys came straight back with me when invited to do so. I'd like you to take that into consideration when deciding punishment, Headmaster!'

The Head turned to the miscreants,

'Anything to say before I pass sentence, Lads?'

Each boy shook his head.

'Taking into consideration all the facts and bearing in mind what Mr Boardman has said in your favour, you will get half of what you would've got, bearing in mind what you were up to with those girls! Agreed?'

The boys nodded their heads as one.

Crossing to the corner cupboard he took out first the cane and then the punishment book.

'Right lads. Let's get to it! Mr Boardman, please stand well back. First boy forward: bend over my desk, put your hand down between your legs from the front and ease your testicles forward lest I not strike true and ruin your marriage prospects!'

Having said all this and with the first one bent over, stiff armed the cane came down and, standing well back as I was, I still nearly lost an eye! Each of the boys took two hard ones! I thought the last and the biggest might give trouble as he shied away like a frightened colt, but the Headmaster's 'Maurice' soon got him into position.

The cane was put away and the punishment book filled in, and I was invited to sign as a witness. With formalities over the atmosphere lifted at once, although the dust from the seats of their pants still darkened the room. The boys were rubbing their behinds hard to try and stop the stinging but they were relaxing by the minute, witness the faces they began pulling at each other and the laughter at the thought of losing their marriage prospects!

Of those in the room I'm pretty sure I was the one most affected. I hated then and for ever after, seeing the cane used but I still believe it did more good than harm.

Now seated, the Head leaned back in his chair and with hands clasped behind his head he reminded the boys that, punishment administered, it was all over and forgotten. He and the boys chatted backwards and forwards like the good friends they were, quite at ease, then with a final joke of 'I bet you won't be showing the girls your battle scars' he dismissed them and off they went, laughing and chattering down the stairs.

Those boys are now men, some with children of their own. One stopped me in the street years later. He was holding his little boy by the hand as he greeted me with,

'Hello, Sir, do you remember me? Do you remember how you used to find me wandering the streets when I should've been at school? Do you remember how you would take me by the hand and take me to my teacher at the Junior school and tell him not to be cross with me? You were always very kind, Mr Boardman. I couldn't understand what you were trying to do for me then, but I do now, and I thank you for it!'

After chatting we parted and as I turned the corner I looked back and saw him still holding tightly onto his little one's hand, leading him gently away. Suddenly, he was transformed back to how I best remembered him. A short, stocky, uncared for, snotty nosed, little boy. I felt proud I'd had a hand in shaping this new, whole man and if these open faced, hardworking, well-adjusted young men I began to see every day are anything to go on then our system of rewards and punishments up to the abolition of the cane, had worked.

Critics of the cane might say, 'Ah yes, but have you ever suffered the indignity of having to submit to this awful ritual?' I would answer in this way.

'As a school boy I was never caned, but I have received the cane in school.'

It came about like this:

I was entering the local Park one morning around 11 am when two boys of about 13 years, who I didn't recognise, came towards me. One white and one Asian. As they weren't known to me I guessed they attended a school or schools other than mine. I didn't like strangers roaming around on my district as they could lead others into their bad habits and so mindful how the public don't like to see boys being accosted by strangers for apparently no good reason, I let them get right up to me before I stepped in front of them saying,

'Hello, I'm the school welfare officer. Do you mind telling me your names, addresses and what school you're supposed to be at?'

Wow, could these kids move! They were off before I could blink my eyes! The white boy just ran whilst the Asian boy ran, but feeling safe for the moment, he spun round and yelled,

'Mind your own f*cking business, you f*cker!'

With that he rejoined his chum and were soon out of sight leaving me absolutely fuming!

'You sods' I thought, 'If it takes me till doomsday, I'll bloody well have you!'

Now, it was my boast that all in good time the 'skallywags' would land back in my lap, but never in my wildest dreams did I imagine I would get my little Asian chummy so quickly or so easily!

The next morning whilst walking on my district I could hardly believe my luck, for coming down the street on the other side of the road was my foul-mouthed little chum from yesterday! He hadn't seen me and so I quickly got out of sight and then followed him. Like a lamb he sauntered past and went on his way, with me close behind. He soon turned into an entry and so did I, just in time to see which of the two gates he went into. With a song in my heart, and no longer bothering to conceal myself, I followed and knocked on the back door. The door opened and there he stood. When he saw who it was, and I could see he recognised me, I thought he'd fill his trousers!

'Right sonny,' I began, 'I'll ask the same question I asked you yesterday' then, not giving him any time to answer, 'and I want your father to tell me!'

Just then the boy's father, a very elderly Asian man, came to the door. Off I went:

'You speak English?' (if he did, he wasn't saying at that point)

I tried again,

'Me school!'

Jackpot! His eyes lit up and a veritable torrent of words poured out. He neither needed or required any prompting from me. The boy was to look even more worried before much longer because I interrupted the old chap's torrent to say:

a) The boy's seemingly very fit today
b) He appeared even fitter yesterday on the Park
c) Who are you!!??

This last question was directed towards a young fellow who'd appeared as if by magic at my elbow and now introduced himself as 'boy wonder's' older brother! (All in near perfect English I might add)

If the boy thought he was going to get any help from his nearest and dearest he was to be sadly disappointed, for this was to be the saga of boyo's sins according to both father and sibling!

'He very naughty boy. He swear at mammy & daddy all time. He won't go to school, Mister. He won't obey mammy & daddy. All time he say school no f*cking good! He pinch money from mammy's purse. He call me a big c*nt. We very, very fed up with him!'

The old chap and the big brother were nearly in tears by the time they'd finished putting the 'bung in' for the villain!

Now, bearing in mind I didn't know which school the boy went to and bearing in mind should it be with a soft touch for a Headmaster, kiddo could well have gotten away with it. I put the question,

'What school does he go to?'

Joy, joy, joy! It was one I knew well, and the Head was not averse to enforcing discipline and backing up the parents if needed!

'Will you take your son into school tomorrow?' I asked father. 'If you see the Headmaster and ask him for help, he will help you! You can tell the Headmaster I will be coming in to see him as well, as your son swore at me yesterday.'

Father thought it an excellent idea and promised me he'd be there!

Bright and early the next morning I pedalled across the sprawling council estate that separated the two districts that were three miles apart. My only worry was that father might not be strong enough to enforce his son's attendance, but no, the school secretary greeted me with,

Ah, Mr Boardman. Do go straight in. The Headmaster is waiting for you to open the proceedings!'

The Head greeted me and asked me to take a seat. We'd met before and no time was wasted on preliminaries. Standing against the desk looking rather worried indeed was 'Matey' and slumped in a big chair against the wall sat father, all comfy and cosy, and as our eyes met he positively beamed! With no prompting, even before the Head could begin, the father chortled,

'You cane him, Sir! Very, very, naughty boy! You hit him!'

The Head looked astonished, as well he might, then answered,

'Now look, Sir, I don't cane to order!' (this seemed to me a very fair comment)

The Head now turned to the boy.

'Right, Sonny. Now listen to what Mr Boardman has to say.'

I recounted the story and at the end the Head again turned to the boy.

'Is that true? Did you use filthy language to Mr Boardman?'

The boy replied with a veritable torrent of denials.

'No, Sir. It ain't true, Sir. He's a liar, Sir!'

The Head now asked,

'A few moments ago your father told me that you call him and your mammy dirty names and that you steal from your mammy's purse. Is that true?'

'No, Sir!! Honest to God, Sir! The old man's telling lies!'

'Hurrumph!' said the Head. 'Did your elder brother not come to me last term because of your bad behaviour at home!? Your lies, cheating and stealing etc'

'No, Sir! It ain't true, Sir! I didn't, Sir! Honest to God, Sir!'

'Did I not warn you about using filthy language in the playground?' the Head went on remorselessly.

'Not me, Sir! No, Sir! It must have been some other kid, Sir! Honest, Sir!'

The Headmaster's hand went up, stopping the flow of protestations. He got to his feet and moved towards the cupboard standing in the corner, murmuring,

'As far as you're concerned, Sonny, Mr Boardman's a liar, your father's a liar, your older brother's a liar and now I'm a liar! Your time has run out!'

With that he took out his cane and the punishment book. Placing them on his desk he frowned and then, returning to his cupboard he took out a slimmer, whippier cane, the balance of which he now tested.

'Right. I want you to touch your toes.'

At this I thought father was going to stand on his chair and cheer!

'Hit him!' he chortled, 'hit bugger till he yells!'

The Head advanced to the centre stage.

'Keep well back' he advised father. 'You too Mr Boardman!'

He positioned himself behind and to the side of the now blubbering boy who, as always at this stage, I was feeling rather sorry for.

My own Head caned with a rigid/ stiff arm but this Head caned in such a way that the expression used by Muhammed Ali (sting like a bee) came to mind for the cane was held loosely, almost casually in the hand. Then, without seeming to use any force, he sort of flicked his wrist and down came the cane. The results were devastating as with a faint 'swish' the cane connected with 'Laddo's' tightly stretched trousers. Our little friend let out one almighty yell and then I swear he jumped up so high he put a dent in the ceiling! The next moment he was screaming, rolling and writhing on the Headmaster's carpet. Father was highly delighted!

'Nasty little bugger' he chortled, 'hit him again, then he not swear at mammy & daddy anymore!'

Ignoring this uncalled for, though I'm sure well-meaning advice, the Head leaned over the still screaming, kicking and writhing boy.

'Now come along,' he said, 'don't go soft on us now. A boy of your undoubted toughness must deserve another stroke! Up on your feet and do let us get this business over and done with once and for all!'

'Holy Jesus! No, no more! Honest to God, I won't do it again!'

In spite of calling on the deity somehow I don't think he was a religious boy. Now the Head turned to me.

'It's no use. He won't get up willingly and I'm determined he's going to get another stoke. You'll have to hold him otherwise he'll think he's got away with it and walk all over us!'

I had to agree with him. Ignoring the father who was still cheering the Head on with shouts of, 'Let me hold him while you hit him!' I moved in and got the boy partly to his feet although he was still a near dead weight and hanging from my arms. He was quite heavy! Suddenly he struggled and tried to swing his behind away from the Head who'd moved in for the 'kill.'

Using as little force as possible I restrained him but he fought me all the way. Although he was as slippery as an eel I'd at last got him balanced across my knee but I was unbalanced, puffing and quite frankly fed up with the whole bloody business!! At last he was in position for that final 'whack' and the Head braced himself. I saw the caning arm twitch and thought, 'thank goodness, it'll soon be all over!'

The caning arm blurred and in that exact split second my arms tightened to hold 'Laddo' to stop him taking off, he wriggled! I went off balance, pivoted around, and my own backside swung into the path of the blur that was the cane descending!

I GOT IT RIGHT ACROSS THE BUTTOCK INSTEAD OF HIM!

Now it was my turn to nearly bounce off the ceiling. It bloody hurt but what cheesed me off the most was that whilst I was manfully clenching and resisting the urge to 'rub hard' that little sod was again rolling around on the floor, screaming and yowling as though it were he and not me who'd stopped it!

I never did tell the Headmaster just how he'd repaid me for conscientiously carrying out my duties but I'll tell you this....as I was cycling back to my own district, bum held well clear of the saddle of my bike to lessen the stinging, I passed two kids obviously playing 'hooky' and heading in the direction of the local Park. I could tell they belonged to the school I'd just left but thought,

'What the hell! I've taken enough stick for one day!'

Chapter 14: Just Another Day!

'I don't know what my son and his friend have been up to,' said the father who spoke very good English.

The Head had requested I call, in an attempt to get an explanation as to why the lad was continually late for school.

'Both of them leave here before 7o'clock every morning, in fact I've asked his pal not to get here quite so early as he arrives when we're still having breakfast!'

This was all said in reply to my request for an explanation as to how come the boy and his pal were so late for school every morning, registration being closed at 9 o'clock. Dad continued,

'Where are they going then? The school's no more than 10 minutes' walk from here and yet you're saying it's taking them 2 hours to get there!'

I was puzzled too. It just didn't make any sense at all. Dad now stood back, waiting for me to suggest some answers. Frankly, I was as lost as he was. It didn't make any sense at all and yet here were two 15 year old boys with excellent school records, clean, smart, very bright and yet neither could explain why it took so long to travel the short distance to school so as to arrive on time. Had they got themselves a job? Not likely. Did they go to the Park to play football? No, I would've seen them. What then?

'Leave it with me' I told the obviously concerned father. 'I'll go and see the other boy's father and maybe he can throw some light on things. Before I do though, just tell me this. Does your son get plenty of sleep at night? Both he and his pal are coming into school and practically falling asleep at their desks!'

Dad was very upset at this but not at me.

'Again, Sir, I'm telling you my son is in bed by 9 o'clock, and he doesn't have to be told to go to bed either. He wants to go!'

I left to interview the other boy's father and to see if he could shed any light on the matter. He couldn't! I received an identical response from him. I was by now a very puzzled man and as my outside enquiries had reached a full stop I went back to the Head to enlist his help and support. It seemed likely a few internal enquiries might solve the puzzle but if not, as the boys were attending school, albeit late, this fell more within the province of the Head. I raised the matter with him that afternoon. The Head and I chewed away at the problem coming up with and then discounting various possibilities, but the sum of our deliberations was NIL.

'Leave it with me,' he grunted.

No time was wasted and the next morning, as soon as our Heroes arrived, late as usual, they were wheeled into the Head's room, not however before he'd made some very searching enquiries among the younger boys and certain prefects. With knowledge gained the right questions were asked, and with no room to manoeuvre, the boys came clean. The Head said later that keeping a straight face was the hardest thing he'd ever had to do as their tale unfolded.

The next day I received a note: Don't leave the school without seeng the

Headmaster first.

In his room I was given a chair and a cigarette. He was dying to tell me the result of his findings and I was keen to know what they were.

'It was just as you suspected,' he began. 'They were working, if you could call it that! I had them in here for 2 hours yesterday and once they realised I was on to them, they coughed the lot. They've been going to this woman's house first thing in the morning' (here he pushed a piece of paper with the address towards me) 'and from 7 – 8am they were doing her cleaning for her!'

'Ah,' I said, 'so this explains it, but why all the mystery? They're both old enough to work after all, so why didn't they say so? It shows initiative to earn a 'few bob!'

'You're missing the point,' he said. 'The chores are finished by 8 o'clock.'

'So, what were they doing between 8 o'clock and school starting at 9 o'clock?' I asked, looking to the Head for further enlightenment.

'They were being paid,' he said. 'Now, look at the address on that paper and tell me if it rings any bells?'

Now the penny dropped with a 'clang' that could be heard across the school yard, and I looked again at the address to be absolutely sure.

'This one's on the game! One of the younger, better looking ones, but definitely on the game!'

Without further ado the Head explained how those young blighters had been doing an hour's cleaning for her and she'd been paying them by spending an hour in bed with them! No wonder they couldn't stay awake in class!

We didn't split on the kids to their parents and I absolutely deny that early the next morning the Head and I could be seen slinking along the road back to school carrying Education Committee property, to wit bucket, mop and scrubbing brushes!

Absences and sick notes:

To maintain contact between school and parents we were forever reminding the kids that if they were away from school, for any reason, they had to provide a signed note from a parent or ask their parent to ring the school if they were likely to be away for more than a day.

Many of the notes were works of art, if forgeries could be said to come under such a heading. What the kids didn't twig though was that we could always check authenticity of these notes against a specimen signature held in the child's report card.

Phoney phone calls were even easier because few under sixteens could mask their own voice and adopt the tone of an adult's voice. Add to that the faint background voices and hissed instructions were a dead giveaway. Off course it came to pass that we had so many parents who could hardly speak any English, let alone write it, that a rethink was essential, and I had to visit with the suspect notes to check they were authentic. I nearly gave up one day when in handing such a note to one Asian parent, I asked whether he had actually written it. He appeared to read the note and confirmed he had but unfortunately for him he was reading it upside down!

An anonymous letter:

The welfare state has often been described as a 'safety net' spread beneath the lower levels of a caring society through which no-one in need of help or protection need ever fall. Unfortunately, the human tragedy is ever with us and the mesh of this was too wide and let many unfortunates fall through.

One of my Heads received an anonymous letter to say that living on the district was a family with three children who should've been, but weren't, attending school. Frankly, the Head and I were puzzled for the address given had, up until a week ago, been occupied by a family with three children who attended this particular school but had now moved to the county. Studying the note I saw that at the top of the page were indentations made by a pen being pressed too hard whilst writing a previous letter. I took a soft lead pencil and rubbed gently over, hoping something would show up. It did. It was the address next to the house reported as having children out of school.

I gave the visit priority and was soon standing outside the house being reported. It still had a note on the front door giving a forwarding address for the previous occupants, which I knew already.

Now to interview the anonymous letter writer and see just what their game was.

The houses concerned were part of a terrace and the two front doors were side by side. I studied the house and door on which I'd soon be knocking. It was beautifully clean and well maintained from the outside and had white lace curtains at the windows. Resisting the urge to make a snap judgement or even to feel ill-will against the person who lived there who'd seemingly dragged me out on a wild goose chase, I decided to knock and see what happened.

I lifted and rapped the highly polished brass door knocker and as I did so a terrible thought crossed my mind. What if this were some elaborate hoax dreamed up by my fifth and sixth formers to make me look a proper Charlie!!

The lady who opened the door was in her sixties, well dressed, very clean and beautifully groomed. A retired businesswoman I guessed. Quickly I introduced myself and without giving the game completely away I told her I had reason to suppose there were children in the area who were out of school and did she have any idea where they could be living as a very public spirited person in the area was concerned for the children's welfare. At once she was at ease with me, and more so when I said confidentiality was always respected in these cases. Visibly relaxed she invited me into her home via the hall passage which led directly into the front reception room. The room was polished and spotless.

'I'm so glad you came to me,' she whispered, taking hold of my arm, 'only they started up their noise just before you knocked, and I don't know how much longer I can stand it!'

Here she paused, held up a finger and whispered, 'Listen!'

I listened, before God I listened, but there wasn't a sound other than the traffic on the main road some six streets away.

'It's worse in the hall,' she went on. 'there's only the dividing wall between the two houses.'

Into the hall we went but it was as quiet as the grave.

'Well,' she said. 'How would you like to listen to that din?

My goodness, I thought. We've got a right one here. A candidate for the 'funny farm' for sure, but I didn't let on what I was thinking, I just went along with it.

'What does your husband and children say about it all?' I asked.

'Oh, I live alone. I'm a single lady,' was the reply.

What to do? Obviously the first thing to do was to reassure her that something could be done to help. My mind was working overtime as I didn't want to say anything which might exacerbate the situation.

'Be patient and I promise I'll set things in motion' was all I could think of to say, but as I was talking I was thinking how she probably loved having the kids next door and when she knew they were leaving she coped with the loss the only way she knew how. By turning her face to the wall as it were.

I left the house and went as fast as I could to the nearest school to urgently contact the Mental Health people at the Leicester Town Hall. I fully explained the situation to the chap on the other end of the line, also giving him the name of the woman's GP which I'd managed to wheedle out of her during our conversation.

I was promised faithfully that the local Mental Health officer would deal with the situation as soon as he was given my message, and so I put the phone down. Silly me. I believed him! Hadn't I done the spade work?! All that was needed was a visit by the MHO with the GP and the woman would be offered the help she so obviously needed. One of the criteria for diagnosing mental illness was whether the patient could hear voices!

I made a full report back to the Head who'd alerted me in the first place. As it wasn't anything to do with Education it was left like that, but not before I gave my Chief Officer the original note complete with my comments and action taken written on the back. I'm so glad I did.

Months later whilst reading the Leicester Mercury I saw a headline:

'Local Woman Found Dead'

I was about to pass on when the address jumped up from the page and hit me in the eye. It was the address of the woman who'd been hearing the noises. I double checked with my log book and certainly, it was her. The newspaper gave very few details other than to say neighbours had been concerned she'd not been seen and alerted the police. They broke in and found the poor woman's body.

It would've ended for me there but a year later I found myself in conversation with one of the police officers who'd forced entry to the property. He told me that as they opened the living room door from the hall they were enveloped by swarms of enormous 'blue bottles!' It was summer and the last few weeks had been particularly warm. Inside the room, lying on the couch, was the lady I'd met. As she'd been dead for several weeks in that heat, the cause of death post mortem couldn't be established. What was certain though, from the dates and times given by neighbours, the last time she'd been seen alive was around the time of my visit; to within a week in fact. I have often thought since whether the person I spoke to at the Town Hall actually passed my message on, and if he did whether the officer concerned took appropriate action with regards to the poor soul's condition and followed it up with the GP as I'd been promised it would. OR, did someone forget, thus allowing another tormented being to fall through the Welfare State safety net. I made no further enquiries. It was too late anyway; the dead can't be brought back to life to testify!

School escorts:

One of the duties for an Education Welfare Officer was to undertake escorts of handicapped and difficult children to and from the many special educational establishments spread around the country. Most of them did a really first-class job, but if popular opinion was to be believed, it cost more to keep a child in a disciplinary controlled residential school than it did to send a boy to Eton. As far as I was concerned though if the school achieved what it set out to do and returned a reformed and stable character back into society then I for one was willing stand up and cheer.

We had a new Chief Officer whose path I was soon to cross. Sending for me one morning I was told I was to escort a child from residential school back home to the family. A distance of 130 miles was involved. With all the basic details of the escort clear in my mind I now asked more detailed questions:

Q. How old is the child?

A. 14 years

Q. Are the child's problems educational or emotional?

A. Emotional

Q. In what way emotional?

A. Likely to try and escape from the escort and strong sexual overtones.

'Don't you think I'll need another officer with me in case the boy tries to do a runner at a toilet stop, and as a witness should he take it into his head to accuse me of over familiarity?' I asked.

'What on earth gave you the idea it was a boy?' said the Chief Officer. 'It's a girl!'

No prizes for guessing who told who what to do with THAT escort!

Another time I was asked to take a most delightful boy and his mother to a specialist residential school I was not acquainted with, so he could be assessed for admission. A maiden voyage if you like.

The clerk in charge of these trips told me the name of the school and advised me to go down to Gloucester, skirt the main ring road and by then the school would be within shouting distance. The mother, boy and I set off, arriving at Gloucester some three hours later. I skirted the ring road around the city as instructed and shouted as suggested! No reply! I then popped into a local garage and asked whether they knew the whereabouts of this school. In return I got a blank look. I tried again and showed them the telephone number, asking whether it was a recognisable area code. That cracked it!

'You're in the wrong bloody county, mate! You want Worcester, not Gloucester! After nearly five hours on the road we finally arrived at the school. The Head was affability itself!

'Ah yes, the boy they want me to assess for suitability for entry to my school! Right, do you play football?'

When it was established that the boy did, and his preferred position was 'goalie', as the good Lord is my judge, the Head turned beaming to the boy's mother and said,

'I'll take him!'

Chapter 15: Edith & Jane

I soon realised that on this multi-racial area of mine the one section of the community on which I could always rely were the West Indian mums. Hand on heart I can never ever remember one of these hardworking, invariably beaming & pleased to see me mums, telling me a lie or even half a truth. They were the ones who maintained discipline in the home and they could always find the time, worn out and tired as they must have been with just coming off the night shift at the local factories and hospitals, to exchange pleasantries with me, even though more often than not I'd been forced to wake them from a deep sleep to answer the door. How did they do it?! Coping with a night job, the 'old man', kids, and home always shining clean and highly polished, and yet never out of sorts with me and my intrusions on their sleep time. In matters of discipline, dad, if around, came a very poor second to his spouse! On many occasion a big strapping West Indian boy was left trembling at the knees and felt his bowels turn to water when he knew the schools' inspector had been to see his mum! Unfortunately, since those days, outside influences have been brought to bear on the West Indian population as they have on other sections of the community, by the more, dare I say, liberally & racially aware loud mouths; those self-appointed experts, and not forgetting my own favourite pains in the arse, the race relations industry!

Within a very short time more and more of these mums were reporting a massive breakdown in family and neighbourhood relationships. I predicted the riots that were to sweep the inner-city areas a good eight years before they came to pass, and it was my lovely West Indian mothers who set the seed of what was to come.

One of my West Indian mothers, who I'll call Edith, was the sole support of her two children. A boy and girl both in their early teens. Mum worked in a laundry at night and during the day, when the kids were at school, she entertained a few 'select' gentlemen, fitting in sleep whenever she could. The family home was a large terrace which was let off into various apartments and bed sits. Edith owned the property and had the best apartment for herself. This was on the ground floor. It consisted of two back rooms for sleeping and a large front room which was used as a living room.

On my first visit, the front door was unlatched and slightly ajar. This was so the other tenants and callers had easy access. I knocked and a West Indian voice from the rear of the house called, 'come in!' So, in I went.

The passage in which I now found myself was very dark, and on turning the first corner it was pitch black! I pressed on though, encouraged by the voice still giving me directions. Finally, I found myself in one of the two back bedrooms, blinking as I tried to get my eyes acclimatised to the faint illumination provided by a very dim red light in the ceiling socket. I found myself in a small room, most of the space being taken up by a double bed. As my vision adjusted to the subdued light the shape of a woman appeared in bed, wearing a very skimpy, very pretty nightie and the widest smile I'd ever seen.

The set-up of darkened room, red light and skimpy nightie gave me the clue as to what I'd walked into and so I quickly explained I was from the school and not there on any other business. She got out of bed, not bothering to ask me to wait outside, and as I watched she took several wigs from wooden wig stands, and after pondering 'which one today' she finally selected one, put it on, adjusted it, and ready to face the world again, took me through into the living room where we had a nice chat about her son who I'd called about in the first place. I instinctively liked her.

Not long after I had reason to call on Edith again. This time she was up and about and so I found her sitting in the 'best' room, furnished as the West Indian mums loved to furnish such rooms with lots and lots of brightly coloured cushions and lace doylies. On the shelf and side board were pictures of beaming black people clothed in their Sunday best.

Like so many of the rooms in West Indian homes it was overheated by paraffin heaters which were used to supplement the gas fire, which was full on.

Poor Edith was very much down in the dumps and tears were coursing uncontrollably down her cheeks.

'Whatever is the matter, girl?' I asked, seeing how upset she was and ever ready to turn a sympathetic ear to anyone in distress.

That did it. The flood gates opened and in between great, near convulsing sobs, Edith managed to blurt out that she'd found a lump in her breast. Although she'd been referred to the Leicester Royal Infirmary for tests which had established the lump was non-malignant, Edith was not totally convinced she hadn't got cancer. As she took me through the biopsy, stage by stage, Edith was tugging at her very bright, very loose kimono under which I could see without trying that she was wearing an equally pretty lace trimmed nightie. Without thinking I asked how big the lump was and before you could say 'Jack Robinson' Edith had pushed her hand inside the kimono, down her nightie and scooped out an enormous breast which she damn near dropped into my hands.

'Here,' she said, 'you feel it; go on, just squeeze here and you'll see!'

I declined with thanks but not wishing to hurt her feelings I assured her that if I were ever tempted to go around feeling ladies 'knockers' I would give hers priority! For a split second she stared at me and then as my face began to crack, so did hers, and we both finished up laughing!

Edith's kids were very good attendance wise so visits on a regular basis were not made. However, whenever I saw her in the street I would stop and have a chat. She was easy to talk to and I was mildly flattered that she wasn't averse to fluttering her eyes at me, but ours was a sensible and professional relationship. I last saw her about a year after our first meeting. It was in the afternoon and I was in the office trying to get through a mountain of paperwork that had built up on my desk, seemingly from nowhere. A fellow officer came into the room and announced a black woman wanted to see me. I corrected him by saying, 'Do you mean a black lady?'

The black lady was Edith who'd come into the office to tell me she was leaving the district. I knew she'd been saving hard to reach this goal because she'd discussed leaving the area several times. It was a question of money though, which seemingly she now had, so I suppose she'd taken on more gentleman friends and was doing less poorly paid laundry work.

Edith was wearing a magnificent new wig and was beautifully dressed. She looked great, but what made her visit most memorable was that when I entered the office to greet her she gave a squeal of joy that made all my fellow officers stop what they were doing and stare. She then threw her arms wide and hugged me to her ample bosom.

'Edith' I hollered, pretending to squirm free but loving every minute, 'Edith, you've been drinking!'

She held me at arms' length and addressed my shocked colleagues thus:

"This Mr Boardman is a lovely man. He likes to laugh and joke with people like me! He never takes advantage. I keep telling him he can come and see me whenever he likes, and he can keep his money in his pocket!'

Her grip on me tightened and eyeball to eyeball she went on,

'But you won't, will you!?'

'Edith,' I said, 'I love you as a person and a mother, and that says it all, but if I ever do decide to go off the rails, well, all I can say is........you'll bloody well have to get in the queue with the rest of the women who fancy me!'

At this we dissolved into hysterical laughter!

Edith and her kids moved away from my district and I never saw her again but from time to time snippets about her filtered back to me.

Apart from Edith, the other black mum I took to my heart was Jane. Jane was very, very black, and although she had several children, I never ever saw a man in her house, nor did she declare a husband when applying for free dinners or clothing. Jane's children carried her name but each had a different father. That way it avoided any complications.

Jane was always pleasant and uncomplaining. She lived on social security and coupled with the free school meals and clothing, Jane did very nicely indeed. Jane's kids were very nice too but you didn't need to be a clairvoyant to spot that as sure as God made little green apples, Elvis Mark, the eldest of her children, was going to be a right pain in the backside to the neighbourhood mothers who didn't watch him like a hawk when he was around their daughters! At 13 year of age, Elvis Mark had a roving eye for the girls!

I'd been working my way around the district on this particular day, listening as I so often did to more silly excuses for being absent from school, when I practically fell over Jane and her brood as they came steaming around the corner. Jane was pushing a huge, old fashioned pram which no doubt had been donated by the local Family Service Unit. Hanging onto the sides were two of her brood, little girls of eight and ten years.

The pram wheels were desperately in need of oil as they were making so much noise and Jane's face was red with the exertion of pushing the darn thing. With time to spare and always willing to chat with my mums, I pulled my bike to the kerb and parked it so I could talk to the little group. Jane greeted me as an old friend and the girls squealed with delight.

'I reckon that old pram of yours came out of the Ark, Jane!' I volunteered.

'Yes,' she fired back, 'I saw that old bike of yours there when I went to fetch it!'

We both laughed.

'Whose baby are you looking after?' was my next question but before Jane could answer the two kids shouted out,

'He's ours! Our mam's!'

'Go on!' I said. Now I hadn't any idea whether it was or wasn't but as always where new babies were concerned, I bent over the pram and peered in. That settled it, for gazing up at me was the most beautiful blue eyed, blonde baby I'd seen in many a long day.

'You're having me on!' I laughed. 'That's not your mummy's baby! That's not your baby, is it Jane?!'

'It is my baby, Mr Boardman,' said Jane, 'it really is! Hadn't you noticed I was pregnant?'

I looked again at the beautiful white baby and then at those three black beaming faces, and I realised they meant every word they said. Without thinking I burst out with,

'But Jane, you're black and this baby's white!'

Jane began to explain.

'About 10 months ago I went to an all-night 'Blues' party and had too much to drink. I was so drunk in fact that a very nice white man offered to take me home in his car. Unfortunately, I must have passed out in the car because the next thing I remembered was waking up in my own bed the following morning! I don't know what happened in the interim!'

'Perhaps you don't know, Jane,' I said, 'but I bloody well do, and there's the proof!'

With that I rode off with us all laughing. What else could I have said!?

Lest anyone should jump to condemn these mothers, forget it, for most of them would cheerfully work their fingers to the bone to support their kids. Back in the West Indies it was quite in order for a man and a woman to live together and have a family whilst saving money to get married. The union was as strong as if sanctioned in church. Unfortunately, after the movement of West Indians to this country the men got involved with some very loose living women and prostitutes, and so began to renege on their relationships. As one of my lovely mums said to me,

'Whilst there are stupid white girls who will go on the game for black men, even turning their social security over to them whilst their own kiddies go without, the black men will let them! Back home they have to earn every penny they get!'

It makes you think doesn't it, for it was our society 'rubbing off' on their men that caused the breakdown in their moral code.

Chapter 16: Racial Mixing and Religious Friction

The racial mix in my schools continued and at no time in those early years did we see any obvious signs of future problems. Boys and girls of all nationalities mixed and played together so happily it was amazing! I realised though, and spoke out so many times, about how it made sense to segregate the sexes into all male and all female schools such as we had. I was thinking in particular of the Asian children when putting my ideas forward on this point, realising that in Muslim homes in particular, the chastity of the young females was of paramount importance, and I better than most realised the impact that a big, outgoing, sixteen year old boy, more often than not sexually aware, would have on a shy, naïve Indian maiden.

In my schools were Indians, Pakistanis, Chinese, Vietnamese, Italians, Greeks, you name them, we had them!

I remember being asked for my opinion on replacing the existing single sex schools with a mixed sex one. I spoke of my fears saying that if the present buildings had to be replaced then at least keep the sex's apart and in separate classrooms.

I was only being asked for an opinion and so what I said carried no weight. The old school buildings were eventually replaced with a single building, the classes were mixed and uniforms abolished. The word 'cane' became a dirty word as the old order was pushed aside and the theorists were given free rein. The rest is now history.

Before all this took place I was invited to attend a school governors' meeting at which a vote of thanks for my work in the community, was minuted. The meeting was attended by local councillors and the proposer was a Tory councillor, with the seconder being a labour councillor. Both were senior members of their respective parties. Two governors were also sitting councillors, with the rest being prominent persons. I think it was the first time such an honour had been awarded to a lowly Boardman. My feelings? Gratitude, but I was only doing my job. We had no racial problems mainly due to the dedication of the Heads and school staff. Integration was taking place but no banners needed to be raised to stress the point. I remember doing a report for the then Education Committee where I made the point that,

'The strengths and weaknesses of the area can clearly be seen because the boundary lines and lines of demarcation between the races can clearly be seen, BUT WATCH OUT, for when these lines and boundaries begin to blur, that will be the critical make or break time.'

I said it then and I still stand by it, this city was unique in its race relations development, but stability depended on separate development being allowed to crumble away at its own speed and in its own good time. In other words, 'don't rush it!' Unfortunately, the meddlers, opportunists and politicals moved in and it all started to go wrong. The status quo could've been maintained a little longer than it was and if it had been, the riots and unrest that lay ten years hence might've been avoided. We will never know.

One bone of contention that got me going at first was the upsurge of religious differences although thank goodness these were very few and far between. I was aware of the strong feelings that could run between Hindu and Muslim, the brutality and slaughter at the time of partition in India affecting both religious groups was still fresh in everyone's mind, but in the main we'd seen little evidence of the rivalry here. Of course we always had the odd clowns squaring up to each other in the school yard but what was most surprising, and to me amusing, was that the protagonists of different religions would not throw insults at each other of a religious nature, but would call each other the sort of names you would expect people of different races to call each other. Eg one Asian boy would call another a Punjabi prick. I also remember a little brown boy calling a big black boy a 'black bastard' before running like hell, and yet both black and brown were West Indian!

Time passed and we in the schools were becoming increasingly aware that undercurrents could be felt, and to give the kids in my school credit where credit was due, the contamination was from outside sources and in their HOMES!

Entering the playground one morning I nearly fell head first over a struggling, writhing mob of Asian children who'd surround a couple of their mates. They were all doing their best to knock the living daylights out of each other but fortunately their wild swings were missing.

Insults of a religious nature were being thrown around and I distinctly heard the words 'Muslim Pigs' and 'Hindu Cow Shit!'

Once I was spotted all activity of a violent nature ceased and the move now was to get the hell out of it before identification was made. I wasn't having any of it!

I put my hands on the shoulders of the main protagonist and without mincing words asked,

'And what the hell are you berks scrapping for?!'

The reply of 'nothing Sir, was to be expected but I wasn't accepting that however much they tried to duck and evade the question and finally they gave me an answer. It was the one I'd pretty much expected. Muslim / Hindu friction had been stirred out of all proportion by the same little mob who were now trying to skip off. With it all out in the open I decided on a course of action which was to go into my world famous, 'Mr Boardman blowing his top' routine.

I told them they were ungrateful little so and so's and reminded them this was England! I went on to tell them we'd got along very nicely THANK YOU VERY MUCH for hundreds of years without any racial or religious friction (praying as I did so that they'd never heard of Ireland) and if they wanted to start a religious war might I suggest, with deepest respect of course, that they clear off back to their own bloody country of origin, start it up there and keep us English out of it! (and if anybody takes exception to my swearing in front of these little darlings, be advised that every insult they hurled at each other had in the middle or ended with, 'Bastard, f*cking or bloody!) It was I who was disadvantaged as they could cuss in two or three languages whereas I could only swear in one!

Finished, showing a red face and seemingly furious, I glared at them.

'Well, are you two going to cut it out or aren't you? Say so now and I can decide if we're going up to see the boss to let him sort you out! To their credit the boys looked thoroughly ashamed as I finished a performance that would've netted me a fortune on the stage, but as my eyes met theirs, I was lost. They all looked as though I'd given them a good kicking, but I knew that to show this would be fatal.

'Alright, I won't tell the Head this time but just let me hear anymore abuse and insults about another's religion and you know what to expect!'

I dismissed them. Because of the religious implications however, I had to tell the Headmaster so he had advance warning of what was brewing up but he was already aware the first stirrings were there and that his own position as school Head was being challenged, as was the authority of other Heads in the city to be challenged, sooner rather than later.

To understand the problem you need to be aware that one of the major religions taught that up to the age of fourteen a child must obey the Father. After that the priest's authority prevailed. With these sort of teachings, and with the 'pull' of being in an alien land (forget being 'British' these people owed allegiance only to their own faith) my first real test would come when I had nothing left to fall back on except the relationships, contacts and friendships I'd already made. I had in card playing parlance 'not much in my hand.'

My talents for being able to be all things to all men was in the balance but I still had some cards to play!

It came about in this way.

A priest, in a bid for, I suspect, power and prestige, declared that no boy of his religious persuasion could be allowed to wear a school tie for, he said,

'When a tie is crossed just before being knotted, that is a Christian gesture similar to the catholic crossing himself.'

Therefore, as far as he was concerned, ties were OUT! This posed a problem as my Senior Boys' School had a uniform and had done for fifty odd years. The tie was part of their uniform and any boy, be he white, black, brown or even pink with two heads, was expected to conform or be sent home. The wearing of full uniform was a must!

I was of the view the priest was looking for confrontation. I had to see him for myself so went along to the local place of worship where he could be found. I tried to explain that the tie was simply an article of clothing and that by seeing it any other way could only create more problems than solve them. I told him we were doing our best for all the kids of all races, and could he leave well alone?!

Even a senior member of the community who was trying to interpret for me was wearing a tie, but I didn't rub this in for obvious reasons. The far-reaching implications of this man's stand were not to be realised until years later, but for now I will continue. In simple terms if the kids of that faith wore the tie then OK! They'd been wearing it for years anyway. If not, do we suspend them from our school which had a long, honourable tradition of uniform, or do we just capitulate and say OK, let them wear what they want? If that happened we'd have every other kid in the school turning up in jeans and whatever else they wanted to wear, with the whole lot topped off with a 'Mohican' hairstyle!! What should be done!?

I called into the Head's room to report on the up to date situation and asked how many of the boys were affected by this man's ruling. I was told about thirty!

I looked down the list of names and could've wept. Good, decent, hardworking kids most of them, and now their education was being interrupted by a man who I gathered from the short time I'd met with him, couldn't speak our language let alone understand school loyalty and tradition.

'So, what do you think? Do you have any ideas?' asked the Head.

As a matter of fact I had, but not wishing to build up his hopes too much I was non-committal and simply said,

'Leave it with me!'

That evening I put my plan into action. In my own time at around 7:30pm I called at the first house on my list, and with that family gathered around me I discussed everything other than what I'd actually called for. I asked about every member of the family and paid particular attention to anyone who seemed to be holding back. With everyone present relaxed and at ease I then tackled the main problem, letting the head of the house tell me just what the priest had ordered and why the tie offended. As they told me I could hear the priest saying much the same thing.

'My son cannot wear the tie as it is a Christian symbol, therefore we will send him to school but without his tie. You must accept him like that!'

Now it was my turn.

'I am a Christian and I love and trust my God as you trust yours. Do you accept that?

Each member of the family agreed to that.

'Now,' I went on, 'Your priest has told you that this tie and its crossing is sacred to Christians, is that not true also?'

They agreed that this also was true.

'Right then, if this is a Christian symbol, sacred to all Christians, would I do this to it?' and with that I tore open my tie (but leaving it still knotted) threw it on the floor, then stamped on it.

This performance took place at every home on my list and at every home, bar one, the response was the same!

'My son will be in school tomorrow wearing the tie!'

As I left one home the father told me I'd truly proven myself as 'a wise man and friend, Mr Boardman!' They kept their word.

As for the one family who didn't, their eldest son was due to leave school anyway and the younger one transferred to a non-uniform school. I saw the younger boy crossing the Spinney Hill Park one day and asked him how things were going. He replied that he hated his new school and wished he could return to his old school. What a shame.

By working late into the night visiting these homes I'd solved the problem and saved the local authority in general, and the Education Department in particular, many immediate problems. The local newspaper tried to make a big thing out of it but it was over too quickly for that. They were too late. I'd like to say I was called before the Education Committee and thanked for solving the problem, even a letter of commendation would've been nice, but nothing! Nothing except for a quiet, 'Well Done' from the Head. That was thanks enough! Oh yes, two days after it was all over, the local vicar came sidling up to me like a punter approaching a 'bookies runner.'

'Ah,' he said, 'I understand we've cured that business of the ties in your school!'

I couldn't resist it.

'Really,' I said (lying through my back teeth) 'I understand that you and the Bishop will need to be involved, after all, basically the problem is a Christian one and each of us must stand and be counted for Christ's sake!'

He paled significantly, then shot off, and I never heard another word on the subject from that 'defender of the faith!'

This reminds me of the white mother who came to me so very, very distressed. She'd confided to her local cleric her fears that with so many immigrant children in her child's class and the fact that so much time was being devoted to them (I believe there were only two white children in a class of thirty Asians) she feared her child's education might suffer. She'd asked whether he, the cleric, would be able to help her get her child into a nearby school where the racial mix was more equal? My goodness! Didn't he give her a roasting! He felt she was being racist and unsympathetic to these poor, poor people and told her she should be ashamed of herself! By golly she was upset but I consoled her as best I could. That afternoon whilst in the office a thought struck me and I looked on the census card for that cleric's address. I make no comment on the fact he had two sons who attended a private school well away from the area where so many of our immigrant brothers and sisters had settled!

Immigrants (and self-appointed experts):

Still they came, and they came from all over the world! I remember so clearly the dark skinned, dark eyed children with their little arms and legs like thin sticks. Every bone in their body showed through but then the miracle of what a good diet, usually the free school meals, did for them! They put on weight and began to glow. What a shame that so many of those with access to the media today scream and shout racist and fascist at every opportunity. Personally, I feel very proud of my English brothers and sisters for I cannot think of any other race or nation in the world who would and could give up so much and yet receive so little in return. When I think of the hours the school nurses, health visitors and I spent with the parents of the new arrivals explaining diet and local customs, rules and entitlements then I wonder, spread thinly on the ground as we were, how we managed to get through so much work, little of it recognised or even acknowledged by our Lords and Masters in the Council Chambers or on the Education Health Committees.

One such Councillor I met took it upon himself to tell me what my goals should be and how to conduct myself with the different racial groups, and how I should cope with any problems HIS way should the need arise. It was then, as he went on and on to explain, carried away with his own verbosity, that I realised the Pakistanis he was referring to were actually West Indians! This man couldn't even distinguish between the two peoples and yet here he was promoting himself as a self-appointed reference point for those seeking information on Immigrants!

In retrospect I think we were too successful in coping with and solving the multitude of problems we encountered, and by 'WE' I mean anybody and everybody within the schools. It was almost as though someone in authority, be it within the service or politically, wanted it to go badly wrong. But why? I certainly don't know. Suffice to say that although our brains were picked time and time again, no public credit was ever given to our efforts.

Chapter 17: A Born Loser

I'd received yet another call from the probation and after care service advising me that another family known to them had come to live on my district. When I visited to ascertain the school places needed I found the little tribe had been housed in one of those tumbledown shacks all too common on my patch.

I was to find out later that the family had been discovered living 'rough' after the father had been sent down for some minor offence that involved no one outside of the family other than the police and judiciary.

They weren't gypsies but close to it. Neither of the two sons, aged 13 & 16 years, had received any education which was a point I intended to raise with their former 'County Boardman', if I could trace the idle so and so! There was also an older sister who'd collected a baby somewhere along life's highway.

My involvement was with the 13 year old who'd run wild for so long that trying to catch up with him would be like trying to catch a wild rabbit with one arm tied behind my back.

First things first was to try to get some empathy with mum, with dad being absent by virtue of being in Prison, but after our first meeting I didn't hold out much hope.

I soon realised that here was another one who thought I'd be an easy 'con' as operation 'cover up' started from the word 'Go!'

I hated having to talk 'prosecution' to women for their kid's non-attendance so

I made enquiries as to how long father was going to be having free board and lodging at Her Majesty's pleasure!

Luck was with me as father had completed his time and was on his way home, and would you believe it, me and him hit it off from the word 'go.' He was one of the few who'd done his time that I really took to.

He was a small, dark, curly haired bloke who was so clean! It was possible personal hygiene had been taught him in the 'Nick', and in those dirty, shabby surroundings he shone like a lantern.

He was such a nice bloke that one of 'the Bench' who sent him down for one minor offence kept ringing me up for a progress report! Unfortunately though, father had one major fault! When the going got tough he was unable to face up to the harsh realities of life and to solve his immediate problem he'd chuck a brick through the nearest window then wait around to be picked up by the police, only to be sent down again! Prison for this father spelt 'sanctuary.'

He didn't have a trade but like so many travellers he was able to turn his hand to most things and at the time I'm now talking about things were going swimmingly!

Laddie boy was attending school reasonably well and father was getting some kit together so he could expand on the few general maintenance jobs he'd managed to get. He'd acquired these items by sheer hard work and not by 'scrounging' them. The more I got to know him the more I realised that in spite of his prison record this man was not a rogue! Patently, he was just one of life's losers! He had one other cross to bear though and that was the bone idle sod with whom his daughter was now 'shacked up!'

The pair of them occupied the front room, the major space of which was being taken up with a bed, and if the father was to be believed this was where the son-in-law put in the only exertion of his miserable existence!

I remember arriving one day to a partially open front door with little space available for me to get through to gain entry to the middle room. Access was just not possible unless I was prepared to scramble over the bed which was occupied, as always, by the daughter! As my business couldn't wait I started to surmount the hurdle and was just climbing over the daughter when the middle door opened and in walked her father. Now, I'm rarely lost for words, but I was that day!

Everything seemed to be going well so I can be forgiven for thinking we'd 'cracked it' with this basically inadequate family, but it wasn't to be.

Calling in one day I found the father with his head in his hands and as down as it was possible for a man to be. He told me the story and I ended up feeling like putting my head in the gas oven, let alone my hands! It went like this:

From minor repairs and maintenance jobs father had graduated to undertaking repairs under one of the inner-city improvement schemes. He was repairing and replacing roofing slates, guttering, digging out & fitting sewer pipes for inside toilets, fitting wash basins, skirting boards and replastering walls etc. Having finished the job the occupier was sent the bill.

On this occasion father had been told he could leave his tools and ladders at the house until the Monday when he was due back to finish off the last few jobs.

Strengthened and renewed after a weekend with the wife, father had returned to the house only to find his key would not fit in the lock he'd fitted. As he was struggling to get in, the door had opened and the occupier, an Asian lady, had asked what he was trying to do. Assuming this was the wife of the man he'd done the renovation work for, he explained he was there to finish off, collect his ladders and tools, and once the council had passed his work he would be paid the £1,500 he was owed.

'Please,' said the lady. 'The previous owner is not here. My husband paid him cash to buy this house on Saturday and he has returned to India. Also, there are no tools or ladders here!'

The facts were checked and were as stated. The house had been sold to this couple and the tools & ladders were gone, never to be seen again. Father was substantially out of pocket........but was he!?

WHEN GRANT AID WAS GIVEN, THE BILL WAS SENT TO THE HOUSEHOLDER WHO SUBMITTED IT TO THE COUNCIL WHO THEN MADE OUT A CHEQUE IN THE HOUSEHOLDERS NAME!

There hadn't been time for the council to have received the father's bill and issue the cheque to our twisting friend in India!

Father hot footed it down to the council offices. It seems all was not lost after all. This was a grant job, and hadn't he been working to council generated plans and specifications?! Once the facts were known right was on his side and the money was as safe as though already in his bank.

The Council's Chief Building Inspector was very sympathetic once the facts were known but unfortunately this wasn't father's day! The office was turned upside down and then inside out in an attempt to find the paperwork for the job. No luck! Then a young clerk arrived and cleared the mystery of the missing paperwork up! He remembered the case very well.

'Mr Patel came into the office and submitted provisional plans for home improvement work so a grant could be given but Mr Patel never came back for the second visit to have his plans stamped as 'approved' by the council. All father's plans and bits of paper were worthless. Poor bloke! As I said before, he was a born loser. Three months later he was released from Prison! (for throwing a brick through a window)

Chapter 18: Old Faces and a Dodge City Transfer

The name of a new admission to my senior school struck a positive chord and calling round I was able to renew an old acquaintanceship with a family I'd met on my first district, Dodge City.

Most of the children, all of whom I'd had dealings with, had grown up and left home, and within the first few minutes of our renewed acquaintance the mother was referring to her fledglings as, 'those ungrateful bleeders!'

I'd had no real headaches from the family whilst living on Dodge City and the home was reasonably clean and so at first, inwardly, I felt the mother had a point for just when the kids were beginning to earn a few bob to help things along, they'd cleared off! I was soon to find out though that things had gone very badly wrong dating back to the day the woman's cohabitee had raised anchor and cleared off. It was he that had given the family stability even though he had a criminal record a mile long. As in so many of these cases it was a case of treat them right and no matter how much form they have they will usually respond. I quite liked him!

Mother had the two youngest still living with her. One was about 15 years and the other 12 years and yet although the mother soon showed herself to be on the slippery slope 'down,' both the children were darn nice kids who never gave me a minute's trouble.

Naturally, with not much money coming in, I was often at the house helping with free school meals and free school clothing forms, and anything else I could scrounge for the children.

It seemed everyone was working to help that family, and even social services arrived on time, but still, all was not well. Mother confided to me that both the children were in serious trouble with the authority and would be appearing before the local Juvenile Court for breaking into the gas and electric meter. I tried to look suitably shocked although this was difficult, as by now I was virtually unshockable, but I made all the right 'tutting' noises.

'Serve the little bleeders right,' said mother, 'after everything I've done for them!'

Now, it just so happened that I had a non-attendance at the Juvenile Court on the day the two were due to appear and whilst waiting to be called for my case I heard the names of the two alleged meter breakers called to go in before me.

Being Juvenile Court it was closed to spectators so I settled down again eager to get my own business over as quickly as possible whilst also eager to hear the result on the two who'd 'gone before.'

In that dusty, musty smelling waiting room no sound came from the closed door itself other than faint muted noises of voices rising and falling, interposed with periods of silence. Suddenly the court door crashed open and some very harassed, red faced social workers, or maybe probation officers, came hurrying out, all glaring at each other and whispering almost frenziedly to colleagues and senior officers.

Following behind the throng and wearing the broadest, happiest beam I'd ever seen on a copper's face, came our friendly court policeman who, I must confess at once, shared with me a wicked sense of humour where the pompous and self-opinionated were concerned. It wasn't to be too long before this constable was taken off court duty because 'the wets' complained he was too harsh with the young thugs and yobs who were appearing weekly before the bench. Apparently, he was telling the young blighters to 'stand up straight before Your Worship and address the Magistrate as Sir or Madam' but all this was to happen later.

Now the story of the court hearing as later recounted to me by the constable. It went like this:

'You won't bloody believe it! You bloody well won't! They stood before the bench with their mother seated behind them making appropriate 'tut-tutting' noises as the charges against them were read out. Representatives of the gas and electricity boards spoke of damage to the meter and coin of the realm to the value of X amount of pounds being missing. Interviews were read out by the social workers and probation officers and a report was given from your boss saying they were good kids who never gave any trouble in class! The lot! Then somebody thought to say to the kids,

'Before the court decides what is in your best interest, what do you have to say for yourselves? Come on, no-one is going to hurt you! Why did you do it?'

The constable had then paused for maximum effect whilst his shoulders shook with laughter. The youngest kid looked helplessly at the Bench which, thank goodness, was a very kind and humane one this day, and said,

'Please, Sir, it wasn't us who broke into the meter, it was our mam! She told us not to tell you she'd done it. We only stood and watched!'

My involvement with this mother wasn't finished just yet. Two years after leaving school the eldest child cleared off like the previous ones had done, leaving just the younger boy at home. His mother was 'on the booze' and I suspect on the blokes too, so although the younger boy wasn't showing any signs of distress, I was watching things very, very closely indeed. Mother gave nothing away though. She was very crafty.

Going into the school office on this particular morning I was collared by a very dedicated member of the school staff.

'Can you spare me a few moments, Mr Boardman, only I have a boy in my class who's told me his home conditions are so bad he's determined to play truant from school until he's taken before the Juvenile Court and taken into Care!'

There were no prizes for guessing who she was talking about.

I sent for the boy at once and we retired to a quiet place where we could talk freely and not be overheard.

He told me how his life had become a living hell. Apart from his school dinner he didn't know where or when his next meal was coming from. I heard all about the booze, the blokes, the sounds he could hear and the 'gentlemen' who were not averse to making advances towards the boy if his mother was otherwise engaged.

As he spoke I was studying him closely and saw that on the surface the boy wasn't that much different from any of the three hundred or so boys in the school. Even so, the tired eyes and almost monotone way he recounted various incidents told of someone at the end of their tether. The picture presented to me was one that no child's eyes should see, and yet he'd been forced to see it all.

Knowing something of his mother, if one could call her a mother, I knew full well she would deny everything and try to hang onto him, not for any maternal reason but because his family allowance was money in her pocket, or rather the pocket of the man at the corner shop who sold the booze!

I can see the boy now: sitting forward on the edge of the chair with his fingers intertwined. I gave him a moment or two to catch his breath, and then he raised his head and looked questioningly at me.

'Son,' I began, 'Before I can advise you I have to clear up one major point. I thought a social worker had been visiting you since the time you and your brother went to court over the meters. Why hasn't she spotted what you say has been going on?'

'That's right,' said the boy, 'but you know my mam. She's a right con artist and cleans up before anyone comes to check up on us, and she always makes sure they only come in when I'M AT SCHOOL! Anyway, it's mam who's under supervision, not me!'

'Right, tell me what you intend to do whilst you're truanting, where you intend to go, because no way am I going to stand by and let you roam the streets whilst you're out of school! OK? Now, tell me!'

To cut a long story short, the boy had planned to go to his sister's place when truanting.

The next question from me was,

'Do you understand that you will be taken before a Juvenile Court and the whole rotten business will have to be brought out into the open? Your mam's not going to like that and I don't think for one moment she will ever forgive you. What I'm saying, Son, is it'll be 'Goodbye mam' forever if she really turns nasty!'

It was as though he hadn't heard me, though I knew he had.

'I'm not going to run away from home or do anything silly. I'm simply going to stay away from school. I know that by doing that you'll have to take me to court. I also know that truancy isn't a criminal offence so I won't have a police record when convicted.'

I gently reminded him that in a Juvenile Court the word 'convicted' wasn't used.

'I don't want a police record like my brothers and sisters,' he said.

'When are you going to start truanting?' was my next question.

'Straight after the school dinner,' came the reply.

With the boy safely back in the classroom I alerted the social workers as to what was likely to happen. I also suggested the boy should be whipped straight in front of a Juvenile Bench, no time wasted, and take it from there. I was wasting my breath!

'Oh no, we can't do that!' came the reply. 'We really must give things a chance to settle down!'

'Right,' I told them. 'I shall be monitoring progress all along the way and as you obviously don't intend to move yourselves I shall get the wheels moving to have him in court with minimum delay!'

This was always my reaction to any form of inexcusable delay.

For the next month I visited the mother every day and told her of her son's absence from school. I even told her where she might find him should she be able to get off her backside, so she could escort him back into school. I thought I might be able to bring her to her senses using this course of action and possibly encourage her to heal the breach, but no way. It was business as usual!

Two months later, and with social workers fussing around making like they were and always had been, totally involved, I went to court and presented the case that the boy had wanted me to present for him. The social worker's report was a gem!

From me, the Bench got a straightforward: this child is here today Your Worships because he set out a line of action to me some two months ago which he prays will culminate in his being taken away from his mother. He sees this as the only way he can get a proper start in life. A decent and honourable start in life. For myself I can only admire the child for his determination. He is, in my opinion, a fine boy!

He was ordered into Care. I next saw him 3 years later when a beautifully dressed, smart young fellow came up to me in the street. It was him, and he came to say 'hello!'

If the sweet young lady on his arm was as keen on him as he so obviously was with her, then stand by Wedding Bells!

These sorts of family cases always upset me very much and no matter how strained things had become leading to the split, I was more often than not emotionally upset for days afterwards. In this case however there was nearly an added complication. You see, after the boy had been ordered into Care I came out of the Courtroom and was just about to go down the stairs to leave the building when a police officer came to me saying,

'Are you Mr Boardman?'

When I answered in the affirmative he went on to say that Roy, the ex-cohabitee who years before had provided a stabilising influence for the family on Dodge City, was on the stairs leading up to the Court, drunk, and telling all who'd listen just what he was going to do to that 'F*cking Boardman' who'd had the lad 'put into Care!'

I realised it was just the beer talking, mainly because the chap had always been alright with me when sober. I advised the policeman that I had a lot of sympathy for Roy but he didn't know the facts and drunk or not, I intended to give him 5 minutes and then I was 'coming out!' It was a bit like that film High Noon!

With the time up, down I went. Roy was gone! He was probably so drunk he'd forgotten what he was there for in the first place, however, I don't like loose ends!

The next day, and for three successive days after, I turned the district upside down looking for Roy. On the third day, and quite by chance, I had need to call on a prostitute to enquire after her child. The door was opened by Roy. When his eyes saw who it was his eyes popped wide open, a close second after his mouth.

'Hello Roy,' I said. 'I've been looking for you! Is everything alright between us or do you blame me for the 'young un' going into Care?'

Almost visibly, the tension drained from him.

'It's alright, Mr Boardman! It was the beer talking!'

'Fair enough,' was my reply. 'I'll always talk to you so long as you're sober. There's no need to make silly threats!'

'Sorry,' he said, 'it won't happen again!'

Roy later went back to his original cohabitee, the boy's mother, and I'd sometimes see them out together. She always looked the same but Roy looked a physical wreck. I think the meths & sherry cocktails did for him.

Chapter 19: Juvenile Court

I wrote earlier how I was prosecuting in the Juvenile Court on the same day two brothers were up in Court for allegedly 'screwing' the gas and electricity meter. This case I'm about to recount was another nasty case, in fact one of the really nasty ones I had to deal with. It came about in this way:

It had all started on the day I had to visit a particularly seedy looking house on a part of the district most favoured by the prostitutes and pimps, mainly because they were old houses Let off into small room units. These were ideal for the prostitutes.

I was asking after a 7 year old boy and the reasons for his repeated absences from school. His mother was an artful dodger and I needed my wits about me but fortunately the child didn't know me by sight. I walked up the paved path to the front door, keeping out of direct line of the spyhole cut into it, knowing that if the mother or any of the other prostitutes spotted it was me then the door would not be opened.

Fingers crossed, and hoping that even if seen I might be taken for a paying customer and thus gain access, I rang the bell then gave the chipped, stained and unpainted front door a hefty kick, thereby imitating the actions of an impatient paying customer and not the approach of a respectable Local Government Officer. With my presence made known I then placed myself to the side of the front door, thus being out of direct line of sight from the letter box and spy hole drilled in the front door.

With my finger pressed against a hole which had formerly contained a doorbell push in the door frame itself, the door was opened by the child in question; a very pasty faced but seemingly well-nourished boy. It was obvious that today he was being used as a 'door man,' as without asking me my business, he said,

'Come in Mister and sit in that room there!'

I declined with thanks and having gained entrance (which was 98% of the battle) I said,

'Can you tell your mammie the School Welfare Officer wants to see her?'

A look of fright crossed the child's face and I couldn't help but feel sorry for the kid as I feared his mam would take it out on him for admitting me. He tried to push me out of the hall but I was 'IN' and intended to stay there until I'd had words with his mam.

Realising the game was up the kid shouted up the stairs,

'Mam, Mr Boardman wants you!'

All was quiet upstairs and then a woman's voice screamed back,

'Well tell him to bugger off!'

This upset me not at all as I'd been insulted by classier whores than her. What did make me cross though was the child's response to all of this, for as he stared at me to see my reaction, which was to grin as I found the whole scene comic in the extreme, he took the grin as a sign of weakness and so without further ado he came towards me yelling,

'Bugger off then! Go on, Bugger off!'

Resisting the temptation to bend down and clip his ear for him, I turned and left the house whilst whistling for joy because that little scene was a dead cert for me to take positive Court action and do something about the whole lousy, rotten, stinking set up! Even as I rode off up the street the kid was running after me whilst continuing to shout,

'Go on then! You Bugger off!'

Joy, Joy, Joy! I knew the Magistrates didn't like any officer being abused verbally by children! I began to lay the evidence and collect all the data I could collate. My intention was to screw this mother down hard in any Court I could get the case into, but in a very short time a social worker was in touch with me to get the figures on the child's school attendance. I told her the up to date position and was asked to go ahead with all possible speed as it was considered the child was in serious moral danger! Now, hadn't I been telling them that for weeks!

With this admission from the social worker I suggested, in the nicest possible way, that as their case was far more serious than mine, moral as opposed to attendance grounds, they should present the primary case and my case could 'run on' if they failed to prove. Having got this far I now suggested that I should be told just what it was that had happened to put them at 'panic stations!' I was told this charming story:

It appeared that whenever the child's mother was going to entertain a client for the first time she would first 'suss him out' and if the client seemed pretty affluent she would hide the child under the bed. As soon as the springs began to rattle, the child would creep out from under the bed and go through the man's trouser and jacket pockets for any spare cash that might be in there and easily disposed of, and any items of value such as pen, cigarettes, lighter etc.

Unfortunately, on this day in question, one such punter had called in to 'blow his tubes' whilst on his way to the bank, and the child's nimble fingers had encountered a thick wad of notes which he pulled out of the pocket just as the bloke rolled off the bed! He'd seen the child looking up at him, open mouthed, with his small fortune clutched in his hot little hand.

The man yelled, mam screamed, and the child panicked! The boy ran to the window, which was partly open, and threw the wad of notes into the street below as he had the sense to know that he had to get rid of the evidence and be sharp about it! (Have I said before that the kids grew up quickly on this district?)

The locals, looking out to see what all the commotion was about, must have though Christmas had arrived early as notes of the realm spiralled slowly to earth!

The man called the police and the wheels leading to the Courts began to turn.

At the Juvenile Court I recounted what had happened culminating in the child, on the mother's shouted instructions, telling me to 'Bugger off!'

At this the mother shouted out,

'It wasn't me who told the Boardman to 'Bugger off', it was.....' and here she named another well-known prostitute who was known to all and sundry on the district as 'The Titless Wonder,' but the damage was done, for in admitting the words had been said, my story of the child's reaction and abuse directed at me and to me, was confirmed. The child was taken into Care.

Over the following few years I used to see the child's mother scurrying along. She was still 'on the game' but she never held it against me that I'd been instrumental with others in getting her child taken into Care. In fact she would stop and tell me about visiting times and what a lovely kid he was growing into.

Then I saw she was going downhill. Whoever was pimping her was working her hard and she was having to take any of the rubbish and probably practice the perversions that the other girls drew a line at. For the last two years of her life she kept what she earned, her pimp having abandoned her. Going through the district one raw and bitterly cold day I ran slap bang into one of my least favourite prostitutes. She was a middle-aged woman who always looked miserable, so much so I wondered how any man could possibly want to do business with her unless the old adage of 'you don't look at the mantelpiece when poking the fire' was true!

On this day she was dressed in black and her face severe and gaunt. It was obvious she wanted to talk so I stopped my bike alongside her. Putting her hand on my handlebar to detain me she said,

'I've lost my very dear friend, I have.'

When I asked who this might be, she named the mother of the child under the bed.

'She's being buried today.'

Had she only said that all would've been well, but she always was a 'yappy' so and so, and she went on and on and on. What finally made me lose my cool though was her saying that she and the rest of 'Les Girls' had clubbed together to buy,

"A beautiful floral 'Gates to Heaven' to sit on top of the coffin!"

For just a few seconds I remembered that poor little mite forced to hide under the bed and listen to what was going on! I lost my temper,

'If there's any justice in this world and the next, the Gates of Heaven ought to fall off their hinges and hit your dear friend right on top of her bloody head!'

In the shocked silence following my outburst I remounted my bike and departed as swiftly as I could. I could only take so much crap!

Chapter 20: How to 'Con' the Local Authority

Part I

I was told to visit a home recently occupied by new arrivals to the district. To my knocking a very pleasant young lady answered the door and invited me inside. Stepping into the hall I paused to let her walk in front whilst at the same time noticing that the slip of paper requesting this visit said the family wanted Free School Meals and Free School Clothing for six children. In total this would mean a cost to the tax payer of £600 for the clothing and about £3 per week for the meals.

The young lady stopped at the front room door leading off the hall, tapped on it and without waiting, threw the door open and motioned me to enter.

First impressions were of a thick pile carpet and a massive colour television. At home I was renting a black & white set! But these didn't hold my attention for more than a few fleeting seconds for, as my eyes swept around the room I focussed on the girl's parent who was sitting, or rather squatting, at a low coffee table behind the door. In front of him, stacked up, was more money than I'd ever seen in one place or at one time! Five, Ten, Twenty, even higher in denomination notes that I did not recognise as most certainly they had never appeared in the meagre pay packets I was used to!

I think I got as far as, 'you wrote to us about entitlement to free......' when he swept the piles of notes and coins under a large cushion and sat on top of it.

I proceeded 'by the book,' filling in the forms for free this, and free that. Rent, insurance, outgoings, incomings. I nearly choked when he declared he was on social security! I then did a quick assessment and told him,

'No way chum! You're way over scale!'

He bristled at this and began to bluster,

'In Bradford, where I come from, I got everything I wanted. Free meals, free clothing, everything!'

Here I stopped him dead!

'Well, this isn't Bradford, Mate, and as far as I'm concerned you get nothing, especially when you have that pile of money in the house! You can appeal of course but we will want to know just where you got that money, and by the way have you declared it to the income tax people?'

I couldn't resist saying the next bit,

'We have to be careful, Sir, because these grants are for people in real hardship need.'

It must have hit home. His eye blazed and he looked like he wanted to stick a knife in my guts but then he realised I was ready for him so changed his mind.

Back in the office later, I rang Bradford. It was as I'd thought. Prior to him leaving Bradford he'd applied for and been granted free school clothing for each of his six children. A total of £515. The clothes were provided on the Wednesday and on the Saturday the family had moved down to Leicester. The greed of some people is unbelievable! Unfortunately, there were more people like him in the pipeline!

Part II:

It was a nasty winter morning and the snow lay thick on the ground. I was glad I was still able to ride my trusty bike through the snow drifts as my shoes let in the wet and I had no chance of a new pair as one of my own children needed new shoes. I had to go to the back of the queue!

I was on my way to another Free School Meals/ Free School Clothing request so was most surprised to find myself outside a huge and imposing house used for private residential use as well as business premises. It was a local independent Estate Agent! Free meals & clothing, I thought, and yet I knew this man was making 'a bomb!'

I decided it must be one of his employees with the same last name that had put in the request. That was the only explanation! I pushed open the swing doors and was met by a blast of warm air which carried within it the smell of cigars, coffee, perfume and furniture polish. The smell of opulence!

The reception area was sumptuous and my poor cold feet revelled in the thick carpet and blast of heat from strategically placed hot air heaters. Overhead were two lovely chandeliers and immediately in front of me was a reception desk of highly polished oak bearing a telephone and intercom.

The two receptionists regarded me with the gravest disapproval as I stood beaming at them whilst dripping slush and melting snow all over that lovely carpet.

'Yes?' said one, 'and what is it you are wanting?'

No greeting, please or thank you! In fact no blasted manners at all! Certainly the lads in my school could've taught this one a few manners. At least my lads knew how to address someone as, Sir!

'I'd like to see Mr 'so and so', I answered, (naming the man concerned) whilst proffering the letter requesting a visit under her nose. She didn't even look at it.

'Mr 'so and so' is a very busy man indeed so you'll have to state your business as he doesn't see just anybody without an appointment.'

The term 'just anybody' really got to me!

'Really? If that's the case you'd better tell your employer he can come to the Education Offices and make his own application for his kids to get FREE SCHOOL DINNERS AND CLOTHING.......!'

In a trice the button was pressed on the intercom!

'A person wishes to see you, Sir, about an Educational matter.'

I was ushered in!

I found a large man seated behind a massive desk surrounded by oak bookshelves and with a roaring fire in the hearth. Had the positions been reversed I doubt I could've looked the caller in the face, but not this guy!

Whilst I stood dripping over his carpet (he hadn't the courtesy to ask me to sit down) he began detailing his family which I wrote down but when I began to ask him about his finances/ income etc he referred me to his accountant!

When I was well clear of the office I pulled my bike into the kerb and with joy in my heart I tore the application forms into pieces. I had no fear of doing this for these were the days before the public had been brainwashed into accepting this sort of pillaging of our welfare state. I knew that if he dared to complain and the facts got out he would've been publicly pilloried, and so did he!

Part III

The Chief Officer came sidling up to me on this particular day. As usual I was up to my elbows in paperwork which never seemed to diminish no matter how much I got stuck into it.

Putting a very friendly arm around my shoulder (which always made me suspicious) he turned on his not so inconsiderable charm and used my Christian name, which made me even more wary.

'What do you know about the gentleman waiting to be interviewed by me, Norman?' indicating a man I'd never met before sitting in the reception area.

Whilst never meeting the man I already felt I knew him as he'd been pointed out to me on the district several times by people of all races who, forced by circumstance to have dealings with him, had lived to regret it! All had basically said the same thing; they were being robbed right left and centre!

I thought carefully before I answered, after all, all that I did know was hearsay, but then thinking again I realised that what I'd been hearing over the months must contain more than an element of truth!

'I know of him,' was all I was prepared to concede.

'Come along then,' said the Chief and into his office we all trooped!

Now seated, I gazed expectantly at the visitor as the boss began his preamble.

'Mr 'so and so' has come today to request an Educational grant for Free School Meals and Clothing, and an additional Education grant for his three eldest children to attend college and then university. Mr 'so and so' has completed this form and I wonder, Mr Boardman, if you would cast your eyes over it and see if any comment you might have would have any bearing on the acceptance or rejection of the application?'

With this my Lord and Master lifted the form between forefinger and thumb as though contact with it may contaminate whoever was foolish enough to come into contact with the same and flicked it towards me. The way he did this was so out of character for this usually very polite man that I knew he too had more than just a 'hunch' to go on.

I took my time reading the form through from beginning to end and then read it again. Finally, I put it down in front of the client and pointed out the first omission.

'You've forgotten to put down the house in Tanker Street. The one converted into six bed sits and Let out per room at £25 per week?'

'Please, that is not so!' squealed our friend. 'I am only getting £7 per week per room!'

'Ignoring for the moment you didn't declare the property on your application, I happened to be in one of those rooms when you called for the rent and saw the lady give you £25, and yet you only entered £7 in her rent book! Now, although it was no business of mine I advised all the tenants in those rooms to go to the Town Hall as what you are doing is illegal!'

The man went pale as I continued,

'Now, let's turn to the matter of another property you own which the neighbours are complaining about!'

Here I gave the number and street of a property on my district which was being used as a common 'doss house' for new arrivals into the country at £1 per night to sleep on the floor.

'I reckon you must be making 30 – 40 quid a night! £1 per person to sleep on bare floorboards! Still, I bet the poor devils are glad to find anywhere that gets them out of this cold!'

I swear he almost fell off his chair at the sensational disclosures of this friendly neighbourhood Boardman!

The same couldn't be said for the boss who was positively beaming! I was certainly turning into his 'blue eyed' boy!

Still I pressed on,

'You also own an 'Out Door Beer Licence' that breaks every 'trading law' in this City, and if rumours have any substance you're also in negotiations to buy a supermarket!'

By now the bile was rising in my throat and turning to my Chief I asked,

'May I go now as this greedy sod's likely to make me sick!'

The Chief and I stood up together effectively bringing the interview to a close, and taking the fraudulent form from me the Chief tore it up under the nose of our guest.

'Perhaps you would like to complete a new application form, Sir?'

With that the Chief showed 'Matey Boy' the door and the client left with his tail between his legs.

'Well Chief,' I began, 'I've certainly saved the Local Authority some money there!'

If I'd expected applause for that day's work I was to be sadly disappointed, for with one of those changes of mood he was so famous for he looked at me and said,

'I haven't had any prosecutions from you lately, Mr Boardman! You're not going soft on us are you?!'

Chapter 21: Workloads and Fathers

I was still reporting into the central office every afternoon where the main task was to get the mountain of paperwork down, a task which I equated with the old boy in mythology trying to clean out the Aegean stables. This guy also had a mountain of crap piling up every day and as fast as he cleared it away another pile appeared!

We had to enter onto the record cards for every house on the district, the names, dates of birth, schools admitted to, schools discharged from, court appearances, results etc. If the family left a district we had to find out where they'd gone, amend the card to the new address and pass it to the Boardman for that district. It was our boast we 'never lost a child!'

Outside Authorities were contacted should the move be away from the city boundary. We even had a large tome dating back to the late 19th century for those who'd left the country.

With new arrivals from the West Indies, Pakistan, India, China, not to mention the East African Asians pouring into the district, all of whom had to be visited, you can imagine that the files containing the aforementioned record cards were bulging. I had 15 boxes near bursting the cards were crammed in that tight whereas the average for other officers was 8 boxes. The traditional lore passed on by word of mouth to new officers remained the same:

Officers calling on a family should always use the front door. The back door was 'out' because of a) dangerous dogs and b) dangerous human beings! If an officer was physically assaulted at the back of the house there was less chance of witnesses seeing what had happened and testifying on his (or her) behalf. Some of our men were thumped at some time or another and we were all threatened. The threats didn't bother us too much because very rarely was there any attempt to carry out threats made.

I remember one such incident. The boy in question was near to leaving school by reason of age. As with so many similar he thought school was a waste of time.

'We aint learning nowt so what's the point!' was the usual response!

I knew the family well. Dad was a regular 'out of work' but basically a nice enough chap. Knowing the family's financial set up was a bit dicey to say the least I decided to visit to try and keep dad out of court and thus save him having to pay a hefty fine. Every morning for weeks I would go into the school and check to see if the boy was 'IN'. If not I would head off to see the dad. At first he would always say the same thing, 'Well, he should be in!' but in spite of dad's threats the boy still wouldn't attend, and so dad 'belted' him.

The routine was the same every day until one day when dad declared,

'That's funny, I took him to school myself!'

(That bloody kid had gone in at the front and then straight out the back!)

'Well, he wasn't in,' I informed dad, 'but tomorrow I'll go into the school, check the register and do a physical check of the classroom myself.'

This I did but there was no sign of the little sod! As a special favour to the dad I visited that evening, hoping to catch the kid in as well, but the boy had gone out proving once again that truants have a special sixth senses which tells them when the Boardman was on his way. Now remember, I was doing this visit in my own time to help the family out.

Dad opened the door and this is how the conversation went:

Me: I checked the register and classroom today and your lad was absent morning and afternoon.

Dad: He can't have been. He told me he was at school!

Me: Well, he wasn't. We turned the school inside out and upside down and he wasn't there.

Dad: Well, he told me he was there and if you're telling me f*cking lies, I'll knock you're f*cking head off!

I looked down at him and nearly laughed but decided not to as he might well have 'had a go!'

Dads do however put up with a lot and I could understand a few flying off the handle as half the time they had no idea what was going on, and mums would tell some awful whoppers to cover up junior's misdemeanours.

Another time I was approached by a fellow officer with a tale of how a colleague had been thumped by an irate father. It was recounted to me how the officer had called one evening on a special visit to see dad and acquaint him of the fact that his wife, the child's mother, hadn't been sending the child to school. Father had just started to eat his tea when the knock came at the door so he wasn't in the best of tempers. Dad had told his visitor to, 'F*ck Off' but the officer persisted and warned him that he, the father, could be prosecuted........ and got a punch on the nose for his pains. Just then the aggrieved Officer came into the office, his face badly bruised. I went over to him and instead of offering sympathy, which he was getting aplenty anyway, I suggested that in future if a parent suggested he 'F*ck Off' that he did just that! In that way he would save himself a lot of grief, could try again another day and, if that failed, he could PROSECUTE!

Chapter 22: The Lioness Headmistress

The years sped by and to say I was ready, indeed overdue a rest from this district, was an understatement. Usually officers were moved from district to district fairly regularly but I seemed to be overlooked whenever a 'normal' area became vacant, so I decided to ask for a move. One reason was that even with my heavy case load the Chief Officer had told me that due to another officer not giving his Head Teachers satisfaction with visits, prosecutions etc that I would be required to take on extra districts and fit part of this man's work in with my own. This was the only time I snapped at my boss!

In all the deliberations and reorganisations involving me and my case load, no offer of extra wages was ever mentioned until:

My senior school Head tipped me off that school staff in inner-city areas were to be paid an extra allowance as compensation for the total involvement and committal needed in every day working. He suggested I should see if I could get an extra allowance too. When I put this to my Chief Officer he said he'd support my claim as I deserved it but I had to get my colleagues' support as the proposal could run foul of NALGO. (National And Local Government Officers' association)

That afternoon, with all the officers together laughing, joking, smoking and generally socialising, I pushed my paperwork to one side and called out,

'If I could have your attention gentlemen!?

I then went on to explain that the boss had told me that as long as they didn't have any serious objections he'd be putting in an application for an extra district responsibility allowance on my behalf, and that this was to compensate for the extra workload I carried.

There was a deathly silence as this was digested and then one of them (the one with the crème de la crème district which was Buckingham Palace to my Soho) spoke thus:

'Oh no! If you get extra money, we want it as well!'

I'd got no chance! When my district was having a house to house census to establish the numbers of children, this self-appointed spokesman was too afraid to go knocking at strange doors and entering ropey looking houses and insisted another officer should accompany him. Perhaps he was afraid he might get attacked in broad daylight!!

The last straw came about in this way.

I'd just walked into the office one afternoon when my name was called and a telephone thrust into my hand. I put it to my ear and heard a voice gabbling,

'Is that you Mr Boardman?'

On hearing the affirmative the voice continued,

'Thank God! Can you get to us fast, only we have a drunken father in the Headmistress's office and he's trying to strangle his daughter! We've pulled him off three times, but he's determined he's going to kill her! For God's sake, please hurry!'

Now anyone else in their right mind would've asked whether they'd called the police but me being the silly bugger I was just said,

'Hang on, I'll be right there!'

Down went the phone and I called out to the room at large,

'Gentlemen, I need a couple of you to help me. There's a drunken parent in my senior girls' school trying to strangle his daughter. I need you to help me eject him. Any offers?'

The room was dead quiet when a moment or so earlier it'd been full of the chatter of my fellow officers socialising. Now though some were engrossed in their paperwork whilst others were exiting through the door with fixed, glazed 'don't spoil my concentration' looks in their eyes! The one thing they all seemed to have in common was that none of them would meet my enquiring almost pleading look.

Undeterred, I tried again!

'Will one of you at least take me to the school in your car? I've only got my bike and the school's 25 minutes ride away! I need some help!'

Well, help I didn't get but there was advice aplenty!

'Tell them to ring the police!'

'Lose yourself until it's all over!'

And one more that's still used to this day,

'It's not our job!'

Too disgusted for words I raced through the streets on my bike and dashed into the school, meeting on the way the school secretary who'd phoned me. She was as white as a sheet and hurrying down the stairs.

'The Head's room, quickly!' she said, 'He's in the Head's room and he's started again!!'

I leaped up the last few stairs two at a time and dashed into the 'Holy of Holies' without bothering to knock!

What I now saw was a young Indian girl of about 14 years with her back pressed up against the wall by the sheer weight of a man who I recognised from district visiting, and who I guessed was the child's father. His hands were around her throat and he was squeezing hard. Behind him was the plucky Headmistress and another female member of staff who up until now had managed to contain the situation but were now as a last resort being forced to try and forcibly drag him off! Considering this plucky Headmistress stood only four foot nothing in her high heels and was obviously fighting a losing battle, my mind flew back all those years and I could almost hear my old 'brickie' boss exhorting me to, 'pull as if you're pulling the bloke next door off your sister!'

The Head's face was almost purple with her exertions but as always she was immaculately dressed as if for Ascot. Even now, with not a hair out of place, she was 'pitching in' like 'a good un.'

I jammed my hip in between the man and his daughter and twisting my body hard, got him to release his grip. At the same time, I was shouting for him to 'leave her and get out!'

He was so drunk the whiskey fumes were getting through to me and I think it was this that saved the day, for he was easily distracted and released his hold on the girl's throat enough that the Head and I were able to bundle him out of the office as his daughter collapsed wheezing and wailing onto the floor.

Outside, the father now took stock of the situation and recognised me as the Sahib who sometimes called at his house or spoke to him in the street, always so friendly. At this point he burst into tears thus allowing us to push him the rest of the way down the stairs and into the street.

For the next ten minutes we pleaded, threatened and finally persuaded him to simmer down. So, what was it all about?

The father had found out his daughter had a boyfriend. The lad was also Indian BUT as the parents wanted control over who she dated and they hadn't been consulted, her people's social code had been broken.

The Head decided that with the father so maudlin drunk she dare not allow the girl to go home that night. The whiskey was still in the father and if he started up again, we wouldn't be around.

I rang Social Services but after explaining the case was told they didn't have anyone available to make the decision to 'take the girl in.'

I managed to wheedle out of them the phone number of a senior officer of theirs and rang his home. After explaining what had happened to his wife I was told to 'hang on', which I did. I could hear muttering in the background and then back she came.

'He's not in and I'm not sure what time he'll be back. Can I suggest the police?'

Within 5 minutes or so a police woman arrived and took the girl away. Ten minutes after that, as we'd guessed would happen, the father was back at the school having had a 'top up' of whiskey. Thank goodness I'd hung on as by this time the staff and kids had all gone home and the Head would've had to face the drunken swine on her own. As I said before, she was a plucky little so and so and she'd likely have slain him!

I took father gently by the arm and led him outside, and with no witnesses present I told him to 'Piss Off!' You see, I was fed up with him as well!

The Head involved was a relatively new addition to the school and from the onset she slotted in so beautifully it was as though she'd been hand tailored to fit the school. She had the widest grin, as opposed to smile, of any Head I'd ever worked with, and she was loyal and expected 100% loyalty in return. This lady worked herself, her staff and me into the ground for the girls in her care. Nothing was too much.

Many times when going into the school I'd find her on tip toe, waving an admonishing finger under the nose of some gawky 16 year old girl who'd be towering above her. With the finger wagging back & forth like a fiddler's elbow the Head would threaten to take the slipper to her if she didn't behave herself. She was, I might add, the only Headmistress I ever worked with who was given her proper name and title by the girls, and some of those girls were tough 'cookies' indeed, both in and out of the school!

With the naughty one disposed of she would slump back into her chair and patting her already immaculately coiffured hair straight she would grin and knowing full well I never drank on duty would offer 'Sherry, Mr Boardman?'

This Head caught me right on the hop one afternoon. On answering the telephone in the office, I found the Head on the other end of the line asking whether I'd be willing to present a few awards at the school that week. She said it was no big deal but the staff thought that as I was so involved in what they were trying to do for the girls I'd be an ideal person for the job. Now, although this request seemed simple enough, I must add that this was the first time any EWO in the city had been honoured in this way. I felt rather nervous, but why? I had no idea but remembering the kindness she and her staff gave me plus the fact these self-same kids were giving me around 95% attendance, I thought I owed them, and so accepted.

On the agreed day I dressed with care, for if they were going to do me the honour of inviting me then I felt I should put in extra effort to look good for them. In my clerical grey court suit and with my shoes buffed to a high shine, I made my appearance. I was ushered into the Head's room where she, beautifully turned out as usual, sat in state. She offered me a 'Sherry' and complimented me on my turn out.

'My girls will be so proud!'

And so we sat, as it were, chewing the fat, until a senior monitor came to tell us that the preliminaries were over (registers etc) and would we now please come along.

With the Head leading the way, off we went up the stairs and through the main doors into the Hall. It was then I thought I would die of shock for the whole school were gathered. Approximately 500 girls plus staff were seated upon chairs in neat, orderly rows. Upon our entrance from the back of the Hall, without a word being spoken or command given, simultaneously they rose to their feet and stood in silence, as beautifully turned out as the Head and I were, and yet with so many coming from pitifully poor homes they were paying us this compliment. I cannot remember walking down the centre of the Hall through those lines of standing staff and girls but I know I nearly staggered as I walked due to the feeling of being thrown off balance by the sheer numbers involved in what, foolish me had imagined would be a simple affair involving no more than 20 or 30 girls. Had I known this ceremony was to be on the scale it was I think I might've tried to duck out of it.

On the stage we sang the school hymn with a beat and rhythm I'd never heard before thanks to the numbers of our West Indian pupils. Notices were read out, changes to lessons etc. Finally it was time and shaking like a leaf I stood to make the presentations. For the first time I was able to take a hard look at those girls, seated now but upright with hands in laps watching me so attentively. Of course so many of them I recognised and realisation came that they were 'with me!' ME, the bloke who chased them into school and told their Mams and Dads off (very nicely, of course), who stood no messing and demanded respect! The same respect I gave them and theirs!

It was though a tap was turned off and I wasn't nervous anymore, and so as the winners of the awards came to me, each answering her name, I took each one's hand with confidence and began to enjoy what I was doing.

Panic stations!!! (but not from me I might add) Someone on the staff had miscounted and we were an award short. Not to worry though, for as various staff members hurried about trying to find the one we were short of, Mr Boardman stepped into the breach and held in conversation the child who was so patiently waiting for her award until it was all sorted out.

Presentations made and mission accomplished, we all sat down. I was expecting the closing hymn to be announced but no, not yet.

'Girls' the Head now started, 'I'm sure you would want Mr Boardman to say a few words to you!'

Honestly, I wasn't prepared for that and hadn't got a word down on paper, but I rose to my feet and for the next 7 minutes spoke to the girls about their school, its traditions in the past, how it was during the War and the changes as I'd seen over the years. I concluded by saying how proud they had all made me feel that day by honouring me so. As I spoke I could almost feel the presence of my old Headmaster and those members of his staff who, like him, had gone before. I hoped they were as proud of me as I had always been so proud of them and all the standards and values they had sent me out into the world with, and which I'd now, hopefully, passed onto these children before me.

Interestingly, to this day I can still remember the outline of what I said but straight after the ceremony my mind was blank. It took ten years to come back.

Chapter 23: A New District and New Challenges

We had come to the parting of the ways in more ways than one. I was tired out, although exhausted would probably better describe my condition. What really decided me I needed 'out' was discovering that in a space of a few weeks the department was to lose the Director of Education, the Chief Officer, (my boss) and the Headmaster of the Senior Boys' School I'd served for such a long time. With this in mind I felt it was now time for me to reconsider my own career and try to shed some of the pressure I'd experienced for so many years. I put in for a move to what in those days was considered a 'normal' district but in reality, as I was soon to discover, there really was no such place.

So I went in to see the Chief and without mincing my words asked whether he could make one of his last tasks that of moving me 'off' my current district and directing another officer, 'on.' In short, I wanted a transfer!

I explained that from the outset no other officer had wanted my district but now I'd proven, when handled properly, my district could give good returns for effort. I was still getting far better than average attendances and that the advantages far outweighed the disadvantages.

With no hesitation whatsoever his reply was,

'You've worked darn hard for the department. Starting Monday you'll be on another district and someone else can have a go at your old patch!'

I didn't tell my old Heads I was going and my leaving coincided with the start of the schools' summer holidays. By the time these were over two months had elapsed and I was well established on my new district.

Oh, what a doddle my new patch was! The only worry was whether I could get to my tea spot before they ran out of milk and the chocolate 'bikkies' I was being offered!

Half my district consisted of council properties and the other half was privately owned. I soon made plenty of friends in the council sector.

I will always remember the first case I got my teeth into: Three sisters who only went to school when the mother decided they could, which wasn't very often and 'that's that!!'

Unfortunately for this mother I'd already reached the conclusion that the officer who'd previously been on the district wasn't the most conscientious of people; witness the number of kids and parents who, for a very long time, had been allowed to 'get away with murder' attendance wise!

The father in this family worked during the day and so an evening visit was called for. At 7pm that evening I arrived on their doorstep and knocked at the door. Mum opened it and was most surprised to see who her visitor was.

'Could you tell your husband I need a quick word with him please?' I said, and as good as gold she trotted off leaving the front door ajar which enabled me to distinctly hear her say,

'Alf, the new Boardman wants to see you!'

A chair could be heard scraping across the floor and then the loud sound of footsteps approaching. Just before 'Alf' hove into sight a loud voice stated,

'We've heard it all bleeding before, mate!'

When 'Alf' appeared, he stopped dead in his tracks. I looked him up & down for a moment then, although it wasn't in the 'School Boardman's Handbook' on how to deal with such a situation without giving offence, I couldn't resist responding by saying,

'Well, it looks like you're going to bleeding well hear it all again, don't it, MATE!'

As God is my judge, from that night I never had to call at the house again!

Judo & wrestling lessons:

I was told by one of my senior school Heads that one of his boys was visiting a gentleman friend. He told me the arrangement was 'quite alright' because the boy was Judo mad and the man was giving him wrestling lessons!

Suspicious old me made a few discreet enquiries and I returned to the Head with my report:

'You're quite right Headmaster. The gentleman and the boy are wrestling together but unfortunately, they're doing it stark bollock naked! I've reported it to the relevant authorities!'

So no, my new district wasn't going to throw up any new surprises, and I immediately felt at home!

Psychopath dad:

I was warned to be wary of a young father who'd been adjudged a psychopath.

The dreaded day arrived but I was only dreading the visit as I was no braver than the next man!

I called at the address and the man was ok with me then, going out through the back door I stopped to admire his garden, telling him,

'Those sprouts could do with some manure around them.'

The next day I took him some vegetable plants from my own garden and made another friend.

During my time on this district and whenever I had dealings with him and his kids, the dad never laid a finger on them or showed aggression towards me. Perhaps the fact I was bigger than him had something to do with it. I don't know, but I always found the hand of friendship to be a great bridge builder between myself and my parents.

Santa Claus and Christmas:

Christmas that year was an absolute 'WOW!'

I'd played Santa before but unfortunately most of the Heads spoiled the fun for the little ones by insisting the kids had to be in straight lines and not to move, and my verbal interactions with them were scripted!

Me! Well, I just loved to see the excitement on the kids' faces and watch them trying to wriggle ever closer as the initial shock of the big man in the red costume wore off. This year it was different! I was Santa at an infant school on my new district!

In no time at all I had the kids singing, laughing and squealing with delight! They especially loved me telling them I'd left my reindeer in the yard. I then stood on the chair to look out of the window and told them how Rudolph had stolen Mr Plod the Policeman's helmet from his head, and he was now chasing Rudolph around their playground trying to get it back! The kids believed every word of it!

One year the Head borrowed a magnificent Santa outfit from a large Department Store in Leicester. Even I was impressed. The wig was amazing!

In honour of the occasion I took my old gardening 'wellies' and painted them in black gloss paint. I then glued patches of cotton wool all over the boots, liberally sprinkled on gold & silver glitter and finally sewed holly with red berries around the top. My efforts received an 'Ahhh' from the Headmistress, and the kids went mad!!

My grand entrance was always made from the rear of the Hall, ringing a large bell as I came. If any kids (now grown-ups) remember Santa coming into the school and ringing the bell so hard the 'clapper' came off, nearly 'braining' a visitor, well that was me!

With Santa's outfit put away for another year and now dressed in my ordinary clothes, I left the school without getting a second glance, passing through crowds of little ones shrieking & shouting of how Santa had been to their school, what he'd said and how he'd danced up & down the Hall with Miss! Ah fame! If only for a fleeting moment!

I played Santa for many, many years and was in much demand! Not everyone feels confident enough to step into those big boots but if they tried I'm sure they'd enjoy it. The time eventually came when I was performing at schools with 96% and more immigrant children, consisting of Hindu, Muslim, Sikh, Jain and Buddhist. In trying to accommodate all faiths I changed my script and had the kids sing 'Happy Birthday Dear Jesus!'

Although not politically correct, these were different times and society was navigating through unchartered waters; we were all learning about inclusion. The race relations industry eventually stepped in to object and I was 'OUT' of a job, so I burned my Christmas 'wellies' and said 'Goodbye' to that part of my career!

Chapter 24: Back to Centre Point

Fourteen months had passed and to my surprise, shock and horror, I realised I was extremely bored and missing the 'belly laughs' I was so used to on my old patch. Even so, I had the good sense to keep my head down and at every opportunity moaned about problems I had on my district!

The new Chief Officer was still feeling his feet and we kept well out of each other's way. I never got under his feet and give him his due, he never got under mine. That is until.......

'Norman, we want you back on your old district!'

Honestly, these were his opening words to me one day!

Now, I'd guessed for some time that all was not well on my old patch from 'dribs & drabs' that filtered through the grapevine and was aware two other officers had fallen flat on their faces after a stint there. My next strategic move was decided.

'That's not on! The old Chief told me I could have a three year break at least and it's just over 12 months!'

What a 'berk' I was! I should have asked how much more they'd be willing to pay me!

He dismissed me with a curt, 'think about it!'

I wasn't given much time to think about anything for within 3 days I was called in again and told,

'I'm not asking you, I'm telling you! You're going back and that's on the orders from the top!'

Fair enough, or was it? I had a right to know why I was being ordered back and I damn well asked the question! The truth finally emerged. Nobody else was willing to have a go!

I'd worked the Centre Point District for seven years and knew exactly how easy it was on an ordinary district, and yet here I was being ordered to go back. It was darned unfair, and I said so. At this the Chief stood up, went to the door and closed it. He then returned and sat down. Speaking very quietly he asked,

'What was your average attendance when you left?'

'95%' I replied.

'You've been off that district for fourteen months. In that time attendance has slumped to the low 80s and is still falling!'

No wonder they wanted me back. It was the old story and one that has bedevilled me all my working life. 'Pull somebody else's chestnuts out of the fire.'

I pretended that hard thinking was needed and so sat in silence for a time with my internal reasoning going something like this.......

Your present district bores you to tears but there are no pimps, prostitutes or delightful big West Indian Mommas, Right! There are no twisting so & so's doing

310

their best to try and outwit you and con you into approving their applications for Free School Meals & Clothing, Right! By remaining on your current district the future looks very dull & boring and with no chance of a 'belly laugh' to keep the blues away, Right! TOO BLOODY RIGHT!

'Ok!' I conceded. I'll go back but just understand it's under protest!!'

So, that's what happened. One week later I was back on my beloved Centre Point!

My first port of call was to the boys' senior school.

The building smelled as so many Senior Boys' Schools did, of floor polish, gym shoes and perspiration, and a number of other odours difficult to identify but most certainly including stale school dinners which had permeated the painted, bare brick walls. In those days the Heads still had some control over colour schemes: brown or green.

The same old council worker was there on his hands & knees much the same as he had been 14 months previously and he was still swearing the same oaths as he struggled to get the 'mankey' old heating system to work. I even made the same old joke as I passed,

'Don't put your tools down, mate or leave them lying around! These buggers'll nick anything!'

I passed through the Hall and began my ascent of the staircase, nearly bumping into a chap coming round the corner.

'Mind your back,' I chortled, 'make way for a working man!'

'Good morning,' he replied, 'I'm the new Headmaster! What can I do for you?'

Now, I was aware the school had a new Headmaster, so I introduced myself and we shook hands. He then invited me to come up to his office so we could have a chat. Up we went, passing kids on the stairs who on recognising me with the Head passed the word back along through the school 'telegraph' that 'the old Boardman's back!'

In the Head's office we had a coffee and he gave me a smoke. It was then he confessed to being the moving light in my directed return to service the area.

'I took over as Head 14 months ago and in that time we've had two different Officers. Neither of these could get the kids to school on a regular basis and attendance is now in the low 80%. All the work various people around here have told me you used to do has gone for nothing and the morale of staff and pupils is at an all-time low.'

The Head went on to explain that truancy was at such a high he'd taken it upon himself to call a meeting of all the district Heads and with their agreement a memo had been sent to the Director of Education insisting they had me back. He ended by saying that if I wanted to blame anyone for being lumbered with a lot of hard work, which included repairing the damage done, I had to blame him because it was he who'd initiated the whole business of my return. This was solely down to what others had told him about my dedication to the kids and parents.

'Any questions? No? Right! So, how long do you think it'll take to get our attendance back into the 90%?'

It was to be years later before I tumbled to the fact I always sold myself short and so it was for this reason, I answered,

'Give me twelve to eighteen months.'

I was way out though for it took no more than three! (and all done by using kindness!)

Incompetence of services:

Now, prior to me leaving the Centre Point District some fourteen months earlier I'd become involved in a case which even today, just thinking about it, makes my toes curl in frustration and anger at the way a family's fragile stability can be upturned, and then the family be broken up, by sheer incompetence and I suspect indifference, by outsiders who were being paid, and well-paid at that, to maintain a watching brief, and should've been ready to spring into action at a moment's notice (in theory) and so prevent further hardship and decline.

One of my infant school Heads, a lady in every sense of the word, had received a tip off there was a child living in the area over school admission age and yet was not on the register of any school. I always took special heed when we got this sort of tip-off and moved very carefully, for as I knew from experience, most parents wanted to enrol their youngsters and get them on the register even if for ever after they ran me ragged chasing their kids into becoming regular attenders. The other reason was that the facts, as presented, needn't have been accurate.

First things first then. I needed to see a birth certificate but perhaps, more importantly, I needed a chance to weigh up the mum or dad, sometimes both, to see how they reacted to me and to also decide whether either or both were stable. The tip-off in this case had alleged the parents were 'emotionally upset'. (whatever that meant!)

In cases like these there was rarely a second chance and any relationship would have to be established, no matter how fragile it might be, on this first visit!

The house was on Diseworth Street, an ordinary terrace type property in a side street off the main road. One thing for sure was there were children living here, for as I propped my bike up against the kerb the net curtain at the front downstairs window was being jerked up and down by a little boy and girl who were beside themselves with excitement, not I hasten to add at seeing me, but because an elderly lady of about 70 years was coming up the street waving a bag which obviously contained something nice intended for them!

It was big smiles all round as I knocked at their door. The kids were going mad trying to get to the bag of 'goodies' through the window, which the elderly lady waved tantalisingly towards them!

'Any minute now and they'll be coming through the glass!' I said to the old dear.

'Aren't they lovely! I bring them some sweeties every time I fetch my pension and they look out for me to make sure I've not forgotten them, and when they run out of coal I let them have a bucket of mine. Their dad's always so grateful!'

At that point the door opened and a man stood scowling at me for some unknown reason. The elderly lady passed over the bag of 'goodies' to the kiddies who were by now pushing and shoving like mad at the back of the man. Seeing the lady the man's scowl cleared and he beamed and gabbled his thanks for the gifts in a language I took to be Eastern European.

I quickly tumbled to the fact that the elderly lady was going to be the key to getting me into the house and so I gently took her arm.

'Can you explain to dad that I'm from the Infant School and want to find him a school place for any of his children I can fit in!'

The penny dropped, and with the children munching on sweeties and rustling the paper bags in the background, she took dad's arm and mine as though completing a circuit and said very slowly,

'This man is from the school. You know, SCHOOL!'

He wasn't completely sold but with as good a grace as possible under the circumstances, in a thick accent he said,

'You fuggin come in!'

In my experience the frequent use of expletives originated from immigrants listening to workmates and so were picked up and used in every day conversation!

We both stood and watched as the elderly lady walked away and entered a property a few doors away.

Dad stood and stared at me, seemingly forgetting his invitation for me to 'fuggin come in' but then as good as gold he turned and led me into the property accompanied by shrieks and excited squeals from the nippers who were comparing who had the most or most exciting selection of sweets!

As we went down the passage I noticed that the children were carrying an extra unopened bag which I now realised was for two other children who were fast asleep on a blanket on the floor of the main living room. Four children in total!

With a hand rolled, saliva stained cigarette between his teeth, (I was never to see him without this comfort) dad now stood patiently waiting. He didn't offer me a chair for the simple reason there wasn't one, so I stood and looked around.

We were in a spotlessly clean living-room consisting of bare scrubbed floorboards and furniture noticeable by its absence. At some point the paper on the walls had been stripped off leaving just bare plaster. This too was so clean I swear the walls had also been scrubbed, but the room was cosily warm thanks to a roaring fire in the hearth protected by an old-fashioned fireguard completely enclosing it, on which were draped spotlessly clean nappies put there to air. Everything in the passage we'd just come through, and in the room we were now in, smelt fresh and clean.

Glancing out of the window I saw a huge, black, hound of the Baskervilles type dog staring at me whilst standing guard over a young baby in a huge, old fashioned pram. The look from the brute was warning enough: 'Come out here, mate, and I'll have you!'

I stayed at the house for over an hour and a half and dad was never still. He finished off a huge copper of washing, all done by hand, kept feeling the nappies on the fireguard and moving them around, gave the little ones a drink, changed the baby, and all the time he watched over the older children, never getting cross with them but telling them quietly and firmly whenever they went over the top.

All this time he was trying to communicate with me and vice versa. Unfortunately, what he tried to tell me was almost indecipherable, but the 'fuggin' this and 'fuggin' that were coming through loud and clear. I persevered as I needed his trust and at the same time wanted to let the children know me and be at ease with me, but I was missing too much information or wasn't getting the full story: Where was his wife, the children's mother? I tried to find out but he became excited and emotional, too emotional in fact to give me a coherent story, so I made my farewells as much in the dark as when I first called round, but I managed to get him to understand I would be coming back.

From there I went down the street a couple of houses to the elderly lady's house making quite sure first that I wasn't observed from the house I'd just left for very obvious reasons.

I was invited in without comment and sat down with a cup of tea. She then poured out the family's tragic story as she knew it.

As I'd expected the father was an Eastern European caught up in the Second World War. He'd met and married a Yugoslavian girl and they'd come to live in England. Neither of them could speak a word of English but she was more out of her depth than him because she'd come from a remote village, and unlike her husband who went out to work and picked up a smattering of the language, she'd stayed at home having babies. She had very little contact with the neighbours apart from the odd smile but this had not helped her to speak our language. Even in this densely populated City of Leicester she was isolated.

Things had gone desperately wrong when the heavily pregnant mum, with the tots hanging onto the pram I'd seen in the yard, went shopping at the local store. On coming out she was stopped and searched and it was found she hadn't paid for some of the items in her bag. The store prosecuted and she'd been taken to court. In answer to the charges, relayed through the children's father (they didn't understand about solicitors) it was pleaded in mitigation that she, the mother, had been and still was, suffering from blinding headaches that clouded her thinking, and that theft was not intended, the offence being committed when she was having a blackout. The court was unconvinced! Guilty......a fine was imposed. Personally, if my experience of dad's English was anything to go by, I doubt whether anything he'd said had been understood, and if it was he would've been 'fuggin' this and 'fuggin' that! Oh dear, oh dear!

Mum had her baby a few weeks later but no sooner was she over this than the headaches became much worse, then late one night she was taken terribly ill. Poor dad had dashed into the street. He had trouble using a telephone and so had run to various passers by seeking their help. Understandably, they thought he was a madman; mental or even drunk, and what with his fractured English and 'fuggin' every other word, he didn't stand a chance!

Eventually help was summoned and mum was taken to hospital, but too late. She died. The post mortem showed she had a large brain tumour.

Now dad was all alone, the sole defender, carer and provider for five children, one a new born baby. He gave up his job and with the very minimal of help had set to raise his children single handed. He was suspicious and would flare up at a moment's notice but by God he loved his kids.

What could I do to help him? He hadn't asked for my help but I was determined he should get it.

I reported everything I'd found out back to the Infant School Headmistress and after she'd shed a few tears over the plight of the family, we started working on a strategy.

First, the Education Department were to be kept in the dark for fear they might insist on our working strictly to the letter of the law. Whilst the older child could be taken into the school full time due to age, the next along the line was too young for a full day at school but we were determined it would be a full day if only to give the dad a bit of a break.

As dad was reluctant to trust anyone with his 'treasures' we held off forcing the issue but I was visiting daily and talking to & playing with the kiddies, turning the mangle and generally helping where I could.

It all paid off when two weeks later I saw, and I confess it was with tears running down my cheeks, dad with his four little mites hanging onto his trouser legs like grim death, pushing that old fashioned pram, sleeping baby inside, as he took the two eldest children to register them at school. It was such a great break through, although I never did manage to win over that bloody dog!

I'd alerted the local Social Services of my involvement and a case conference was called to which I was invited. It seemed to me, and I could quite see how it had come about, that some of those present were quite wary of dad, however, I spoke up for him and said that if any time I could be of help they shouldn't hesitate to contact me as he would always let me through the front door.

There were both statutory and voluntary social workers at the case conference, health visitors, nurses and social security people all promising help and support. It was agreed with no abstentions that dad would get maximum support. He had no debts and had used his own money to keep his head above water but now his savings were almost gone. It was confirmed that as long as the social security money arrived on time each week (and I felt this was the weak link) he should be ok. A careful eye was to be kept on the little brood.

One of those present who I didn't know by sight told the assembled gathering that his organisation would do something about getting the bare walls wallpapered, supplying the materials etc. 'Just leave it all to me!' were his words.

Five weeks later when doing my weekly visit to keep an eye on things, the father took me into the still clean and fresh smelling living room to where a number of rolls of wallpaper were deposited on the floor. No paste, brushes or pasting table, just a pile of wallpaper.

'Last week, man bring that 'fuggin' paper and dump on 'fuggin' floor. I ask man are you gonna stick 'fuggin' paper on 'fuggin' wall and he say no. We give you 'fuggin' paper and you stick on 'fuggin' walls. How they think I have 'fuggin' time? I have four kids and baby. All day I washing 'fuggin' clothes and napkins. I scrub floors. I 'fuggin' iron. I do shopping and take kids to 'fuggin' school. I go bed when children go bed I so 'fuggin' tired!'

The dad paused, 'How the 'fuggin' hell do these people think I have time to stick paper on 'fuggin' walls?! I think these people 'fuggin' mad!'

I couldn't have put it better myself!

I phoned the agency concerned but it was as I'd guessed. With others present they'd talked 'BIG' but in reality they couldn't come through.

Next, as I'd expected, the social security cheques failed to arrive on time. I shudder to think what dad must've sounded like on the phone trying to explain that no money meant no food, no food meant hungry children and all interspersed with 'fuggins.' I was only surprised someone didn't get thumped in his frustration.

It was about this time I changed districts but before leaving I'd briefed my replacement. Now I was back after just 14 months and the address was the first I visited. The house was empty. In social worker parlance there'd been a breakdown in communication and all the kids were in Care!

Fifteen years later, on my way to court, I ran slap bang into dad. He was so excited to see me he didn't talk as much as 'gabbled!'

'Yes, the kiddies are all right and Erica is getting engaged!'

He gave me all the up to date news on his little family and it really made my day.

'So, where are you dashing off to in such a hurry?' I asked.

At once that well remembered look of frustrated tension crossed his face and his eyes flashed as of old.

'Fuggin' housing people 'fuggin' say I owe them 'fuggin' rent but I got a 'fuggin' rent book here that shows I pay them 'fuggin' rent every 'fuggin' week. I bet they try to blame on 'fuggin' computer saying it not their 'fuggin' fault, but I tell you my fren (and here he put his hand into mine) you my fren are very 'fuggin' good!'

A high accolade indeed!

I felt rather sorry for the housing official, the Clerk to the Magistrates and everyone else in the Court he was on his way to see. With his still fractured English it just wasn't going to be their day!

Oh yes, on a final note, that dear elderly lady who lived a couple of doors away from the little family, well, she was MY mum!

Chapter 25: Medical Certificates and Absences

The issue of medical notes caused me and my colleagues more headaches than I care to remember. When absences went on and on it was quite in order to suggest to the parents that in everybody's interest some sort of medical cover note should be obtained, after all, this was normal procedure when the individual reached working age so why not when they were younger. Sometimes in reply we'd be told,

'My doctor doesn't give medical notes for children' or 'I can't afford to pay for one.' Invariably, most of the time when a note wasn't forthcoming and the pressure was being put on, we would get,

'My doctor says if you don't believe me you can get in touch with him direct.' This was usually said because the parents knew full well this was the last excuse left to them before I found out there was nothing wrong serious enough to merit, say, a two week absence from school. Time after time I explained that a medical note could save all sorts of unpleasantness but there's no doubt about it, 99% of the time the mother was the fly in the ointment. Now, I can understand a mother being loyal to their own offspring but if that meant the poor old dad, out at work all day and believing that his kids were in school, was now going to be threatened with a summons for something he knew nothing about, then my sympathies were with him. For this reason, no matter how much a visit to dad impinged on my time, I always made damned sure, as best as I was able, to get to speak to dad, eyeball to eyeball. Even with night visits it was still a battle of wits to get him because should mum or the child get to the door first, even though I'd seen dad through the curtains sitting having his tea, I would be told, 'No, he ain't in yet!'

I had a boy in the senior age range who missed school for a good part of every week by reason of stomach pains. A local GP was complicit in his absences, giving him a sicknote at the drop of a hat, and it was widely rumoured a young scout who'd asked for something for 'Bob a Job' was excused school for a week! I was well and truly stumped!

Unfortunately, at this same school was a school master who was very vocal and in with the 'politicals' which he believed gave him the right to supervise me and my work. Not to put too fine a point on it he was one of those interfering sods we could all do without. His opening gambit was always along the lines of,

'I want you to go and play hell with this mother' or 'tell this father his kid's a thicko' and he'd then go on to tell me a number of other home truths about the family which to my mind just wasn't on! This wasn't my way of working and so in the main I ignored his advice and went along my own road.

On this day the boy in question was again absent from school and my Nemesis came bowling up to me demanding to know what his excuse was this time as to why he wasn't in!

I didn't answer but simply handed over that week's sicknote, all duly signed and dated. The teacher hit the roof,

'I'm bloody well fed up! How can I be expected to teach a blasted boy if he's never here?!'

I tried to get a word in but he was red faced and in full flood as he continued to rant,

'It just won't do! I demand he be brought in by force if necessary!'

By this time the teacher's raised voice had alerted the Head to a problem and he came out of his office to see what all the noise was about! He opened his mouth to intervene, but I forestalled him.

'I'm sorry, very sorry, but this boy has us by the 'short & curlies' and his dad's in league with him! I can't contest a sicknote. The BMA would have my guts for garters!'

'Sorry indeed,' said our friend! 'Right, I'll go and see his blasted father. I'll tell him a few things!'

He paused to see how I would react to this threat but I wasn't biting.

'That's quite alright by me but when dad does come to the door, and I warn you now he's a 'rajjy' old sod, don't forget to duck as he'll stick one on you at the drop of a hat. Oh, and don't forget you're not insured for such risks either!'

The room suddenly went quiet and with no further comment our friend became thoughtful and wouldn't meet my eye. Two weeks later I passed him in the Hall.

'How did you get on then? I asked. 'Did you go and see that father?'

He gave me a sickly grin.

'No, I haven't had time yet!'

Sodding liar, I thought, for I knew he practically passed the family's house every day! I'm glad he started making a detour though because if he'd happened to see the boy's father I would've been in a spot as he was so short he'd struggle to punch anyone, even in the navel!

On another occasion a mother told me that her husband couldn't come to the door because their dog was having pups. I then proceeded to write on the form for recording why the father was unavailable how 'mother told me her husband could not see me because the dog was having pups.' I then looked up at her and said,

'When your husband's standing in court being made to look a bloody fool when this is read out he's not going to thank you but I do for winning my case for me even before we get there!'

In two seconds flat he was at the door and it was as I'd guessed. He hadn't even been told Mr Boardman wanted a word!

I couldn't resist it and told him what his wife had said about their dog having pups, to which he exclaimed,

'We haven't got a dog!'

Patrick:

I'd always had a very soft spot for the 'naughty boys' I dealt with on an almost daily basis. I don't mean the nasty or vicious boys, nor the thief or liar, no, I mean the 'Just William' type of character who, when his misdeeds were found out just scowled and audibly told anyone who cared to listen that adults just didn't understand, before looking around for fresh fields of devilment to conquer.

One of my families was lovely, and large, and of Irish descent. They consisted of mum & dad, a number of girls and several boys, the youngest of whom was Patrick.

Patrick (never Pat) had clear, innocent grey eyes that were a warning to me to 'watch him!' He enjoyed school if the subjects taught that day suited him but for the rest he was always on the alert for new ways of skiving off. Once located & caught he'd scowl, kick the ground and with head cast down exclaim, 'it ain't fair' before a quick clip round the ear from his doting mum or dad had him toeing the line UNTIL THE NEXT TIME!

It was about 10am when I spotted a seemingly familiar figure 'duck' into an entry just after I'd turned the corner on my bicycle from main road into side street. Whoever it was, was darned quick, but my eyes, after years chasing kids, was attuned to any sudden movements such as chummy boy made. I was so good I could instinctively tell if a child was out of school legitimately for a doctors or dental appointment just by their body language or eye movements but the best give away of all was when they nipped down the nearest entry or behind a parked car.

Without undue haste I carried on pedalling, glancing casually around, seemingly without a care in the world and certainly with no idea that I had a 'runner' on my patch who, at any excuse, would be up and away over the connecting garden walls like Red Rum clearing the Grand National hurdles.

As I came closer to my 'sighting' I received amused glances from the locals walking along the path. They didn't miss much either and guessed I had a quarry in sight.

Without slackening my pace, I passed the entry into which 'me boyyo' had gone and resisting the urge to glance towards it I passed and pulled into the kerb, parking my bike outside the newsagents on the corner where I entered and purchased a newspaper.

Coming outside again I retraced those few steps quietly back along the street to where my quarry was hiding, counting in my head as I did so: 5,4,3,2......1. Just as I reached 1 out he popped right on cue, and straight into my, dare I say it, welcome arms!

'Patrick, me darling! Sure, it's yourself, and why is it you're not in school then?!' I said in my best Irish brogue!

Brick red in the face he had his answer ready!

'I've been to the doctor, ain't I!' then, playing his 'trump' card again he repeated, 'I've been to the doctor!'

To hammer his message home he added, 'He gave me a medical 'sustificate' din he!'

'Did the doctor tell you how long the note was for?' I asked, and with this he pushed an already grubby and creased piece of paper under my nose which, on inspection, proved to be a medical note duly dated and in Patrick's name. He'd played his unbeatable master card and nobody, and I mean nobody in my job, ever argued with a medical 'sustificate!' Why then, if that medical note was real, had 'Wonder boy' tried to hide from me? The answer was, on this lawful occasion, that Master Patrick liked nothing more than thumbing his nose at Mr Boardman!

'Well then Patrick me darling,' said I, continuing with an Irish twang, 'Let's walk back home together!'

To this suggestion our hero showed a marked reluctance to comply but under the circumstances had little option. I couldn't help but notice he became agitated the closer we got to the property and on arrival at the well-polished front door my knock was answered by Patrick's mum.

She spotted me instantly and her face lit up but for some reason, Patrick, her pride and joy, stood well back and out of sight.

'Hello Mr Boardman, and how's yourself?!' she greeted me cheerily!

'I'm fine thank you, Maureen, and how's himself?' I answered back, referring to dad who by now had appeared beaming at his good lady's shoulder.

'It's Patrick I'm asking after, Maureen!' to which both parents chanted in unison,

'You can be sure he's at school, Mr Boardman!'

To their obvious surprise I replied, 'Indeed he's not!'

'Then where the 'divil' is he?' the chorus continued.

'He's hiding in your entry, look, here he is!' I said stepping backwards so they could get a better view.

At this Patrick's mum screamed 'WHAT!?' in a pitch that nearly burst my ear drums then, sticking her head around the door frame she came eyeball to eyeball with her treasure. Again, that awful screech, 'WILL YE GIT OUT OF THERE YE DIVIL!' to which he emerged further only to have his ear gripped so tightly that even I winced!

Dear oh dear, she WAS cross!

'Why are you not at school?' she began and then, without giving him time to answer she landed him a couple of slaps around the ear. (which any parent will tell you is far better than any medicine for getting the blood pressure down)

By now our Patrick was ducking and weaving as good as Mohammed Ali whilst hollering, 'I've been to the doctor's, mam, ain't I?!

'But there's nothing wrong with ya! YET!' chimed in dad.

Patrick now played what he'd so far held tightly to his breast. His trump card!

'If there's nothing wrong with me then why did the doctor give me this medical sustificate?'

At this mum ripped the doctor's note from his grasp and quite landed him the mightiest clout around the ear! Quite beside herself she was!

Dad, with an 'if it's turning to violence' look on his face hurriedly retreated back inside and with more and more neighbours coming into the street to see who was being murdered I decided that maybe it was time to beat a hasty retreat myself! Getting between mum and her punchbag I said,

'Let me have him for now, mum, and I'll get him back into school!'

'You can drown the little bleeder for all I care!' was her reply, and with that she went inside slamming the door so hard behind her I thought the hinges would snap!

With 'Laddo' in tow, shuffling and bemoaning his plight at the side of me, we ambled off to where he should've been in the first place. School.

'Taint fair. Me mam's a rotter!' Was all he'd say to start with and then after a few seconds of silence, he continued,

'Can I have a go on your bike, Mr Boardman? Go on, giz a ride!'

'Like heck you can!' I replied, with visions of a speeding Patrick shooting off down the street with me in hot pursuit!

Saying the only thing he could to save face Patrick wrinkled his nose in distaste before declaring, 'It's a rotten old bike anyway!!!'

He really was a likeable kid.

Arriving at the local Catholic school we went into the Headmaster's room. Patrick was by now very quiet as at this school the strap and cane were still regularly in use. However, this Head, who I'd met before, was down to earth with a neat sense of humour and it was difficult to tell whether he was cross or not. I recounted the whole story, and listening intently, fingers steepled under his chin, he clearly enjoyed my version of mum's Irish brogue, in fact his eyes twinkled and several times he laughed outright, exclaiming as he did so, 'Patrick, you really are a little divil!' At this Patrick, took heart and positively glowed. Story fully recounted I sat back whilst the Headmaster, still smiling, pondered. Then he spoke. For at least five minutes he lectured on the evils and dangers of truancy and the fraudulent misuse of official documents ie medical certificates. (I nearly corrected him with 'sustificates') Of wasting the Boardman's time, his parents' time and the doctor's time and then, seemingly finished, rising to his feet, which I took as a signal we could go, as did Patrick who turned to depart with me, but the Head restrained him gently by taking his shoulder.

'No, not you Patrick, not yet anyway. You see as well as wasting your mum's time, doctor's time, Mr Boardman's time and even the school secretary's time because she had to fetch me from assembly, you've also wasted my time and that I cannot forgive!'

With that the Headmaster crossed the room to a wall cupboard and taking out a very supple and lethal looking cane, indicated to Patrick he should bend over the desk, and as his arm bent back for the first strike, I hurriedly left the room knowing how Patrick's fun & games were going to be curtailed for at least a week!

I had one further visit to make, the secondary cause of all this commotion. The doctor! Across the district I pedalled, cursing the waste of my time, but the visit had to be made.

I introduced myself to the receptionist praying the doctor would be approachable. You never knew with some of them and the issue of a certificate being issued was dicey to say the least.

The doctor was as broad Irish as they come and for the third time in the space of an hour I found myself recounting the story, missing nothing out, and he listened entranced. Being Irish himself his first comment was predictable.

'Well, the little divil, would you listen to that now!'

Young Patrick had totally taken him in with a story of stomachache and vomiting. When asked why his mum hadn't accompanied him to the surgery he'd explained how 'mammy's legs are bad again' and so in all innocence he'd been given a note to cover a morning's absence from school.

The doctor and I had a good laugh about 'the con' but as I left the surgery I bet the same thought was going through his head as was going through mine,

'HOW MANY OTHER KIDS PULL THE SAME STUNT?!'

Big Andy:

One of my favourite 'pains in the arse' was Big Andy, a great loud mouthed slob of a man whose voice could and often was heard three streets away. In general I must admit Andy and I didn't get on too badly. However, whenever I pressed the issue of school attendance too much for his liking, he wouldn't meet my eyes whilst ignoring the fact he'd just sent the kids running up the street for a packet of 'fags' and telling me how ill his kids were!

I'd met Andy a few years previously on another district and in those days his children had presented no problem. However, over the years news of his exploits had filtered through to the office and in plain language he'd managed to 'put the wind up' several of those who'd had dealings with him over various matters to do with his children. This I could understand as he came over as a 'hard man', and now he was on my patch again! The officer who passed him over did so with these words:

'Big Andy's back with you! You'll have to do something about him as his kids are never at school!'

Andy had come to me only three days previously and yet here I was being told 'you'll have to do something with him!' That particular Officer got a right earful from me for a start!! If something had to be done about Big Andy then why hadn't HE done something?! No prizes for guessing the answer to that one!

I made the first of what was to be many visits and the door swung open to reveal the Lord and Master of the house. Framed in the doorway he looked HUGE, which he was! He glared at me as did the two huge Alsatian dogs appearing behind him. Both were licking their lips in anticipation and as the house was raised up from the pavement, their faces were at eye level with mine.

Andy's greeting was typical.

'Who the f*cking hell are you??!!'

I smiled at him knowing full well that if I backed off now I'd be making a near fatal error, so I answered him thus,

'When we get to know each other better and with your kids' attendance record at school much improved, I'm quite sure we're going to get on fine but if you speak me again in that way I will, in all probability, tell you to 'BALLS!'

I'd certainly got my man weighed up right for his face immediately relaxed as he said,

'Christ, it's the f*cking Boardman already! You're quick off the mark, mate, come in!'

At this he stepped backwards and took a kick at the dogs which, as we were talking had taken the opportunity to sidle past Andy and were now forcefully sniffing my crotch causing me, not for the first time that day, to tense up.

I wasn't over fond of dogs at the best of times and my least favourite ones were those that made a beeline for my crotch and leisurely sniffed away. All those assurances from doting dog owners that 'he doesn't bite' or 'he won't hurt you' held no sway with me for I reckoned most dogs that bit were probably doing it for the first time anyway, and those big Alsatians seemed to be choosing a soft spot in which to sink their fangs. If it was where I suspected it might be, and they did, then I'd be single treble in the church on Sunday!

Dogs in full retreat I was led through to the front room which wasn't a front room any longer due to the fact that although he'd only had the tenancy for three days, Andy had got himself a sledge hammer and had bashed the dividing wall out! There was rubble and dust everywhere. I had to ask,

'Have the council said you can do that?'

I should've guessed what his answer would be.

'F*ck the council!'

I deduced from this that he hadn't!

Andy was a man who loved the sound of his own voice and so choosing a spot to sit where, should the ceiling fall down as it had no visible means of support, the least damage to myself would be caused, I prepared to listen, hoping to pick up a clue as to his 'anti' attitudes along the way. One hour later he was still in full flow and all I'd learned was that all visitors: police, rent man, council employees, teachers, social workers etc., etc., came under his main heading of 'C*nts!'

This, plus his moaning at how the DHSS (Department of Health & Social Security) didn't give him enough money to hold body and soul together, didn't exactly bode well for the future! Incidentally, Andy hadn't worked for over 20 years.

Although he claimed money was short Andy was chain smoking all the time I was with him, lighting one cigarette from another, but this time they were my smokes! A fact that seemed to bother him not at all!

'Do you want a drink, Mr Boardman?' Andy asked.

Now, you can say what you like about Andy but his home was always clean (barring brick dust of course) and as by this time I was parched from breathing in all the brick dust floating about, I was happy to accept.

'I'd love a cup of tea, thanks, Andy!'

'Tea!' he shouted, 'who the f*cking hell mentioned tea?! I mean a real drink, Mr Boardman!' and with that Andy swung open the door to a corner cupboard which revealed whisky, rum, gin in fact every type of spirit and ale you could imagine! It was so full I swear he had more alcohol than the local pub. I could now relax though; he'd offered me a drink which was a definite breakthrough for a first visit.

As I'd expected the children were a school attendance problem right from the word 'GO' so I wasn't too upset. What did surprise me however was that Andy seemed to genuinely like me even though, as the weeks passed, I would break into his long-winded stories more and more often to tell him,

'Andy, me old darlin, you and I are fast coming to the parting of the ways if you don't do something quick and get them into school! Every visit now is another nail in your coffin. If you do get 'nicked' it'll be your own bloomin fault! Now, be a good lad and send them to school!'

It was a waste of my breath! Finally, the day arrived and with a heavy heart I went to his home and told him, with no frills,

'Andy, that's your lot! You're going to Court to answer the charge of why you don't send your kids to school!'

Now, it's a fact of life that I readily subscribe to the view that if you're going to do a job you've more or less been forced into against your own wishes, that you do it so there's little chance of you having to do it a second time or, to put it another way, if you're going for the throat you need to go for it hard! So, rather than mess about with the Magistrates' Court who would possibly only impose a nominal fine, I plumped for the Juvenile Court to try for a Supervision Order on the kids. The social worker tried all ways to block me on this as no way did she want to have 'our Andy' and his tribe on their hands.

Andy blew his top! In fact he displayed a sense of fair play that up to then I never knew existed in him.

'It's my f*cking fault the kids haven't been going to school so take me to the Magistrates' Court!'

The penny dropped! He knew that if he'd told the kids to go to school they would've done! He was ready to take his punishment in the Adult Court and saw Juvenile Court as being the kids being punished, which of course was nonsense! I was using the Juvenile Court to help me make sure the kids got an education and should things 'go to pot' again we could enforce the Order and whip Andy into the Adult Court! I'd got him by 'the balls' and he knew it, but the anticipated punch on the nose didn't materialise! He just went very withdrawn and quiet.

In the Juvenile Court I had to sit and listen to him raving and shouting abuse, much of it being directed at me, for by his thinking, he had to maintain the front of being a 'really hard man!' He didn't moderate his language and several times I thought he'd gone too far. He really was a 'one off' and again, I felt the sneaking respect I'd felt for him in the past. In a tight spot, could I choose, he was the one I'd have opted to stand with. Then Andy made a big mistake. He called me to the box as he wanted to cross examine me. He hoped to make me look a fool but my 'blood was up' and I gave him as good as I got. The Bench deliberated and then made Orders on all the children. Now Andy had to let the social workers have access. When the Bench had finished speaking Andy turned to me and screamed,

'If that bastard comes to my house again, so help me I'll set the f*cking Alsatians on him!'

I came out of the Courtroom after him and found him in conversation with a social worker who was having the law, as per Andy, read to her by him! He saw me and glared!

'Hard Luck, Mate' I thought but I refused to run away. Without hesitation I walked straight up to them both and said,

'You're a lousy shit, Andy! Nobody tried harder than me to get your kids into school! I got them Free School Meals, and Free Clothing and always came to your door as a friend but you took that friendship as a sign of weakness and thought that when the chips were down I'd back off as so many others had done in the past. Well, Hard Luck, Mate and 'up yours too!'

I walked away trying to decide whose mouth was gaping the widest: Andy's or the social worker's!

Exactly a week later I was riding my bike along the street where Andy lived when a voice boomed out,

'Come here! I want you, you f*cker!'

'This is it,' I thought and getting off my bike I parked it against the kerb preparatory to taking off my coat and swapping blow for blow! Talk about High Noon!

Andy walked slowly down the street as I walked equally slowly up to meet him. I swear even the birds stopped coughing! Then the moment of truth and we stood face to face, chin to chin and at that critical moment my lousy sense of humour crept in and my nose began to wrinkle just as I saw his nose doing the same. The next minute we were both hanging onto one another in hysterical laughter!

'You f*cker,' he burst out. 'I've always liked you! Why ain't you been round for a cuppa?'

As I said before, how on earth could you dislike a 'bleeder' like Andy!!?

Prolific non-attenders:

The Junior School Headmaster, normally so cool, detached and aloof, was going through a stack of school registers with me. Every so often he would pause, closely study the lines of marks which denoted attendance or non-attendance, clinic visits or verminous heads, ponder a moment then sometimes comment as to whether I knew anything about this one, or that one, before reaching for a form from the pile of made up absence records in front of him.

He looked thoughtful as he paused on this particular occasion then said,

'I admitted two girls this morning. Sisters. I haven't got very much to go on but I feel you'll be involved with them before much time has passed.'

'It makes little difference to me!' I replied, 'If they do go to pieces they'll just be another cross for me to bear! If you like I'll make a courtesy call to the house after dinner and see where they've come from. See if I can get some background information! Leave it with me and once I know where they've come from I'll make some enquiries!'

2pm that day found me knocking on the front door of a terraced house just off one of the major roads running through the district. No reply. This wasn't that unusual for often such summonses were ignored for the simple reason so many of these doors wouldn't open due to the damp wood swelling, and then other times many of my parents just ignored the front door being knocked, expecting the caller to go round the back or go away.

So, round the back I went via the shared entry with the next-door property and knocked on the back door. I heard movement and whispering but my knocks went unanswered. I knocked a little harder, with the same negative response, and was just about to take a monumental kick at the door when I heard the patter of tiny feet coming down the entry I'd just walked. Into the miniscule back yard appeared a pert little miss of about 9years old who, on seeing me coloured up slightly. Without me having uttered a word the young lady began telling me, a complete stranger, why she wasn't at school that afternoon which rocked me back on my heels! This told me a) she was well versed in dealing with a schools' attendance officer from whichever town, hamlet or village she'd come and b) her sister was also absent as well for it was 'our Tracey' this and 'our Tracey' that.

'Alright sweetheart' I broke in, flashing my photo identification, 'Just open the door and tell 'our Tracey' and whoever else is in there with her that Mr Boardman would like a quick word!'

Of course, she had no alternative than to do just that although, bless her, she did try.

'Our Tracey and me mam have gone up town to buy some shoes' she warbled, looking me straight in the eye all 'po' faced.

'Now, that certainly can't be right because I've just heard them talking in there. (and here I told a little fib) They said they'll answer in a minute!'

I'd got her then as she didn't know whether they had or hadn't! IN I WENT!

Mother was a 'tidy' little woman and 'our Tracey' was a very similar little Miss, but perhaps a little younger than the sister I'd just been speaking to.

Mum had a slight Irish brogue. I was informed that the family had moved from another county, that the girls loved their school and the teacher idolised them, that dad believed in education above all else and the reason they were not at school that afternoon was because they had a tummy upset and the mother had it as well. Mum said it was so lovely I'd taken the trouble to visit and reassured me that the girls would most certainly be in school the next morning.

I checked in with the school the next day, but were they in? WERE THEY HELL!

I received a report from the girls' previous school two weeks later and, missing out the glowing testimonials to their excellent attendance (I have to as there weren't any) what in effect it said was 'BLOODY GOOD LUCK MATE!'

Visit after visit, assurance after assurance and promise after promise were never kept. Those girls' absence forms were in and out more times and faster than the proverbial 'fiddler's elbow!'

I would night visit dad but he, in my opinion, was another 'con man!' He'd mention the connections he had with the police and City & County Councillors but he never fooled me for an instant. Finally, I had to warn him 'send your daughters to school OR ELSE!' I might well have saved my breath!

With the evidence laid in the Court Brief I'd prepared, in due course the Summons came through for me to serve upon dad, but without going into too many details it was an impossible task, for not to put a too finer point on it this father scented what I was about and dodged me at every turn. I spent hours staking out the house but to no avail then, having done all I could to serve it on the defendant, I served it on his wife!

Come the date of the Hearing, I turned up, the Clerk to the Magistrate turned up, the Court Bailiff turned up and the three Magistrates turned up, in fact everyone turned up except for the dear father and so the case was adjourned, but not before the Clerk to the Magistrates (for it was an Adult Court and not Juvenile Court) had asked me for proof of the Summons being served. On being told I'd been unable to serve it on the father and instead had served it on the mother I was told, 'I'm sorry Mr Boardman, this is not a good service and so it'll need to be served again, upon the DEFENDANT! (ie the father!)

Well, I knew what it said on the back of the Summons Form and so did nothing but turn up for the next Hearing two weeks later. The case was again called. I rose but before I could say or do anything the Clerk to the Magistrates addressed the Magistrates thus:

'I do apologise Your Worships for the previous Hearing of this case. I told Mr Boardman that he had not made a good service when in fact he had. It stresses on the back of the Summons that if the Summons cannot be served personally then it may be left at the Defendant's last known address.'

This is exactly what I'd done. The case went ahead without the father putting in an appearance and the case proven. He was fined £55 in his absence, but did this make any difference? Not a jot!

I made out a second Court Brief and again he didn't appear. Another fine was imposed but still those girls did not attend school.

I'd had enough by now. I made out another Court Brief but asked for Juvenile Court in an attempt to enforce attendance via a Supervision Order.

The appointed Hearing date arrived but dad did not, so I addressed the Bench thus:

'Your Worships, I managed to serve the Summons by hand on the children's admitted father personally, however, from experience, I have no reason to suppose he will attend this Court voluntarily.'

Now Magistrates aren't daft and I was asked whether I had a recommendation for the Court.

'Yes, Your Worships! I would ask for a Warrant for his arrest!'

Two weeks later I called in to one of my schools to see if there were any messages when the phone rang and a colleague who was in Court that morning gabbled,

'Get down here quickly! The police have just brought in that father and his kids! He's under arrest!'

I cycled madly back to the office, grabbed the case papers and tore round to the Juvenile Court, arriving all hot & sweaty and out of breath. Dad and the girls were in a side room along with a police constable who was keeping an eye on them. I sat there all morning until the Court was adjourned until the afternoon. I heard the constable telling the two girls they would be taken and given some lunch but to the dad's question as to whether he'd get any, the reply came back,

'No, you bloody well aint!!'

Finally, the case was heard and a Supervision Order was made to the Social Services, but if I'd thought this was to be the cure then I had to think again for now I was not only chasing the girls, their mother and the father, but I was now chasing the Social Worker as well! It just went on and on!

By now both girls were on the Senior School Register but that was about all. They certainly didn't attend! My lovely Headteacher was getting very fed up, and who could blame her? Certainly not me, for I'd had it up neck with the whole business. I rang the Social Worker and gave him an ultimatum, 'Either he took these girls back before the Bench or I would and risk the consequences!'

To my surprise he said he would but asked that I appeared too to collaborate his evidence. In other words, the case would stand or fall on figures of attendance supplied by yours truly. Oh well, not to worry, and so back and forth to Court we went.

Those hardened little liars told a wonderful story and this time they had a solicitor to represent them. I can see it now: I was being questioned by the solicitor, and not doing too badly I might add, when without him realising it he played right into my hands.

'Are you aware Mr Boardman that one of those children was in fact a patient in the City Hospital suffering from a chronic back complaint, and does your authority put children who have been so incapacitated as to prevent them from attending school, into a Juvenile Court?'

I turned to the Bench:

'Your Worships, I am well aware the child was admitted to the hospital and was discharged one week later. In fact, Your Worships, I rang the hospital and spoke with the Ward Sister where the child was. She gave me certain information which I would willingly repeat to this Court, if you so wish, or I could ask for...'

Here the solicitor, very flustered, butted in,

'No, Mr Boardman, that will not be necessary!'

The Bench deliberated and then found in my favour, or rather the Social Services favour, although I'd done all the work. I was in like a shot!

'There is a record, Your Worships!' and here I trotted out the non-appearances and Warrant for dad's arrest. The period of Supervision was extended.

Outside the Court room in the passageway the father had the Social Worker by the throat, literally, threatening what he would do to him if, 'my kids are taken off me by you bastards!'

At this stage all that talk was nonsense so I got between the two and warned the father off, but as I went to move away the solicitor came up to me. He was white and shaking with anger as he spoke:

'Thank you, Mr Boardman, for a most interesting session in Court. I can only admire the way you shot me down but now, please excuse me for I want to see that bastard of a client of mine so he can explain, if he can, why he allowed me to go into Court as if it were his first time, and not telling me beforehand of his previous convictions.'

One of those girls left school and the other still had a year or so to go but was a 'no go.' Her Supervision Order had run out but she was a full stop non-attender, so I took her back to Juvenile Court. Really, she was a most accomplished, rotten little liar but then joy of joys! The Chairman of the Bench spoke up.

'You don't remember me, my dear, do you?'

The girl shook her head.

'Well, I remember you, my dear. I was on a previous Bench in the Adult Court and I decided then that you had no intention of attending school regularly and this afternoon has proven me right. Well, I tell you Miss, YOU WILL GO TO SCHOOL or you will be brought back here, and you will be taken into Care!'

Well, she still didn't go to school and was taken back. Her mother appeared minus the child and refused to say where the child was in hiding. That Magistrate wasn't on the Bench that day and the mother was allowed to walk away scot free.

Chapter 26: School Escorts

Many handicapped children were transported to schools located in open areas near to the outskirts of the City on a bus hired by the Special Education Department and with lady and gentlemen escorts being specially employed. A route was laid out and followed, with children being picked up as the bus went along.

On this day one of the escorts went sick and so ignoring the fact I was already the most overloaded officer in the Department workwise, guess who was dispatched to be the temporary stand in!?

I reported to the private bus depot as instructed and the driver put me in the picture. Off we went for the first pick up following the agreed route and reaching the pick-ups in good time so as not to keep parents or children waiting. The kids who boarded the bus ranged in age from 5 to 15 years. All old hands at the game they displayed no shyness towards me or the driver, greeting us both like old friends, and good naturedly calling out the names (some not very complimentary) of new passengers each time we stopped to pick up.

It was brought home to me that handicap, be it physical or mental, hits all types of classes whether rich or poor. The houses at which we stopped ranged from large detached with swimming pool, to grey council houses on large estates.

The parents helped load the children on board amid plenty of chatter and banter and me, liking nothing more than a good old socialise, made new friends in seconds flat.

I'd been told about the last pick up beforehand. Siddy was a little lad below statutory school age who was hyperactive and had epilepsy. This was to be his first day at school and the only reason he had a school place was to enable his poor mother to have a break. He was wearing her out as I was soon to find out for myself! No sooner was he aboard than he took off like the proverbial 'blue arsed fly', zipping around so fast I feared the driver would become distracted and put us into a ditch, but in a flash the child lost energy, momentarily tired after exhausting himself.

Siddy came and sat on my knee for the journey without saying a word, which gave me the opportunity to look around and take stock. The children had minor physical problems with sight, hearing, delicate etc and yet, as the hubbub of sound they were making echoed around the bus, each child seemingly trying to outdo his or her neighbour in volume, they were no different to any other child.

The eldest child, Angie, a girl of around 15 years who had problems with her sight, appointed herself as my 'mentor'. She sat at my side describing each child's problem as we travelled along. I looked down at little Siddy who was by now flat across my legs, a round faced, rosy cheeked, little cherub with freckles. A child any parent would be proud of, but as he lay exhausted he was on the 'twitch' all the time as the driving force within him gave no rest. Looking down I was praying, 'please don't have a seizure' as I'd never had to personally deal with one of these attacks and was petrified at the thought of one so young having one whilst in my care.

For three days of escorts all was well and Siddy soon became a firm favourite of us all. The other kids loved him as he zoomed up and down the bus in spite of my repeated calls for him to 'sit down Siddy or you'll hurt yourself!' Unfortunately, short of sitting on him there was no way to contain him! There were no child seats or seat belts in those days!

Then it happened. I'd gone to the back of the bus to stop two of the kids from trying to kill each other leaving Siddy, who'd gone quiet, at the front with Angie, my mentor. The quietness should've been the clue for in my book quiet children were either up to no good or sickening for something.

Engrossed in separating the two kids who'd been thumping each other, I was brought back to the here and now by the sheer volume of kids pressing up against me at the rear, hemming me in as they pushed away from the driver's end whilst pointing and displaying scared faces, Angie among them!

I could see no fair hair sticking up from where I'd last seen Siddy and so with a sinking heart I ran to where I'd left him in Angie's charge. He was lying slumped across the seat. Thank goodness he hadn't fallen off! My heart sank. He was having a seizure, a bad one! Instinctively I moved to help him, my own silly fears laid to rest once and for all as I moved to help that tiny, defenceless mite. I made sure his airway was clear and tried to straighten him out into a more comfortable and safe position.

'Do you want me to pull over to the kerb and ring for an ambulance?' called the driver over his shoulder.

Mulling it over I decided that would be pointless and so I called back,

351

'No, keep going, I'll manage. I'm going to let him get on with it!'

Siddy was still fitting when we arrived at his school and because he'd had my full attention the other kids had been left huddled at the back of the bus. As he started to come back to the 'land of the living' I carried Siddy in, realising that my fears about epilepsy were based on ignorance. I decided there and then on a course of action to help the other kids should Siddy be ill again in my care.

The next morning and as full of beans as ever, Siddy was waiting at the pick-up with his mum. My goodness, that little boy sure did love his school! Mum however looked very worried and was most apologetic as she put him aboard.

'I understand he had a 'baddy' yesterday. It won't stop him going to school will it?' She whispered, 'only I know how upsetting it can be for other children, and if their parents complain my Siddy might lose his place!'

I hurried to reassure her, 'Don't worry my girl, I'll see to everything' for I knew it would be a major tragedy in her life if she lost the little rest and ease that having her boy at school meant, plus, she was afraid the other children would reject him.

Not ten minutes into the journey Siddy, who I'd persuaded to sit by me for a few minutes, suddenly lurched forward, grunting, and with arms and legs flailing. At this I gently laid him across the seat, made sure he could breathe, and then with one hand, prevented him from falling from the seat.

By now all the kids, with the exception of Angie, had fled to the rear of the bus with squeals of 'Siddy's having a fit!'

Angie too looked frightened but remained close to me.

'Angie, sweetheart, will you help me to make Siddy a bit more comfortable? That's it, just hold his hand and he'll feel much better!'

Angie was still frightened of Siddy who by now was in the full throws of his seizure but God Bless her, she came forward all wide eyed and nervous, to help.

As I watched a near miracle occurred, for over her face came such a look of love and tenderness and with no further ado that lovely girl perched on the edge of the seat and took the tiny, convulsing hand into her own.

'Siddy's like a broken dolly, isn't he, but he'll soon be better again!'

Now a further miracle, for seeing their leader and friend involved and unafraid, the others at the back of the bus pressed forward, and I let them come, one at a time, a little closer to their 'bus mate' who was 'being poorly.' As they came forward I explained what was happening and reassured them Siddy would be ok. From that day on and until I was relieved of my bus escort duties, whenever Siddy had a bad turn I had twenty willing and eager volunteers helping me to get him better again.

Siddy didn't lose his bus place, mum got a bit of relief from caring for him and I learned a bit more, in fact a lot more, about children!

I never delved too deeply into any child's problem, however, on my last day of escort duties I found out what one boy's problem was without even asking. First let me explain that he was the one boy the other children didn't seem particularly 'pally' with. He was very clean and smart and from what I'd seen of the parents he was from a very good home indeed.

We were on our return trip home and I was seeing the last few passengers off, one at a time, as we came to their destination. I was now left with this one boy who appeared to be around 12 years of age. I was seated in the seats to the left at the front and the boy, who'd been seated at the rear of the bus, now stood up and came forward to sit at the side of me. I was completely relaxed now as the day was warm and my escort duty was all but done, the journey almost over.

I sensed the boy looking sideways at me and with no warning at all, he leaned over and without a 'bye your leave' or even 'may I?' he took a firm grip of my 'Goolies!'

'What's this then?' he said.

Dear Lord, I almost took off, in fact I think I would've done if it hadn't been for the fact my 'crown jewels' were in a grip of steel!

'Gerr-off!' I hollered, fighting to disentangle that hand and fingers from sinking any deeper into the roots of my most vulnerable and sensitive parts.

The bus driver was laughing fit to burst as I struggled to free myself but he couldn't really do very much at that point to help me, being in control of a moving vehicle and all that!

We dropped the boy off at his home and I limped across the road with him to ensure he was returned safely then we set off back to the depot.

'I should've warned you about him,' laughed the bus driver.

'Well I wish you bloody had,' I retorted. 'The little sod near on emasculated me!'

'He got me once,' he went on, 'and I hadn't got a spare hand to fight him off! The female escort had to come and unpeel his fingers from my privates. I don't know who enjoyed themselves the most, him or her!'

The 'Grab em by the Goolies' syndrome was to crop up again sooner than one might have dreamed possible but isn't that a fact of life in general!? What happened was this:

After my stint as school bus escort I carried on where I'd left off in my schools and it was here, in the school secretary's room of the Senior Girls' School, that the Headmistress burst in all red faced and fit to burst from laughing. She slumped into a nearby chair and gave way to uncontrollable laughter which was quite normal in this establishment. We'd collectively agreed many, many times that if we'd put down on paper some of the incidents we'd encountered, nobody but nobody would believe us!

'Poor Alex' she began, referring to one of the few young male teachers in the school. He's just had the most horrendous experience! One of the girls has just sexually molested him, and one of the younger, quieter girls at that!'

Agog, we all gathered around, dropping everything we were doing and asking for details.

It emerged how, with growing unease, Alex had noticed how a particular 12 year old girl would stand at the side of the teacher's desk with her eyes fixed very firmly on the young man's crotch whenever she was called to the front of the class. Being a bachelor, and a very charming and gentle young man, he began to feel very embarrassed indeed, not knowing how to respond. As the Head had a very wicked sense of humour and likely would've kidded him along anyway, he was hoping against hope that she'd just grow out of it. It wasn't to be though and on this day things came to a head!

Sitting in front of his class marking papers whilst intermittently asking the girls to 'keep it down' he'd glanced up to find the girl advancing towards him with her face set and a purposeful look in her eye. He confessed afterwards to a feeling of the inevitable but he didn't know why! He was soon to find out though as events moved on with remorseless speed as she stood at the side of him with her eyes glued, as it were, to his crotch. Nervously, he'd ordered her back to her desk but ignoring his demands she'd shot out her right hand and with the speed of a striking Cobra the young 'goolie grabber' got a firm grip on his pride and joys!

It was Alex's screams of agony that brought help rushing from every direction to break the strangle hold exerted on him. 'Like the jaws of a vice' was how he later described it, and for days afterwards he walked about with a very pronounced list to starboard! I couldn't resist my own silly comment to those he was already having to endure, 'You should thank your lucky stars they were able to break her grip for you'd have looked a right silly bugger being carried out on a stretcher with her still locked on!'

The girl was moved to a class where a female teacher was in charge, and the teacher was given strict given instructions to 'wear a skirt only, no slacks or trousers whilst this young madam's around!' It was the trousers you see that were such a 'turn on.'

Another day, another escort:

It was escort day again and the weather was ominous. Heavy snow had fallen and road conditions were appalling. I rang the AA for advice and was warned to travel only if the journey was essential. By 10am the police were calling for extreme caution when travelling and by 10:30am, whilst the motorway was considered reasonable, further heavy snow was forecast by mid-afternoon.

'Right, if I set off now' I reasoned, 'I can be back here before the really nasty stuff comes down.'

Arriving at the residential school some 2 hours later, I dashed into the office and asked,

'Can I have my three escort children please, only the heaviest snow is due to fall in about 2 hours' time. If I leave now I can get them home before it's impassable!'

'Certainly not!' was the reply, 'You'll have to wait until 1:30pm!'

'But why?' I persisted, 'Why can't I have them now?'

'We're having an end of term assembly and the Headmaster's going to sing a solo. They can't be allowed to miss that can they!?'

Chapter 27: Hazards of the Job

Mrs R, a mother in her early forties, had piercing blue eyes and a complexion like a peach. Unfortunately, on the minus side, she also had lank greasy hair, wore stockings like Nora Batty and carried with her a constant aroma of stale urine.

She was a gentle soul with no harm, wickedness or malicious bone in her body but she wandered around in a seemingly perpetual trance. The front door was never answered when I knocked and the only way to access her was to risk life and limb by going down the entry into the yard, dodging dog turds and piles of rubbish as I went, skirt around the toilet with its filthy & encrusted bowl which was open to all weathers, having no door, and over the stream of water emanating from the cracked & rusty toilet cistern hanging by one screw, and running to the drain, blocked since the year dot!

Now, if the conditions as described so far sound pretty awful then I have to tell you that worse was yet to come. At some time the ground around the blocked drain had been dug up, supposedly to clear the blockage, and the soil and slabs never replaced, so if entry through the back door was to be gained it was necessary to wade through a deep pool of water in which could be seen all manner of things best left undescribed. How then did the occupants of the house get out into the yard to use the toilet facilities such as they were? There was no inside toilet at this house! Simple! They climbed out of the never closed downstairs window! Actually, it wasn't simple at all because over the months, rather than put 'wellies' on to wade outside, Mrs R and kin threw all their household refuse through the aforementioned window rather than deposit it in a dustbin for collection on bin day! Although they didn't get wet feet very often another feature to the landscape was therefore added, being that of a great sloping mound of fire ash, tin cans, pieces of timber, newspapers, contents of slop pots and other unmentionable filth which began at the window ledge and sloped down into the yard.

With so many doors and windows permanently open to the elements one would expect that the risk of the family being robbed would be great but then I think any would be robber, seeing that mess, would actually 'back off!'

Mrs R had opted out as far as the kids and school were concerned, as had her old man, but although Mr R was in employment he spent so much time dodging the rent man, tally man, milkman and me, the Boardman, I was surprised he found the time to lift a shovel or do a day's work! He did however, have time for 'a bit on the side!'

Don't ask me how I managed it but I got their girls through school with an acceptable level of attendance although with the youngest it was touch and go. Not to put too fine a point on it she was a bloody nightmare, so morning, noon and night I'd be at the house trying to get someone, anyone, to speak with me. Usually it was Mrs R and then one day I realised to my horror that she was quite misunderstanding the regular visits I was making to her home. It came about in this way:

I was cycling down the street on my bike when I saw her, shoulders sagging from the weight of the shopping bags she was carrying. They were full of such goodies as pieces of rotting timber and nuggets of coal picked up from the road at the bottom of her street where they lay after falling from coal lorries negotiating the corner. So, there we were. Me and herself! When she saw me some life appeared in her normally glazed eyes and she waved me down. I pulled in alongside, and as always with Mrs R, I began the conversation in an Irish brogue, thus observing the little courtesy she looked for and enjoyed! She really did think I was from the land of her birth and had once asked me what part of Ireland I was from!

'Good morning Mary! And it's glad to see you, I am!'

'Good morning to yourself, Mr Boardman,' she replied, 'and it's wondering 'oive' been. Are you a married man?'

'Indeed I am,' I replied.

'And do you have any children?' was her next question.

'Indeed I do,' I responded.

Mrs R 'otched' forward and lowered her voice before asking her next question,

'And is your wife on the PILL?'

'Indeed she's not,' I replied, suddenly beginning to feel very worried and vulnerable, for her hand had crept forward and was now covering mine with a gentle, stroking movement which alerted me to a line being crossed! She then looked deeply into my eyes and whispered,

'Oi am, so you can stop calling me Mrs R, and call me Mary........'

My goodness, I was on my bike and up that street like a rocket!

The power of faith:

Another of my catholic families who also had a marked reluctance to let me near the father of the household, were taking so much of my time with few positive results that I decided I needed to go round in my own time in the evening to see him. As I've said before, no way was I nicking any dad without he knew in advance what his kids were up to and had a chance to put things right. Many times I'd visited homes at night always with a 'nil' result, the door being answered by mother or the kids with the same story. 'Me usband/ dad ain't in from work yet!' Of course, I'd tumbled to the fact the man of the household might also be in on the plot, but I needed to put this to the test.

One evening I waited down the road, keeping the house under observation, and eventually my patience was rewarded for I saw father go in through the front door. I gave him time to take his coat off then bounded up the step and rat-a-tatted on the door. The door was opened by one of the tribe and on seeing who it was had smirked and said,

'Me dad ain't in from work yet!'

'Oh yes he is,' I retorted, 'I've just seen him come in!'

The child looked bothered but went inside for a few minutes before re-emerging with,

'Me dad's just got in the bath. Can you come back in an hour?'

Yes, I thought, and when this silly old bugger comes back I'll be told 'me dad's just gone out!'

I realised drastic measures were needed and I'd have to go to the top. Although the family were Catholic I decided God shouldn't be bothered at this early stage. I'd have to do the next best thing though. No, not Jesus and all his angels and no, not even the Pope, I mean the real power in a Catholic Community! I would have to see the Parish Priest!

At 'The Manse' (the Priest's house) the housekeeper opened the door. She was the double of Mary R. The same peach like complexion and piercing blue eyes but there all resemblance ended, for this lady was immaculate, in fact had she been dressed in blue I would've said she were the Holy Mother herself!

I introduced myself and she took me into the waiting room before going off to find 'Himself' who she referred to as 'Father Mother'.

The waiting room was lined with dull, unpolished panelling whilst on the floor the faded carpet was threadbare.

A picture hanging on the wall caught my attention. I'm sure I would've missed it altogether but for the fact the reflection from a red lantern, a prominent feature of all Catholic establishments, bounced back through the dusty haze of glass. I could only dimly discern through years of fug from cigarette smoke, grime and dust, something which at first I thought was the Parish Priest visiting the outside 'loo' at midnight! Curiosity broke the spell which held me motionless in that silent room. I rose to my feet and, tiptoeing across the carpet, I took out my hankie and vigorously rubbing, I found that underneath the muck was a wonderful portrayal of 'Our Lord' holding a lantern in the darkness. It was William Holman Hunt's 'The Light of the World'. I was still polishing away when the door opened to reveal the Good Father catching me, an absolute stranger, polishing the picture with a hankie! The dear man must've thought he had a right lunatic visiting him!

The Father proved to be a lovely man and kindness itself as he listened to my outpourings as to how I'd reached a 'dead end' with certain members of his flock, including the family whose home I'd just come.

'So, that's the way of things, is it?' he murmured as I finished the saga. 'To be sure, he is indeed a terrible hard man to pin down as I've found meself! Many times I tort the divil had seen the error of his ways and was going to genuflect until I realised he had a pint of beer in his hand and he was only going to hold it up to see if the beer was clear and not cloudy. Now, just you leave him to me and to be sure, won't I be giving him a hammering the next time he comes into the social club!'

I have no idea what particular threats of leverage the Father used against him but from then on those kids never gave me a moment's trouble. Doesn't this prove what God can do if one of his lowly Parish Priests can work such miracles!

Mrs G:

Mrs G had seven children of different colours by different men. She also had a view like so many in her circumstances that the state owed her an easy living! Mrs G never asked for or requested anything politely, she always demanded! 'Please' and 'Thank you' did not feature in her vocabulary and consequently, without ever trying, she managed to put 'everyone's back up!'

Her boyfriends, if that's what you'd call them, were equally lacking in good manners. They were spoilt by having all the pleasures and privileges of married (or rather unmarried) life, with a home provided by the Council for which the rent was permanently in arrears. Mrs G could always think of something better she could spend their social security money on and unless a woman was prepared to disclose who the father of a particular child was, the social security people couldn't force him to maintain the child.

Mrs G, who was first class at expecting others to give freely away, wasn't prepared to disclose who'd fathered each of her brood and so each time I called I'd be greeted with an outstretched palm and demands of, 'I want! It's my right'

Now, in my own family when clothes or warm coats were outgrown or needed they were passed down to the next in line, including cousins, but not with Mrs G. Anything her brood grew out of was sold to the neighbours and out came her hand and demands for more new clothes, and don't forget in those days we were spending £100 per child of the taxpayer's money!

Elaine, the eldest of Mrs G's children, at 14 years, had started to miss school regularly and I was in a quandary as to what to do for this reason. Although no medical notes were forthcoming the senior school medical officer had advised me that the child was being seen regularly by a Hospital Consultant. More than that I couldn't find out! Meanwhile, the shocking attendance continued and the girl's Headteacher was on my back! What to do?

Fed up to the teeth of getting nowhere, and yet knowing the blasted mother was laughing at me behind my back, I took the bull by the horns and rang the hospital concerned. I was put through to a social worker based at the hospital who knew the case and I was invited to go and see her at the hospital.

I did exactly that the following day and remember we chatted about the child, the mother and the rest of the family. What came through was that the social worker was just as fed up with the whole lot of them as I was, as the mother, true to form, was demanding more of the hospital's time than any other parent. To my surprise I was then told the family were at the hospital at that moment and, 'come with me!'

I trotted after her with no idea where I was going. Up the corridors, through the waiting room, in and out we went until finally we finished up in a room equipped with an examination couch and stainless-steel trollies shrouded in sheets. It was clearly a consulting room but quite empty of people. Putting a finger to her lips signalling me to keep quiet, the social worker crossed to a door set into the adjoining wall which she gently and slowly eased open very slightly. Beckoning me forward she then tip-toed back across the room and left via the door we'd just entered.

Highly bemused I moved forward and peeped through the crack the social worker had left in the door. I nearly died for there, sitting sideways on to me, was Mrs G and Elaine and facing them, the consultant, who was addressing them. With no hesitation I crept away, eased myself out of the room and left the hospital thinking as I did so, 'what on earth is that social worker playing at?!' If anyone had found me listening in on a private consultation I would've been drummed out of the service, and rightly so, however, even as I rode away from the hospital the words of the consultant, which I couldn't help overhearing, kept coming back to me:

'Madam, I can only repeat what I've said so many times to you before, that is, I can find nothing whatsoever wrong with your daughter! She's a perfectly normal and healthy child!'

So, that was that then. I had the evidence but couldn't use it, and mother's reply?

'I want another opinion! It's my right!'

Soon afterwards the family left my district and not long after word filtered through the department that Elaine was pregnant. Ah well!

The little Princess:

Special Education dropped a problem into my lap and no mistake. They'd discovered that living in my district was a little mite from one of the immigrant families who they felt was in urgent need of some form of supervised care for as much of the day as possible. The little one wasn't being ill-treated in the sense she was being abused or harmed, no, rather her form of deprivation was that having slight learning difficulties she was being ignored by her parents and extended family. The problem was that the child was only just 4 years of age and therefore we had no real responsibility or jurisdiction over her. If for some reason the father decided to play hard to get when it came to sending his child to take up the place we'd found in a special school for her, and he was, things could get a little tricky. One bright spot on the horizon was that dad didn't understand he had the final say, yea or nay, over her attending school until she was of statutory school age. Now it was up to the great persuader, (or bluffer) ME!

I visited the family knowing if I was told to 'hop it' that would be that, but those magic words 'Me school' worked yet again! I was welcomed in like a long lost brother and ushered into the house by a bearded dad wearing a lacey skull cap! His welcome was so profuse I began wondering what all the fuss was about in the first place!

The living room was packed with men and women and a sprinkling of children. It was most noticeable that the men all sat around a roaring fire whilst the women huddled together for warmth at the back of the room. It was my first encounter with gender discrimination.

Without any trouble at all I immediately identified the little mite I was there for. She was a dear little thing, vacant of face, dressed in a thin cotton shift, bare of foot and occupying the least coveted spot in the room right next to the back door where she was entertaining herself playing with a ball of paper tied to a piece of string which she'd throw and then retrieve by pulling on the string.

Unfortunately for her, her aim wasn't very good, and the paper ball hit a young boy sitting with the men folk. For this he ran at the little girl, pulled the string and ball from her grasp and pushed her so hard she fell and hit her head. She didn't turn a hair or cry and I supposed she was used to this treatment. He on the other hand returned to the men folk and tossed her ball and string into the flames.

I began to explain the purpose of my visit, that I was from the school and we had a place for the child. A taxi would call each morning to take the child into school and free dinners would be provided etc etc. The parents were overjoyed, and so was I considering what I'd been expecting, until I realised the little boy who moments earlier had destroyed the girl's makeshift toy as the one they were all crowding around and congratulating! Too late I realised this was also the parents' child and they thought the place was for him. From the expression on the women's faces I guessed they couldn't wait to get rid of him due to his unfortunate habit of kicking the women, but never the men! He was obviously spoiled rotten by the men.

Hurriedly I broke into the celebrations to explain it was the little girl who was being offered the school place. At this daddy wasn't at all pleased and junior's fury knew no bounds. It was kicks all round!

The women's attitude to this was that although they didn't want to lose him they felt he should be the one offered the place! This was understandable if their shins were black and blue from his repeated kicking.

I was surrounded by protesting adults, all of them trying to get me to change my mind and take the boy who was also under statutory school age.

'He's been on nursery waiting list for very, very long time, Sir! He very bright boy. Girl not good. You take him and leave her with women!'

They really did go on but finally, my patience broke.

'Look, it isn't the boy whose being offered a place and I'm not arguing anymore. I'm telling you! Tomorrow morning at 8:30am a taxi will call at your front door. You will put her into the taxi and she will be taken to school. At around 4:30pm tomorrow afternoon she will be brought back home. She will have her dinner at school which won't cost you a penny and neither will the taxi. SO, HAVE HER READY!'

I must've made an impression as they all went quiet, so I left. The next morning, I was contacted whilst on my rounds. The taxi had been sent away and the child hadn't arrived at school.

Round to the house I went to be greeted by the same pleas and arguments I'd faced the previous day. I was nearly foaming at the mouth as on arrival I'd seen the little girl playing alone in the freezing and filthy back yard. A little mite I'd already taken to my heart and was now mentally referring to as 'the little princess.'

Whilst the rest of the family provided the background noise prevailing upon me to change my mind and take 'the boy wonder' I concentrated on the dad.

Lying through my teeth I told him he would be held responsible for the cost of the taxi should it ever be sent away empty and he'd be required to pay for any unconsumed school dinners. Furthermore, I had further powers under the Act (but don't ask me what Act) to hold him accountable for non-school attendance!

'While I'm about it' I continued, 'why is your little girl outside in the cold and shivering whilst your son is in front of the fire drinking hot milk and eating biscuits? Fetch her in at once!'

And he did too, like a lamb!

I finally left after dad promised faithfully his daughter would be in the taxi the following morning.

Next day, after hearing nothing from the school, I took it upon myself to phone the school concerned to ask whether she'd arrived.

'You've done a great job,' chirped the school secretary, 'the child is in school, all present and correct!'

The next morning it was the same, and the next, indeed for a whole fortnight until I changed my wording!

'Is the little princess in and is she settling down ok?'

'Yes,' came the reply, 'he's in, and he's getting on very well, but don't you know the difference yet between a boy and a girl, Mr Boardman?!!'

Quite stunned I confirmed that I did, but the voice on the other end of the phone blithely continued how she couldn't understand why the child had been allocated a place at the school as he was quite a normal, albeit naughty little boy, who had a tendency to......' and here I butted in and we both said together 'KICK!'

The telephone line went silent, deathly silent, as I groaned, 'Oh no' and then answered myself with 'Oh yes!'

I was round the house like a rocket and there she was, as before, same yard, same filth, same pile of dirt, same child, blue with cold. I'm not exaggerating when I say that when I got into the house my finger was wagging so hard under the dad's nose it's a wonder it didn't disappear up it! I was so blinking mad I frightened myself let alone him!!

'I want her in NOW!' I hollered! Not tomorrow, not next week but NOW!'

All the old bugger could do was nod his head weakly.

Once inside my car I realised I had a problem. She was so tiny the seat belt was useless and remember these were the days before children's car seats were available. Having got this far though, nil desperandum!

I drove slowly and carefully to my Senior Girls' School and with her safe in my arms, went into the secretary's room where I asked if I could borrow one of her senior girls who could hold the mite on her knee with a seat belt around them both for safety. Whilst a reliable girl was being sent for I sat with 'the little princess' and was soon surrounded by teachers, secretary and school girls all of whom took my little charge to their hearts and started to spoil her rotten. I glanced down at her by now radiant and happy little face (and she was hanging onto me like a limpet) as she munched on biscuits, sweeties and other goodies produced for her to enjoy, and I knew that no matter what, this one would never

371

be an attendance problem!

I only ever saw her again once. It was years later but I immediately recognised the nicely dressed teenage girl waiting at the bus stop. She was a pretty girl and although dressed traditionally, her veil was open. Just then a young chap, instantly recognisable as her brother, passed by. He was as thin as a rake and quite unlike the chubby boy I'd encountered years earlier. He spoke to her and she replied, and I saw they were now as close as any other siblings, for when he spoke, she laughed, and when she replied she playfully threw a punch at him which he easily ducked then continued on his way laughing. I found myself laughing too at their capers and at that point her eyes locked onto mine. They were still slightly vacant but then for a split second they changed to quizzical as though she half remembered her former champion. I smiled and nodded acknowledgement before continuing on my way.

Poor living conditions:

I was now standing inside the front door of a very large house that judging by the standard of renovative work, had been completed by a one-armed bricklayer, partially sighted plasterer and mentally unstable decorator! The poor dad with whom I was now engaged in conversation had been forced by circumstance, like many other families, to live in this monstrosity, and I, as a representative of the local authority, was now being asked to intervene and bring pressure to bear on the housing department to get him and his brood rehoused.

I had a lot of sympathy for this bloke because a) he wasn't trying to blackmail me by threatening to keep his kids from school and b) he had a vicious sense of humour which quite appealed to me.

He took me upstairs to see what his living conditions were like and as we went I could see that in better days this house would probably have been occupied by professional people. Unfortunately, the war and several near misses by bombs had given the foundations and structure a hell of a bashing as seen by the great tie rods extending from wall to wall, stopping the walls from falling outwards. With plywood partitioning making three rooms out of one large one, and dark unlit passageways, the place was a maze. An added complication was that the front door was never locked and so not even the owner, who didn't give a damn anyway as long as his money kept coming in every week, knew who was roaming around the house at all hours.

We went into the family's quarters and sat down. Dad began to explain something that I'd heard many times before about these places, namely that many nights the kids couldn't have a bath because with free access some of the cheaper whores would bring their clients in through the unlocked, open front door and, putting one or two cushions in the bath, would use that as the bed on which to entertain their clients to earn a few quid.

As dad and I sat talking in his living room cum kitchen, cum bedroom, we could hear the other tenants talking, washing pots, snoring, with no sounds being filtered out as the walls were so thin. I felt sorry for the little family but could do little other than point them in various directions for rehousing.

I stood to go and as I did so dad tapped the paper thin partitioning that served as a wall close to where he was sitting and said,

'This is a corridor out here and just at the end of it lives a 'Pro'. In the normal course of events when she has a client, she lays a three section mattress in the bath and her clients 'shag' her there, however, if our kids get in the bath first her clients have to make do with a 'knee trembler' right up against the outside of our wall so it gets a bit noisy in here when she's got her arse hard up against the wall and the bloke's shagging away like a rattlesnake!'

Dad then held up a six inch nail and went on,

'One of these days I'm going to let the buggers get into their stride then ram this straight through the wall into her arse! I swear she'll jump and scream so hard the bloke 'shagging' her will think he's brought her off like she's never been brought off before!'

The picture he conjured up had me chuckling for the rest of the day! See what I mean about a vicious sense of humour!

Chapter 28: Truanting & Absent Kids

I have often wondered how kids from the most ordinary of homes and with the most ordinary of parents can, at the drop of a hat, become the most accomplished of manipulators and liars and, once it's been proven to the parents that their child is on the 'downward path' they cannot see they're being 'conned?'

The majority of us, once we know that our child (especially a girl) has been ducking school and giving no plausible explanation as to where she's been spending her truanting hours, immediately revert to panic stations and watch the wayward child like a hawk! One of my stock in trade suggestions to parents was when in doubt don't hesitate to ring us at the school. We'll not only check the register but also do a physical check of the classroom. This last service was because we'd learned from bitter experience that kids would often register then 'do a bunk' at the first opportunity! When I suggested to a Head at a school other than one of mine that spot register checks should be carried out, the Head and staff vetoed this idea and yet knew their kids were regularly 'bunking off' after getting their mark. I suppose they thought it was all too much trouble!

I'm reminded of one child who started on the downward path as described and inevitably started to regularly truant. I visited the home two or three times but got no reply to my knocking even though I suspected the child, aged around 12 years, was in the house all the time. Then the Head of one of my junior schools alerted me to the poor attendance of one of his pupils who I discovered was the younger brother to the girl. No good, it would have to be an evening visit.

It was winter time and the street where the girl lived was ill lit. I knocked on the door and the girl answered.

'No, me mam and dad aren't in. It's only me and me little brother. We haven't been well but we'll be at school in the morning!'

When I asked what time her dad got in from work, the girl told me,

'He won't be in for hours yet, nor me mam, but as I said, we'll be at school in the morning!'

Just then I glanced down the street and saw a dim shape in the distance.

'Is that your dad?' I asked.

'Oh no, he won't be in for hours yet!'

'Alright, Pet,' I said, and moved as if to go down the street.

The girl went back inside and with her out of sight I came back and waited. The dim shape I'd seen moved closer and materialised into a man who, as he came closer I approached with,

'Good evening. Do you live at this address?'

'Yes,' came his reply, 'and who might you be?'

I introduced myself and asked whether he was aware his daughter and son had been missing school.

'Missing school, missing school?' he parroted!' But they go every day!'

I then put the record straight, ending with,

'I'll expect them to both be at school tomorrow and don't hesitate to check by ringing. I'd sooner keep right out of things at this stage especially as you now know they've been skiving!'

The next day the boy was in and I'm pleased to say he stayed in, but the girl had an 'O' against her name.

'Has dad rung the school?' I asked.

The reply was in the negative.

'Right,' I thought.

I got the girl's record card out and looked for dad's place of employment. Nothing! I then rang the Junior School and enlisted the help of the Headteacher.

'Can you get the younger brother to tell you where his dad works?'

Simple, or maybe not so simple! Either the child didn't know or, as I suspected, he didn't intend telling us where he worked!

There was nothing for it. Another evening visit was called for! Dad was quite shocked as his daughter had told him she'd been to school.

'She'll be in tomorrow,' he promised.

'Well, she'd better be,' was my threat.

The next morning, as before, no attendance! As I'd found out the night before where dad worked I visited the Foreman and asked if I could speak to him. Dad made the same promise that she'd be in the next day, but was she? Was she hell!

The next day I rang the dad at work.

'Not in? But she promised me faithfully she'd be in school, attending regularly, just like she's been doing all along!!'

Attending regularly!!?? What on earth was the man talking about! Dad then apologised for not being home when I telephoned. Frankly, I was now totally lost and it must've shown in the tone of my voice for he enlarged on the matter.

'When I got home from work my daughter explained how you'd telephoned and left a message that it was all a mistake. That the register was wrong and she'd been attending all the time. As I was a bit suspicious I asked my son if what his sister had said was true and he confirmed that it was!'

Two months later the father appeared before the Magistrates' Court to face charges!

School phobia:

In twenty years of working with children I was only to see one genuine case of school phobia, genuine that is to my way of thinking. Since being involved with that one child I've heard 'school phobia' being diagnosed in several cases, however, I'm convinced these other cases were simply a refusal to accept the benign discipline of school life or was a crafty intent to 'play the system.'

From the other side I also consider a diagnosis of 'school phobia' as a cure for all ills or an unadmitted admission of failure by adults, social workers and education welfare officers who see this diagnosis as an easy way out when all their theories based on getting a working relationship with the child have been blown to dust. But, to get back to this particular child.

As usual I'd inherited him from another officer. Making my first call I wasn't at all impressed by what I saw of the home. Mother was present and she was a very large, domineering type of person who made it quite clear she knew all about mental illness and there was no doubt in her mind that it was this (in a very mild form) which was causing the school phobia from which she alleged her child suffered. Any point she made was backed up by frequent references to a book on child development and mental disorders in children which she'd obtained from goodness knows where and quoted at great length.

Upon my arrival the lad, who I judged to be of Junior school age, was playing quietly with a toy car on the table, not concerned about my presence one little bit but as his mother went on and on about 'my poor boy this and my sick child that' I could see he was beginning to disintegrate from the inside out. I hurriedly changed the subject, or at least tried to, by bringing up dad.

'Would it help if dad took an hour off in the morning and walked you to school?' I asked the boy but before he could open his mouth the mother absolutely exploded with a tirade of how dad was inadequate, most of the boy's problems stemmed from dad underachieving, dad was useless as a husband and as a father etc., etc. At this I cut her short and told her I would call back the next day. To the boy I said,

'Don't worry, don't worry at all. Nobody, least of all me, is going to try and force you. Just relax and we'll have a nice chat tomorrow.'

That afternoon I put 'feelers' out to the schools psychological service and school medics. Whilst waiting for them to reply I went in to both the Infant and Junior School the child had previously attended and asked some searching questions. As I guessed, and feared, the child's reluctance to go to school on a regular basis stemmed from Infant school days and both Heads and teachers put most, if not all the blame, on the mother. Everyone knew the mother but nobody had ever met or seen the father.

I waited until all the local children were safely in school before visiting again. I spoke quietly to the mother and chatted away to the boy who, apart from being rather quiet seemed perfectly normal. Finally, I asked,

'How would you like to come to the school with me? If you don't feel you can face going in, we can always come straight back.'

At this point I'd gained his confidence enough and he was willing to give it a try but what came in the next 10 minutes was quite horrific. As we approached the school building I saw the child slowly but surely crumble into pieces under my very nose. It began soon after we left the house as a tremble in his voice and by the time the building was in sight he was shaking so hard I thought his arms & legs would fall off, and he couldn't speak. With NO hesitation I gently took his arm, turned him around and took him home again. That afternoon I had some replies to my enquiry. Everybody on the medical and psychological side knew of him but not one of them (and remember these were highly paid experts) could suggest any course of action that would help the child. I even rang the 'cruelty man' to see if anything was known from that side and was told by a very sympathetic inspector 'don't touch it'. The child had been known to that department for years and yet nothing had been done.

I was very tempted to take that advice but I couldn't get the boy out of my head. If I did nothing then that was fundamentally what the boy's future would hold. Nothing! That night I went to the boy's house and waited until the father came home. He was a very nice bloke and we had a good talk punctuated by his wife's voice booming in at every opportunity. At first I thought I was going to manage to get father to take some time off work so we could take the child into school together but as we conversed I realised she was doing the same with dad as she was with the boy that morning! Destroying his confidence! My goodness it was cleverly done. She'd got brain washing down to a fine art. I'd failed, and the miserable, hopeless look on dad's face proved that.

Next morning I went into the Junior School to find the mother had got in there first. She was lecturing the school secretary on what a waste of time it was me going to see the father, he being such a poor specimen of a man and all that. I could tell the secretary was fed up to the nines and so I collared the mother, and whilst continuing to talk non-stop, I eased her out of the office and into the corridor. The next move was to get her out of the school as her voice was booming out and was easily heard throughout the whole building. I was just succeeding when the Headmaster arrived and told us in no uncertain terms to,

'Get out of my school! I don't want you quarrelling in here!'

Once mother was out of the school I went back to the Headmaster to tell him to get his facts right before accusing me of bringing problems into his blasted school! Fortunately, the secretary had beaten me to it and had put the record straight. Well, I never got an apology from him but I never ever needed a champion in that school. I'd made a friend for life!

So what to do? Did I say like the rest of them, 'Sod it, nobody else wants to know! The kid will have to take his chances in later life,' or did I try to force the Authority's hand and risk their displeasure? No contest!

That afternoon I wrote a Court brief and taking it to the Chief, laid it under his nose. He didn't quibble, he simply read what I'd written, grunted and then counter signed it! Two months later, feeling like the rat of the century, I faced the parents and their child across the Juvenile Court. I gave my evidence such as it was. School Health were noticeable by their absence. The Bench were obviously perplexed and I thought they were going to throw the case out of Court but then dad saved the day. He saved his son, as events were to prove, and he saved us all a lot of time.

His missus, overawed by it all, had the good sense to keep her mouth shut but dad, the darling, suddenly stood up and without being asked said something along the lines of:

'Please don't take the lad away from us. I realise I should've done more, much more to get the boy into school.'

It was here he could've really dropped his missus in it by laying the blame on her and her medical books, but he didn't.

'Give me a chance, a last chance, and I promise you that my son WILL go to school!'

Now believe it or not, he was given that last chance and I never had to visit that home again. The boy went back to the same school he was used to but the damage had been done. Eventually he went to a Special School and did marvellously well. A footnote to this is that 6 years after this took place a booming voice that I wished I'd never have to EVER hear again, hailed me in the street! It was SHE, and she hadn't changed! She loudly went over the same old ground and I shut off, that is until I came to with a jerk as I realised she'd changed tack, and it was now SHE who'd persuaded the Magistrates to give the boy another chance. It was SHE who'd restored the state of equilibrium and thanks to HER the boy was now at work and had good prospects. Hypocrite that I am I told her what a great mother she was and how appreciative I was to all her efforts. It all goes to show, doesn't it, that the powers that be were focusing in on the wrong problem when it only needed one visit to the home to identify the real cause of all the trouble.

Raggle, taggle gypsies:

My four 'Raggle Taggle Gypsies' were in trouble again. I dare to bet that had there been no such thing as mischief in the world they would've invented it. Each one of them came from the poorest homes on the district so the cards were already stacked against them. Had I not understood how tough and resilient these kids can be from the meaner environments I would've despaired, thinking that they would be sure to go under. Not them. They, like so many others similarly placed had learnt long ago how to bend with the prevailing winds. Scrape after scrape these four beauties got themselves into. Nothing really bad, mean or vicious, just devilment. Time after time I would go and see their parents, trying to get them more and more involved in their children's moral and social development. It was like bashing my head against a brick wall. The kids themselves, all cheeky faced and bright eyed girls, never ever seemed out of sorts with me. Me, the bloke who often put a stopper on their fun and games. The world had nothing more to teach them and though they could shock, in truth they were unshockable.

Once again, they were up again in the Headmistress's room, standing in a straight line in front of her desk. Tatty blazers, torn pockets, dusty & stained tunics, scuffed shoes and wrinkled 'off white' socks. Whispering and shuffling they tried to put together a story that might just ring true enough to be believed by 'Miss' when she came down from assembly.

The Head arrived and the interrogation began:

'Now girls, you must tell me why you are so late for school each day and why on some days you've been truanting?'

'Please Miss, we aint!' came the reply.

Four mouths opened in unison and then quickly closed as the class register was placed before them clearly showing the late and absence marks.

384

'Please Miss, we aint been doing nuffink except help this poor old man who lives on his own and aint got nobody to help him!' offered one of the girls.

'Now, let me get this quite clear girls. Am I to understand you've been helping an elderly gentleman cope with his day to day living? asked the Head.

'Oh yes, Miss! We do his errands and fings!' they chorused, heads eagerly bobbing up and down.

'That's very commendable, girls,' began the Headmistress, 'but apart from errands, what are the other things you help him with?'

At this I saw a quick glance pass between the three girls who were the leaders of the mischief before they turned towards the fourth who was, from past experience, the most likely one to 'blab', and she didn't let us down!

'We help him have a bath!' she blurted out helpfully.

They most certainly had been helping him. Each day they'd been visiting the old man who they'd met on the park, and twice, sometimes three times a day (depending how much pension he had) they'd give him a bath. He must've been the cleanest 'dirty old bugger' on the district!

The old gentleman:

Over the years one of my most regular visits was to a crumbling, three storey, terraced house which, from the outside was a monument to Victorian standards of the worst kind. The immediate area smelled of a combination of steam locomotives from the nearby railway goods depot and very irregularly cleaned public conveniences, the latter being likely due to shared entries near to a local pub being used by the regulars as a urinal at chucking out time! Added to these aromas was the odour of dirty socks and cabbage water!

The occupants of the house were led by an elderly gentleman who always seemed to be harassed to death, although it was clear he'd seen better days and in racing parlance, 'came from a good stable!' He had a beautifully modulated voice and a very English accent which was in stark contrast to that of his immigrant neighbours.

In my view it had been his bad luck to have met up with and married a young widow with several children who he was now raising as his own. They'd been married a few years but as so often happens when an elderly man marries a young wife, he couldn't keep up with her (if you get my drift) and so his rather attractive wife had acquired a succession of regularly changed boyfriends who would 'scratch her itch!'

Her older and seemingly disillusioned husband had taken this all in his stride. He'd taken over the running of the household by doing the cooking, cleaning and raising the kids. Unfortunately, he wasn't very good at cleaning and his child rearing skills weren't much better.

The one fault he had which caused me to make such regular visits was that he didn't start his day off at the same time as other, better ordered households, so the kids rarely, if ever, arrived at school for the closing of the register, and often not at all, and so, after fighting my way through the pack of stray mongrel dogs always to be found waiting outside his house for his bitch whippet to come out and play, I was to be found on most days thumping on his front door to see just where the hell his kids had got to this time.

My reception was always the same. I would hear the old gentleman's swiftly pacing footsteps coming up the passage on the bare, echoing floorboards. The door would swing open and all the stray neighbourhood dogs would attempt to gain entry whilst his female whippet tried her damnedest to get out! All hell would break loose as he and I joined forces in aiming wild kicks at these almost feral strays and the air would be blue with our mutual cussing and sounds of combat! The hounds would then retreat up the road yelping and howling with whatever missiles we could find and throw hurtling after them.

Red faced, panting from his exertions, totally puffed out and causing him to spit chunks of bacon sandwich over me as he spoke, he would then say one word as though he hadn't a clue as to why I'd called in the first place! 'YES?'

On this particular day I'd been beaten to the door by a salesman type of bloke and so I stood well back to watch the fun! I heard the old man's hurried footsteps along the passage, the door bolt being drawn and saw the door open. Again, the pack of dogs charged forward and the air was once again filled with curses and yelps as we joined forces to fight off the dogs for, correctly reading & assessing the situation, the salesman fought on our side and it was three against the pack! We won!

With the hounds in full retreat and the old man breathing less heavily than normal, he acknowledged my presence with a nod then turned to the salesman type chappie and, in his beautifully modulated voice asked the standard question, 'YES?'

To my amazement the salesman introduced himself thus:

'Good morning, Sir! I'm from the local Education Department. I'm doing research into learning in the home and with the backing of the Department of Education and Science I'm empowered to offer you and the lady of the house text books for use in the home by the children at a greatly reduced price!'

On hearing this I 'bit my tongue' hard, for this man was good and I wanted to see and hear chapter two of his selling routine.

It must have been heart breaking for the bloke because the master of this house showed no reaction at all except once, and that was when, quite unbeknown to the poor salesman, two of the curs so recently beaten off, crept back and with the bloke still in full flow each in turn after sniffing at his trouser bottoms, had cocked their leg and 'peed' over his turn ups! At last, running short of wind, he stopped. The old gentleman sort of jerked himself back to the here and now and resumed the slow mastication of his bacon 'sarny' then, facing his caller he said,

'Mister, the only use we have for books in this house is tearing the pages out and wiping bums! Bums we have aplenty, but few books! Sometimes we use the pages for lighting fires but as we can't afford coal very often we don't often use them for that purpose either. As for the lady of the house, she isn't home and, as most of the slanderous sods round here will tell you, my wife is no lady!

Twice those bloody dogs have come back and pissed up your leg and you haven't noticed, and this gentleman standing here beside you, listening, happens to be a real Education Officer, although around here we have more descriptive words to call him so, if I were you Mister, I would 'sod off' before he sends for the coppers and has you done for impersonating him amongst other things! So, go with my blessing and bugger your bloody rotten luck cos it just isn't your day, is it!?'

The poor devil gaped at me as I waved my warrant card under his nose and then turning, he fled!

As the man disappeared down the street at a rate of knots, I turned to the old gentleman who was leaning against the door frame picking his teeth with the business card recently presented to him by the salesman.

'That must be the funniest thing I've seen in years' I said, 'especially when those dogs cocked their legs and pissed on him!'

At this point the old man's face which had retained its customary dead pan expression, cracked slightly and, just before closing the door on me he said,

'I'm glad you found that funny, because they've just pissed up yours as well!

'

Chapter 29: The Lowest of the Low

If ever the extremes of difference between east and west needed to be demonstrated, then this was a perfect example. The home I was visiting was one of many such dwellings which lay off the main road. Even if I'd been blind-folded I would've known I was in a house occupied by an Asian family, or at least, had been. Now though the only occupant was a broken-hearted mother of around 19 years, an unknown female and myself. The visit had been requested by one of my Infant School Heads who was concerned that one of her pupils had gone back to Bangladesh under what she'd been told were distressing circumstances. Distressing they certainly were as I was now finding out. That poor woman, squatting in the middle of the bare room, dressed in traditional Asian costume, absolutely breaking her heart and her frail frame wracked with sobs. She was unable to speak even a few words of her host country's tongue and had been treated in such a rotten despicable manner that, if I could've laid hands on her husband, I think I would've killed the swine. Certainly, in all my years of serving the parents and children I had never heard such a story to match what I was hearing now. The relator of events was the very nice, westernised, young Asian visitor occupying a broken stool which was all the furniture the room boasted. I'd carried it in from the yard where it had been put for the dustbin men to take.

This is the story the lady visitor interpreted for me:

The young woman squatting on the floor was married with two young children. The eldest was six years. Everything in her life was good. They had a nice home, a car, a television and video. One day her husband had complained that the picture quality on the tv wasn't good enough and he was going to take it in to the repair shop for adjustment. Next he told his wife that he was going to sell the most expensive items of their furniture and replace them with new. He even brought in a man to inspect what furniture was to be sold. The poor mum didn't understand any of what was going on as she had a six year old and two year old to look after but anyway, she lived in a male dominated society and she did what she was told without question. Then one day, right out of the blue, the husband told her he was taking the children to visit friends in London and she was to stay behind. She accepted this. What else could she do! That night her husband failed to return. The following day, still alone and frightened, there was a knock at the door. At last! She'd rushed to open the door to greet her family but no, it wasn't them, only the man who'd visited to value their furniture. One of her own people. He explained he had a van outside and without any further time being wasted he and a helper systematically loaded the contents of her little home aboard. Just before they'd finished two white men arrived and, with the furniture man acting as an interpreter, they told the by now totally bewildered mum they were from the gas and electric board and were disconnecting her supply as per her husband's instructions. This they did, leaving her with no heating, lighting or cooking facilities. With these men gone one can only guess what was going through that poor young woman's mind. If only her husband could come home and explain it all to her! For a week she'd squatted there on those bare floor boards with no food. That bastard had even taken the child benefit books, the ones that had a space for her to mark her name with a 'X' for she couldn't even write her name, and he'd taken every spare penny in the house. The final blow came when one of her missing husband's friends had turned up asking, 'when did she plan to vacate the house?' Her husband had sold the house to him prior to returning to Bangladesh with his children, a place from which he did not intend to return. He no longer wanted her!

I was now totally involved! Social workers, Housing Department, Social Security etc.,etc. I even contacted the Post Office and got any 'pay out' on the Family Allowance Books stopped, after all, only an 'X' was required on the signature space and 'Bingo!' With the father out of the country he wasn't going to be collecting the money but anyone who'd bought them off him wouldn't get the money either! What the outcome to it all was I never knew, nor did I ever enquire, but I did what I could for my conscience would never let me 'pass by on the other side!'

Chapter 30: The Don't Cane Brigade

One of the most vocal of the 'don't cane the little dears or you'll drive one devil out and twenty in' brigade, came into the secretary's office when I was there and was handed a parcel addressed to her. The parcel had been left in the reception area, obviously delivered by hand as no stamp was affixed.

'Watch out,' I joked, 'it could be a bomb!'

Inside, when opened, was a second parcel of greaseproof paper and in this lay a severed chicken's head, two chicken legs and a bouquet of blood stained feathers wired together. A note inside, obviously written by a child and smeared with gore and other unmentionables, promised, 'we're going to get you!'

For a woman noted for her hostility to the forces of law and order her reaction was unpredictable to say the least! She now collectivised the pupils of the school who up until then she'd described as 'victims of a hostile environment,' as 'Those Little Bastards' and yet there was no proof our kids were responsible! (and she really did go on)

'Why don't the police spend more time catching these sods instead of sitting around on their fat arses doing 'sod all!' Bloody kids like these need cane, cane and more CANE, degenerate little bastards!'

With all her ideals destroyed in one fell swoop she glared around challenging us to contradict her if we dare! I could've done but what was the point!? A year later she was gone to pastures new to put her half-baked theories to the test again!

Karl:

Karl, a most handsome boy of West Indian parents, ran the Head of his Junior School nearly into the ground which didn't surprise me at all because this particular Head didn't believe in physically punishing even the naughtiest child. Prior to his taking over as Headmaster I was never pulled in on internal disciplinary problems. These were always sorted out within the school's four walls. How? I don't know, nor do I want to know but since this chap had arrived and taken over I was having to visit parents of children of Junior School age and tell them their son or daughter was being naughty in school and they'd have to do something about it! But just what the heck were the parents expected to do? We'd just passed from the old Children's Department being disbanded and the Social Services set up was coming into force. Parents were being threatened that if they smacked their children the child and Social Services would take them to Court!

I was already in the Headmaster's bad books, for having been told by him that he didn't believe punishing a child did any good because it was too traumatic, I'd replied that in my opinion it was far better to administer a 'short, sharp, shock' than to do nothing and risk exposing the child to the trauma of a Juvenile Court later on.

Karl wasn't vicious, just very, very naughty, and the Headmaster was sending me on a daily basis to the house with messages and notes for the parents, reporting just how naughty Karl was being. As soon as he walked through the door Karl's mum would give her son 'what for' but as soon as he was in school the next day Karl would be up to his old games! After a while mum lost patience, saying,

'When that child of mine is naughty, I smack him! If the Headmaster would just do the same at school he would have to behave! I've given my permission for Karl to be smacked and smacked hard but all he does is talk, and talk, and talk. Doesn't he know Karl's just laughing at him!'

When I passed this message back to the Headmaster I got a 'snort' in reply. Somehow we managed to get through to Karl leaving the Junior School and then it was time for him to go to Senior School. Mum sent a message through to me,

'I don't want that boy of mine to go to the same senior school as his older brother. He's a good boy and getting on fine with everybody. I'm pleased with him, but Karl with his naughty ways, will spoil things.'

It was a funny old thing but I'd been thinking along the same lines.

'Would you trust me to get him a place at another senior school? I know a Headmaster who'll get on fine with young Karl!'

'That's fine with me,' said mum, 'but understand, I don't want you coming here every two minutes if he gets up to his old tricks at the new school!'

It was the first day of the new term at the nominated, and accepted, new senior school and I went to see the Headmaster to warn him of the sort of behaviour he may encounter with young Karl. 'Leave it with me' was the response.

The following day Karl tested the boundaries for the first time and the member of staff involved, having been warned in advance by the Head, wasted no time in sending the boy to him. In the Head's room the Headmaster spoke thus:

'I've been told that in your Junior School you thought you were King. I have to tell you that in this school, I rule!'

Crossing over to the corner cupboard the Headmaster took out the cane and very quietly, he showed it to Karl.

'Sonny, just step out of line once more and with your mother's blessing I will use this on your backside, so don't push me!'

Five years later Karl left that school. He'd enjoyed every moment of it and never been caned! Don't get me wrong, he wasn't a 'goody, goody' boy and we wouldn't have wanted him to be, but the last time I saw his mother she told me,

'My Karl's doing better than his older brother!'

Chapter 31: If It Aint Broke

My senior, single sex schools, were still generally turning out young ladies and gentlemen, but change was in the air. Whereas previously my Heads and school staff had been fobbed off by promises of more money, which in the main were never kept, now it seemed a tap had been turned on and there was money, money, money and more money just there for the asking.

At one meeting I was invited to attend we were told the schools had been allocated thousands of pounds of additional monies and we had 10 days to come up with ideas as to how we wanted the money spent!

I sat dumbfounded for, apart from one or two Headmistresses and Headmasters, not one senior representative from the Education Department had bothered to attend and put in a bid for some of the 'lolly!'

Most of this money was quickly snapped up by the 'Empire Builders' whilst we small fry from Education, sent in with no briefing as to what was up for grabs, didn't get a look in, thus supporting a point of view I'd held for a long time that certain 'High Ups' didn't want us to succeed.

After being forced to sit and listen to some of the more crack pot suggestions put forward by the more vocal, but complete strangers to me (where did these people come from?) I got up and walked out in disgust. The next day a Head who'd been present, congratulated me on having the guts to make my displeasure clear. But what else could I have done? (and why hadn't she joined me!)

It had been on the cards for some years that a new Educational Establishment was urgently needed to replace two Victorian schools we'd been forced to make do with for so long, in fact several years previously I'd been invited to go before the Governors of both the Boys and Girls Senior schools to make my opinions clear on various proposals. When I said that in my opinion we needed to retain the single sex status of the schools, even though they might share the same Community College Building, my proposal caused some concern. However, I stuck to my guns saying that the Muslim community, who I felt were becoming very vocal indeed, would not want their female children mixing with sexually aware boys of all nationalities, and I also pointed out there was pressure from the Mosques for the girls to be veiled in the presence of the boys. Boys being boys the least the girls could expect would be taunts along the lines of, 'she must be ugly if she has to keep her 'fissog' (face) covered!'

They only wanted my opinion, and then they voted. A mixed sex Community College was ordained.

Within a year the Muslim girls were being withdrawn to be educated within the confines of the Mosque. I make no further comment.

The new community college was eventually built and the Headmaster with whom I'd worked with and for, was passed over for the new post of Principal. I met the new chap and found he didn't intend to retain a uniform or use the cane. The college was now mixed sex and informality was 'IN' with the use of teachers first names being encouraged.

My request for a transfer came through.

The area of the city I was now to work was miles away from the areas I was used to but whilst most of the housing was new, I still had many old terraces.

On the first day I visited my allocated schools to introduce myself, feeling very much like a 'new boy.'

The school staff were suspicious of me and it was made very clear the individual year tutors wanted to tell me who to visit, and when. Now my objections to this system, whether they're willing to admit it or not, is that many teachers have favourites and some kids would always 'get away with it' whilst others would be harried from pillar to post. Two examples:

1)   The child who rarely attended and yet I was never asked to visit because the mother would go into school twice a week to make excuses, therefore the absences must be genuine. Mostly they were not, as my threat to prosecute soon proved with the child subsequently making a 100% attendance.

2)   The demand I should prosecute a boy one month before his official leaving date. The boy by then was 16½ years. The pressure to prosecute was because the father was a police officer and an example needed to be made.

I thought my sense of humour would see me through but even that was quashed when I was asked to make a visit to enquire after a 13 year old boy. The absence form was absolutely clean and apart from first thing in the morning, the boy hadn't missed school all year.

When I arrived at the address I made to go to the front gate and up the garden path when, lo and behold, there sitting on the front doorstep was the biggest, nastiest, growliest Alsatian dog I'd seen for a very long time. Now, as I've said before, I don't like big fierce dogs, especially those that slink towards you, teeth unfurled and making deep growling noises as they proceed, and so I hurriedly closed the gate and stood making whistling noises, hoping that someone inside would hear me and come out, but it wasn't to be my day!

'Visited 9:45am. Large dog obstructed entry. Mr Boardman doesn't like big fierce dogs and the feeling was reciprocated. Will call back pm today.'

Well I did go back and the dog by this time was safely inside. A very irate mother came to the door and accused me of wasting her time, ratepayers' money etc., etc. She said she'd rung the school the day before and explained the boy had to see the dentist. I apologised for the inconvenience and soothed her feelings. We chatted and laughed together for a few minutes during which time we agreed that whoever had taken the message was 'a prat', and we left best of friends.

The next morning the deputy Head called me in to complain that my humorous comments on the absence form were not appreciated, the teacher concerned having complained. For me this was confirmation that this teacher was also 'a prat.'

I still had a very large Asian population on my district and was to renew some old friendships. Knocking at one door I was greeted by the lady of the house who was wearing traditional dress. She recognised me at once, although at first I didn't recognise her until I was invited into the house without introducing myself. This told me she was one of my 'old girls' for normally I would never have been allowed over the threshold with her husband being out, as I was to find out he was.

Suddenly, it was as though I'd been transported back to a small terraced house in a street of identical terraced houses, occupied by a newly arrived family from Pakistan. If I remembered correctly there were three daughters and a son that needed enrolling in school. Looking at this young woman it all came flooding back.

Her father, who looked more Arabic than Pakistani, had invited me to be seated and take tea with him and as by this time I'd developed a taste for tea brewed in their particular style, I accepted with 'many thanks.' The girl, who according to her passport was thirteen years but appeared much older, was sent out to do the honours. I remembered how nervous she was as she placed my cup in front of me as I sat in solitary splendour with all the family around the table waiting for the Sahibs approbation of his refreshment. Father didn't touch his tea. His having one was just a token gesture. I'd taken the first sip of the aromatic brew but nearly spat it out it was so salty. I'd guessed that the girl in her fluster at being asked to wait on the guest had put two spoons of salt in my tea instead of sugar, but what to do? I realised how upset the father would be if he realised what his daughter had accidentally done. He would feel his guest had been insulted and, as was their way, the girl would be soundly beaten. Nothing for it then but for yours truly to drink it down like a 'good un.' It was awful!

When dad got up to fetch more documents and with everyone's attention distracted, I caught the girl's eye and leaning forward tapped the 'sugar bag' clearly marked 'Sifta Salt'. At first she looked very puzzled but then 'tumbled.' Reaching forward she wet her finger in her mouth and then like any child stealing sugar, dipped her finger first into the salt bag and then into her mouth. Her expression of horror spoke loud and clear. I smiled reassuringly at her and left as soon as I decently could to wash my mouth out.

It was the young woman who now raised the incident again and, after all those years, we laughed about it. Our laughing disturbed an infant in the next room.

'Is that your first?' I asked.

'No,' came her reply, 'I have another of 5 years!'

'Good gracious!' I exclaimed, doing some quick metal arithmetic. 'You were thirteen years of age eight years ago which means you're twenty one years now. You must have been married at fifteen years of age!'

'No,' she corrected me gently. 'I was seventeen years of age eight years ago but thirteen years on my fake passport. It was awful being seventeen in a classroom of thirteen year olds!'

This state of affairs wasn't uncommon for I know of one Headmaster who'd admitted a very big lad who was alleged to be fourteen years on both his passport and birth certificate but what made the Headmaster suspicious was picking up a photo the boy had dropped and looking at him complete with full beard!

Even after several months on my new patch I was still a 'lost soul' at times. I just couldn't settle or feel 'at home.' A vital ingredient was missing but then all at once the sun began to shine thanks to, and I won't say the naughtiest boy in school, but one of them, and it came about in this way:

'Our Arfur' had been a right pain in class all morning. Just before break though,

Arfur had been rocking backwards & forwards on the back legs of his chair and sticking up two fingers in a 'V' to his newly qualified teacher. Without the knowledge and experience to deal with young 'scallywags' that saw newly fledged members of the teaching profession as 'fair game,' the boy was now encouraging his classmates to join in with the fun & games. What Arfur didn't realise though was that whilst he was in full flow a senior and very experienced member of staff just happened to be passing the classroom and, on hearing the hub-bub had peered over the glass partitioning. Seeing what was going on he'd crept in. Quite a few of the class spotted him at once but like all kids, they hadn't bothered to audibly warn Arfur about the alien presence. After hurling a particularly nasty, 'you're bloody useless', Arfur found himself on the receiving end of a 'clip round the ear' and momentous bollocking!

As if by magic peace was restored and after glaring at the young villain for a few moments more, the senior member of staff left the classroom a darn sight quieter than when he'd found it.

Come playtime and along with his peers, Arfur was dismissed for break but after wandering aimlessly into the playground for a moment or two, whilst the other girls and boys drank their milk and ate whatever snacks they had, Arfur alighted on a pile of builders' rubble.

Arfur carefully sorted through the dross and extricated a chunk of concrete which, after he'd weighed it up for balance, he sauntered the length of the playground and lobbed it straight at the staffroom window which, as sheer bad luck would have it, was closed! CRASH! CLANG! The 'clang' was a dent being put in the staff room tea urn!

Arfur made no attempt to run away after committing the foul deed and so he was quickly grabbed and put under close guard in a spare room until such time the police could be sent for, as no doubt about it, Arfur was caught 'dead to rights!' Criminal damage to school property, to wit, one large chunk of dried out sand and cement aimed with malice aforethought through a closed school window.

Along came our friendly neighbourhood policeman, a Sergeant no less who, having been suitably refreshed with coffee and biscuits courtesy of the Education Department, proceeded to take statements from all and sundry. This part of the enquiry was a 'doddle' as there were plenty of witnesses who agreed unanimously that Arfur had thrown the concrete. The only dispute was whether it'd been thrown underarm, overarm, yacked or bowled!

Satisfied that all those wishing to help the police with their enquiries had been interviewed, 'our Arfur' was sent for.

Arfur stood in front of his inquisitors rather like that child did in William Frederick Yeames', 'When did you last see your father' and answered all his inquisitors' questions calmly and respectfully: Name, address, age etc. They soon reached the 64 dollar one, namely,

'Arfur why did you throw a missile, to wit, one large chunk of concrete, through the staff room window?'

Arfur momentarily looked puzzled before asking,

'Would you mind repeating the question?'

Again, the charge was repeated.

'Window, what window?' was his reply.

At this the Sergeant, who'd been writing it all down in a bored 'I've seen and heard it all before way,' now began to take notice and look interested and, laying aside his pen said,

'Look Sonny, we've got umpteen witnesses who saw you pick up that missile and throw it through the staffroom window which not only did the window no good at all but you also put a bloody great dent in the tea urn!'

Arfur looked at the Sergeant in amazement and surprise with his mouth gaping open and then in a weak voice said,

'Oh no, Sir. I don't remember doing that!'

Here Arfur swayed to the extent that thinking he was going to faint, Matron nearly, but not quite (cynical beggar our Matron) rose from her seat to fetch the boy a glass of water. Arfur went on,

'You see, Sir, I don't remember anything at all after Sir here, (and here he indicated the senior member of staff who'd clipped him round the ear) hit me across the head just before playtime!'

The silence was deafening until the Sergeant spoke, very, very quietly,

'In view of this new development I must ask whether this boy was hit across the head immediately prior to committing the offence?'

Up chirped the Head,

'Come on now, it was only a little tap!'

Fixing the senior member of staff with a firm gaze the Sergeant said,

'You hit the boy across the head. That is admitted. The boy says that after you struck him, he had no recollection of what he did next.'

Turning, the Sergeant addressed the room in general.

'In view of what has been said, do you wish to go ahead with your charges?' and then as though the matter was already finished with, he closed his notebook and put his pen into his breast pocket. Once again he looked round at the gathered assembly of the accused and his accusers in the deathly silent room. Hardly anyone breathed, let alone spoke, then, carefully putting on his helmet and giving a last loving look at the biscuit tin marked 'Education Committee Property' he walked slowly and ponderously to the door. Those present thought he wanted to sneeze as his nose was twitching so hard.

At the door he turned and facing the assembly he raised his hand in a general and respectful sort of salute. I'm sure it was coincidental that he happened to be facing directly towards Arfur as he did so. Suddenly the world seemed a brighter place and it went through my mind,

'You know, I might just get some laughs out of this blasted school after all!!!'

Norman Hastings

If you liked reading this book, you might like to read Norman's first book which gives an insight into how Norman's own childhood experiences moulded him into the man he became. In *Norman: Through My Eyes. A social and personal history of Leicester*, Norman recalls his parents' turbulent marriage & subsequent separation and life growing up in the poorest neighbourhoods of Leicester during the 1930s & 1940s. Sometimes poignant & sad, but mostly nostalgic & humorous, Norman remembers his own childhood with fondness & understanding, even though his sanity, at times, was tested, but one has to remember when considering these 'Good Old Days' that what Norman & his family experienced wasn't unique. Whether recalling his days as a St Barnabas Church choirboy and singing at the now closed Towers Mental Hospital, his confinement in Groby Road Sanatorium with TB or life as a Moat Boys school boy in a Leicester at war, the subtle way Norman's own story evolves gives a unique insight into a world now gone but not actually that far from living memory.

Norman passed away aged 84 years following a short battle with cancer. Whilst he never lived to see his books published the drive to tell his stories remained strong to the end. I am proud to now be doing this on Norman's behalf.

Norman & Joyce with grandson Glyn

Printed in Great Britain
by Amazon